Here Comes the Clown

Also by Dom Joly:

Look at Me, Look at Me
The Dark Tourist
Scary Monsters and Super Creeps

Here Comes
the Clown

A Stumble through Show Business

Written by Dom Joly

(Honest)

**SIMON &
SCHUSTER**

London · New York · Sydney · Toronto · New Delhi

A CBS COMPANY

First published in Great Britain by Simon & Schuster UK Ltd, 2015
A CBS COMPANY

1 3 5 7 9 10 8 6 4 2

Simon & Schuster UK Ltd
1st Floor
222 Gray's Inn Road
London WC1X 8HB

www.simonandschuster.co.uk

Simon & Schuster Australia, Sydney
Simon & Schuster India, New Delhi

A CIP catalogue record for this book
is available from the British Library

Hardback ISBN: 978-0-85720-767-8
eBook ISBN: 978-0-85720-769-2

Typeset in the UK by M Rules
Printed and bound by CPI Group (UK) Ltd, Croydon, CR0 4YY

For Stacey,
without whom nothing would have been possible

'Fame is a fickle food upon a shifting plate'
Emily Dickinson

'Some call it fun, some call it mayhem'
Cabbage

Contents

Prologue

I loathe prologues. Everybody loathes prologues. Why do prologues exist?

Here's my prologue.

In 2004 I wrote a spoof autobiography called *Look at Me, Look at Me*. It pretty much documented the real events of my life up to *Trigger Happy TV* and used these as a basis for some fantastical storytelling. My intention was to write a sort of Munchausen-Zelig-type story of my life but I think some people might have been confused as to whether it was fact or fiction, despite the early appearance of a talking dog.

In *Here Comes the Clown* there will, I hope, be no such confusion. I take up the story from 14 January 2000, when the very first episode of *Trigger Happy TV* aired on Channel 4 and everything changed. Suddenly, I was famous and there was no need for fanciful storytelling. Reality was now weirder than any fiction I could conjure up. This is the story of what happened next (and just before).

This is *not* an autobiography, more snippets of recollections (most probably inaccurate) from my adventures in show business. I read a lot of biographies and the weird thing about them is that they tend (apart from the ones written by 19-year-old starlets) to have an arc in which you already know the ending.

However wonderful things appear at any particular moment, you know that life is probably going to throw some terrible spanner in the works – a marriage breaks up, you get addicted to drugs, you contract a case of West Nile disease, you are knocked over and killed by a milkman … It rarely ends well.

As I write this I have no idea of my arc – so far, so good, but life normally doesn't pan out like that. In fact, you probably already have the benefit of hindsight and know what happens to me. I wish you could tell me … Or maybe I don't … I don't know anything. It's like William Goldman said: 'Nobody knows anything.' So you already know more than all of showbiz and me. I hope that makes you feel good.

Dom Joly
January 2015

Chapter 1

Mr Gund

Fame, when it came, was on a train. Coach no. 3. Standard class. Whilst travelling from London Paddington to Oxford. It's all been pretty weird ever since.

It was Tuesday, 18 January 2000. Four days after the first episode of *Trigger Happy TV* had aired on Channel 4 and I can't remember why, but I was going to Oxford. I was seated to the rear of the carriage and reading a newspaper when *that* mobile phone ringtone went off. Without knowing I was on board, three random strangers all shouted, 'HELLO, I'M ON THE TRAIN ... NO, IT'S RUBBISH ... CIAO!' I sat there, dumbfounded. What the hell had just happened? Part of me wanted to stand up and shout, 'It's me. I'm that Big Mobile guy off the telly. That's my catchphrase you're all doing ...' But there was also a part of me that was frightened. I had suddenly stepped into a whole new world – a world whose rules I really didn't understand and in which I was pretty sure that I didn't belong.

My first ever job in comedy was as a researcher on *The Mark Thomas Comedy Product* on Channel 4. I'd got that job after I was fired from being a producer for ITN in Parliament, for paying someone to kick a football into David Mellor's face. You know David Mellor? Former member of the Cabinet, Queen's Counsel, award-winning broadcaster? That's how he introduces himself to black-cab drivers ... But I digress. I'd organised for some friends to have a kick-about in the background as I interviewed Mellor on College Green. I might have mentioned that it would not be totally unhelpful were the interview to be interrupted in some way. One minute in, the ball came flying towards us and struck Mellor hard on the side of the face.

Personally, I felt that this was just the sort of television that the UK public was crying out for. ITN obviously felt differently. So I sent my CV to a bunch of production companies in an attempt to move into documentaries. By chance one of these CVs landed on the desk of the production company making Mark Thomas's first show, a kind of pre-Michael Moore political satire show in which Mark did some live stand-up interspersed with some anarchic, silly VTs.

I was asked in for an interview and assumed it was for another political show. I put on my best (and only) suit and up I went to Ham Yard in Soho. I quickly surmised that this was no normal political show – far from it. This sort of show was going to suit me much more than the rather stifling, nerdy atmosphere of Westminster. They asked me what I would do if I were to play a joke on Westminster. I told them an idea I'd had about Cabinet reshuffles. They don't do it now, but back then, whenever there was a Cabinet reshuffle, MPs would sit near a phone for a couple of days desperately hoping to get the call to come into Number 10. I'd found out that it was just the Number 10 switchboard that made the call and so it wouldn't be difficult to fake. My idea was to ring as many Tory backbenchers as possible pretending to be Number 10 and to ask them all to pop over at 2pm. The result would be a confused and angry scrum of ambitious, chinless wonders all trying to get past the Plebgate police

4

officers with no record of their supposed appointments. The interview went well and they told me that the next step was for me to meet Mark himself. As I was getting up to leave, Joanna, one of the heads of the company, took me aside. She seemed nervous about mentioning something: 'Uuhhmm, Mark is a bit ... judgemental. It might be better if you didn't wear your suit when you come in to actually meet him.'

She seemed worried that this request might somehow offend me. It was the best thing I've ever had said to me in television. I was in TV for two things: not to wear a suit and not to have to get up too early. I got home, threw off my suit and have never worn one seriously since. Overnight, with minimum effort, I'd jumped from politics into comedy.

There were two researchers on the first *Mark Thomas Comedy Product* – me and another Dom, Dom English. Dom E was the real deal, a proper telly-head. He was a smart Essex boy schooled in telly at the university of *The Big Breakfast*. He wrote sitcoms and knew exactly what he wanted to do. I could tell he thought I was a lazy, floppy-haired, posh chancer, which I was. We got on like a house on fire. We were supposed to do 'research' and help set up ideas for some of the VTs that Mark was going to film on the show. If I am honest, I was a rubbish researcher. In hindsight, I should have mentioned this at the job interview. Fortunately, Dom E was brilliant at it. I just mucked about and hoped nobody would notice. As the show didn't have the biggest of budgets, I soon found myself volunteering to be in some of the VTs. This was easier than going to the trouble of hiring an extra who would come with restricted work hours, a stage-school attitude and annoying demands for endless coffee breaks. I did exciting things like having lunch with a foul man who was making legal snuff documentaries. I'd tried to conceal a hidden camera and a microphone in my trousers but the base unit got hotter and hotter until I had to run out of the restaurant screaming in pain with second-degree burns on my arse.

One time, Dom E and I had to dress up as a penis and a fifty-pound note. The idea was that Mark was taking a confused group of Japanese tourists on a tour of locations of political scandals. The penis would indicate a sex scandal and the fifty-pound note meant it was financial. Guess who got the penis costume? My first appearance on television in a comedy capacity was dressed as a six-foot latex penis waving at Japanese tourists. Very little has changed since.

Later we would take the same penis costume and try to persuade various Tory MPs like Jerry Hayes to put it on. Looking back, it seems so unnecessary – trying to get a monumental penis to dress up as a penis. At the time, however, it seemed cutting edge. Last I heard of the penis costume it was borrowed by Stewart Lee, who then used it on his BAFTA-winning TV show. I'm so glad that everything worked out for the penis – I always had a feeling that he would make it. Penises tend to do well in telly.

I came up with a simple idea for the show that Mark was totally uninterested in. It was a schoolboy kicking his football into weird places and then asking for it back. I can't remember why but Lawless, the production company, said that Dom E and I could go and film it. So we both dressed up in *Just William*-type schoolboy outfits and off we went. We kicked a football over the wall into Wormwood Scrubs, Kensington Palace, Buckingham Palace and, finally, Number 10 Downing Street. Each time, we would either ring the buzzer or speak to the security people in very high-pitched voices and ask for the ball back. Wormwood Scrubs told us to sling our hook. No one replied at Kensington Palace and the police at Buckingham Palace looked mystified but did retrieve the ball for us. Downing Street was a different kettle of fish, however ... I booted the ball over the wall into the garden but, before we could approach to ask for it back, we were challenged by an armed guard. He was not a man to mess with. He approached us with gun raised and told us that we were lucky that we hadn't been shot – we could have been the IRA throwing a bomb into the garden … Still in my high-pitched voice I queried this tactic as being very improbable and quite ineffective in the retrieval of Ireland for the Irish. We never got the ball back but nobody shot us, so overall it was a good day.

I'd have worked on the show for free. In fact, had I had any money I would have happily paid to take part. I'd had my first taste of something I could possibly be good at. It was about time. I was fast approaching my thirtieth birthday. I'd been a journalist, a diplomat, a waiter, a barman, a bookseller and something in the City that I never really understood. It appeared that I'd finally found something that I could do with my life. Now I just had to work out how to keep on doing it.

Help came in the form of the director of *The Mark Thomas Comedy Product*, Andy De Emmony. He, Dom English and I made a little pilot show called *Dog Bites*, in which we filmed four of us driving around in a VW camper van doing stunts like dressing up as a hungover penguin and trying to break back into London Zoo after a night out on the town. It wasn't great, but it was different and it briefly got the interest of Jon Plowman at the BBC before, like most things in telly, it disappeared. This was not to be the last I heard of Jon Plowman.

I'd started experimenting with animating prank phone calls. It allowed you instant access to anywhere in the world with a phone – ideal for the lazy prankster. I would listen to my favourite prank-call protagonists, The Jerky Boys, for hours on end. My favourite call on the *Dog Bites* reel was one I made to a TGI Friday's restaurant in which I tried to organise a wake for a recently departed patron of their establishment.

7

Me: 'He really loved your restaurant, the happy smiles, the fun that the waiting staff imbue ... If, however, we had the wake there, would it be possible for the staff to wear black armbands and not smile at all for the whole evening, as it would be disrespectful?'

Manager: 'Uuhhmm, I'd have to check with head office.'

Me: 'I was thinking we could have an unhappy hour instead of happy hour.'

Manager: 'I'm not sure we could ...'

Me: 'And you know when it's someone's birthday all the staff come to the table with a cake and sing happy birthday? Would it be possible for them to sing "My Death" by Jacques Brel ...? Obviously, without a cake ...'

I loved phone calls.

But with *Dog Bites* not going anywhere, I was unemployed. Dom E got another job immediately. I didn't, and was starting to panic when I saw an ad in the *Guardian*. It read:

Do you have a sense of humour? New comedy channel looking to employ energetic, bright people.

I wasn't entirely sure about 'energetic' but it was the first ad in a newspaper I'd ever seen that was of any interest, so I applied.

I got the job. It was only much later that I was told that somebody had recommended an amazing researcher on *The Mark Thomas Comedy Product* called Dom to Myfanwy Moore, my unnervingly young boss at the channel. I think it had never occurred to her that there might have been two Doms on the show, the good one and me. So I got in – thanks, Dom E, I owe you.

The Paramount Comedy Channel was the right place at the right time. In the next year or so they had Sacha Baron Cohen, Matt Lucas, David Walliams, The Mighty Boosh, Leigh Francis,

Armstrong and Miller, Simon Pegg and me all doing stuff there. It was a playground for people to try weird material out on the telly. It was heaven.

I was hired to be an assistant producer on a weekly show called *Man Made News* (a great title thought up by Leigh Francis, who worked in the art department at the time). The presenter of the show was a Scot called Dominik Diamond, who presented a show about video games called *GamesMaster* on Channel 4. Diamond was, to put it mildly, an arse. He was rude, unpleasant, self-obsessed and remarkably untalented. He was perfect for telly.

Diamond had previously hosted a show on the channel called *Dom 'n' Kirk's Night O'Plenty*, in which future *Little Britain* stars Matt Lucas and David Walliams appeared as guests in an early incarnation of theirs, called Mash and Peas. It quickly became clear that they thought the same of Diamond as everybody else. They proceeded to muck about and utterly destroy him until he finally lost his temper and called them 'complete arseholes' live on air. It was top, unintentional telly and the recording was passed around Paramount like a samizdat whenever Diamond was not rampaging around the office like some ludicrous fame monster.

The series producer was a woman called Alex Jackson-Long and we soon bonded in our loathing for Diamond. Despite this we had a show to make and we didn't want to disappoint the six thousand viewers that the show regularly attracted. This was the big time. One of the joys of having a *selective audience* (in the immortal words of Ian Faith, Spinal Tap's manager) was that nobody really cared what you got up to, so you could experiment to your heart's content. I came up with a character called Hey Hippo – essentially a purple hippo glove puppet that I turned into a budget Dennis Pennis (who was my big hero). Armed with the puppet and a cameraman called Stuart, I would scour a fax-sheet called *London at Large* that listed which celebs would be doing what that week in terms of signings and appearances. We would then go along, stand in a queue and wait for our turn for an interview.

The basic joke was that I would say hello to the celeb, show him the puppet as though embarrassed by my job and explain that Hey Hippo was a hugely popular children's character and would they mind just saying hello to him on screen? I would then adopt a weird Fozzie Bear-type voice and start the interview. It would normally go like this.

> Hey Hippo: 'Hey kids, I'm here with Bill Wowman who used to play in a big band about, like a hundred years ago. Hey Bill, say hello to the kids.'
> Bill Wyman: (awkwardly) 'Hello kids.'
> Hey Hippo: 'So, Bill, are you a big fan of mine?'
> Bill Wyman: 'Uuhhmm ... yes, sure I'm a huge fan.'
> Hey Hippo: 'Really!! You're a big fan, do you watch my show all the time?'
> Bill Wyman: 'Uuhhmm, yeah, I never miss your show.'
> Hey Hippo: 'Oh yeah! What channel is it on, Bill?'

There then followed a long awkward silence as Bill, or whomever I was talking to, would look around for their PR person to come and save them, the PR person that they paid specifically to keep people like me away. It never failed and I harassed an eclectic bunch of people from Billy Idol to Sir Steve Redgrave. Rod Stewart was my all-time favourite – he was just really lovely and unfazed by anything.

I discovered that Barry Manilow was booked to open the Harrods Sale. The plan was that he would get into a horse-drawn carriage at the Harrods Stables in a little square behind the store. Manilow would then be horse-drawn to meet 'fugging' Mohamed Al-Fayed and his adoring public. Stuart and I got to the square early and awaited our prey. About half an hour later another camera crew turned up. It was Dennis Pennis. There was now a little queue of people waiting to take the piss out of Barry Manilow. I'd met Paul Kaye, the man behind Dennis Pennis, when he'd used my roof to film a Pennis sequence in which he kicked a football over London. That was probably the exact moment that I realised what I wanted to do with my life.

An hour later and a carriage appeared from the stables with Manilow and a couple of Harrods flunkies ensconced within it. As we had got there first, prankster etiquette dictated that we kicked off proceedings. I chased after the carriage as it made its way round the square and thrust Hey Hippo into Manilow's face. I/Hey Hippo asked him whether he was a big fan. Manilow looked very confused but nodded and indicated that he never missed a show. I was then punched hard by a flunky and forced to give up the assault. This was the cue for Dennis Pennis to begin his attack. It was way funnier than mine. He simply ran after the generously nosed singer holding up a large white sheet: 'Mr Manilow, Mr Manilow – you've dropped your handkerchief . . .' It was one–nil to Pennis.

The worst moment of my Hey Hippo period was when I joined a queue of journalists to interview Jennifer Saunders, who was promoting a series of *Absolutely Fabulous*. As we waited, someone tugged on my sleeve. I turned around to see a girl that I'd known at university and that I had had a massive crush on. She was even more gorgeous now.

Girl: 'Hey, what are you doing here?'
Me: (lying my arse off as it was too 'complicated' to explain Hey Hippo) 'Oh, I'm interviewing Jennifer Saunders. I'm an entertainment journalist . . .'

Girl: 'Hey, weird, me too. Who do you work for?'
Me: 'Uuhhmm, the BBC.'
Girl: 'Wow, that's great. I'm with Reuters ...'
Me: 'Cool.'
Girl: 'What are you doing after this? Fancy a drink?'
Me: 'Sure ... Great ...'

I couldn't believe my luck. This total babe had just asked me out and I was working for the BBC. Life was good. Then I remembered that I didn't work for the BBC and I was about to talk to Jennifer Saunders using a purple glove puppet. It was a terrible habit of mine that I'd never been able to shake. I'd lie at the drop of a hat to avoid embarrassment and always end up in a complicated web of deceit from which I could never escape.

I decided to let the girl go first and made up some excuse about waiting for some lighting equipment to arrive. I hoped that she would do her interview and then not see me doing mine. Fat chance. I was halfway through asking a bemused Jennifer Saunders, in my weird voice, whether she was a fan when I spotted the girl staring at me. Her mouth was hanging open and not in a good way. When I finished I looked everywhere for her to explain that actually I was a cutting-edge punk comedian beaming to literally hundreds of people on a weekly basis ... but she'd scarpered.

There was a rather scary production manager at Paramount called Ping. After a couple of weeks of me doing Hey Hippo she approached me and said that we might have a trademark issue using the puppet. I told her not to worry, that I'd contacted the manufacturers and that they had said it was alright. This was complete bollocks and she knew it because she asked me what the name of the company was. I looked down and spotted the tag on the side that read Gund Toys.

'It's Gund Toys,' I told her confidently.

'Where are they based?' asked Ping.

'The UK ...' I replied.

'And who did you speak to there?' She wasn't letting go.

'Mr Gund ... I spoke to Mr Gund himself and he said it was fine ... no problem at all.' I smiled at Ping. Ping did not smile back but she did back off.

Alex Jackson-Long had been listening to the whole exchange and leant in.

'You are a bloody brilliant liar ...' I took this as a compliment.

From then on Mr Gund became my default alias whenever a fake name was needed for anything.

Man Made News rolled on with nobody very interested in it. We had a phone-in section of the show where viewers were supposed to ring in. Nobody rang in. Eventually I had to go into another room and use the office phone and pretend to be random members of the public. I had an Iraqi character who never understood anything that Diamond said and who wound him up terribly. We never told him that all the phone calls were fake. It would have been too cruel. When the series ended, the whole thing was quietly wound up. This was bad news for me as it meant that I would probably be getting my marching orders. I started filming as much stuff as I could before I lost access to equipment. I made a little series called *Snapshots* that mainly consisted of me dressed as a giant cat chasing Leigh Francis dressed as a giant mouse in and out of cheese shops in Central London. Nobody was very interested in these and I was getting desperate when salvation came in the form of a man called Dan Brooke.

Dan was from an advertising background and had been brought in to promote the Paramount Comedy Channel. He had the idea that, rather than use his budget to pay for advertising, he could finance me to do funny stuff that would get the channel publicity for what it was supposed to be – funny. He called me in. Could I get the channel into the news? Oh yes, I replied with the confidence of a man who had personally spoken to Mr Gund. 'Go and do it,' he said. So I did.

My first problem was that I couldn't afford a proper camera crew. It was prohibitively expensive for my kind of off-the-cuff, seat-of-the-pants filming. What I needed was a partner in crime. I went out for a celebratory drink with my then girlfriend Izzy at a pub called The Engineer in Primrose Hill. Izzy and I lived together in my flat in All Saints Road. We were pretty anti-social and didn't go out much. Her best friend was a girl called Dido, and she and her boyfriend Bob were regular guests to the flat. I knew that Dido was a backing singer in her brother Rollo's band Faithless but I never paid much heed to this. I dimly remember her playing a demo of her debut solo album one night but I think I rather rudely talked all over it. Then her song 'Thank You' was used on the end credits of the film *Sliding Doors*, Eminem heard it and the rest, as they say, is history. I shall long remember the hedonistic nights we all spent together – we'd play bridge and I'd cook meals from the *River Café Cookbook* – the very epitome of the crazy rock 'n' roll lifestyle that Dido went on to define.

Anyway, I met Izzy in the pub and I was buzzing, I couldn't stop talking. I had this amazing offer to go and film weird, funny stuff but I had this problem. I needed a cameraman. It was frustrating and I didn't know what to do. Suddenly, the barman, a long-haired, blond, rather intense-looking guy, leant over.

'I could do that,' he said, staring at me slightly threateningly.

'Sorry, do what?' I replied.

'The camera stuff. I could be the cameraman you need.' He was still staring manically and I had to break the gaze.

'Are you a cameraman?' I asked him.

'Oh yeah, I do it a lot and this sounds right up my street.' He looked very confident as he dried pint glasses. I had very few options.

'OK ... Do you want to come to Paramount Comedy Channel on Rathbone Place on Monday morning and we'll give it a go?' I had nothing to lose.

'Sure ... See you then. My name's Sam.'

Sam was Sam Cadman. He was an artist and had never used a camera before. In the best Gundian tradition, however, this was not going to get in his way. He borrowed a camera over the weekend, read the manual (a very Sam thing to do) and turned up on Monday morning ready to go. Where I was lazy and unfocused, Sam was hyper-motivated and organised and we soon discovered that we had a very similar sense of humour – very dry, slightly surreal. Dido would have approved – it was a *Sliding Doors* moment. Had I not gone to that pub, that night, everything in the last fifteen years would have been so different.

So now I had Sam, his camera and a radio mike ... but what to do? Paramount decided to air an interstitial (a telly word for the stuff between programmes) show called *World of Paramount*. Up until then, the channel showed a lot of US shows and didn't make much itself. Now we had a three-minute weekly slot. The year was 1997 and there was a general election in the offing – Tony Blair and New Labour were coming. So I set up a fake political party called The Teddy Bear Alliance and we used this as the basis for an anarchic election campaign in which we pestered everyone in sight. I organised two hundred teddy bears to march on Parliament brandishing signs with random slogans like 'Single European Honey' and 'Say No To Fleas' on them. We kidnapped the Tories' chicken mascot that was following Tony Blair around and I stood for election in Kensington & Chelsea against Alan Clark. The official in charge of the election really did not want me standing and ruining his big night. I was standing as Edward Bear and he said that, as it was not my real name, I was ineligible. So, off I went to some solicitors and changed my name to Edward Bear by deed poll. I never bothered to change it back so presumably my legal name is still Edward (Teddy) Bear.

We mainly targeted the Tories in the election as they were in power but I have no particular political affiliations. We were bipartisan nuisances. Once the election was over and New Labour swept into power, we knew who we had to go for. I had a copy of the famous *Vanity Fair* edition in which Patsy Kensit and Liam Gallagher lay in a Union Jack bed – 'London Swings Again' read the headline. Tony Blair was rebranding Britain as Cool Britannia. I'd always been anti on-trend stuff and so we targeted Cool Britannia. I called the project *War of the Flea*, after a book about guerrilla warfare by Robert Taber. It seemed to encapsulate just what I wanted to do.

War of the Flea – the guerrilla fights the war of the flea, and his military enemy suffers the dog's disadvantages: too much to defend; too small, ubiquitous, and agile an enemy to come to grips with.

My first target was Peter Mandelson, the oleaginous mastermind behind the New Labour project. Mandelson was known as a master of the Dark Arts and so I thought it might be fitting for him to have a large following in the underworld. *London at Large* informed us that Mandelson was due to attend the opening of some modern, trendy furniture shop in Tottenham Court Road that very week. This was only two minutes' walk from our offices. It was fate. We dressed up as Frankenstein's monster, the Grim Reaper, assorted vampires and the Devil himself. Then we booked a paparazzo to turn up and take the pictures. There was no point in doing a publicity stunt without documenting the thing properly and you couldn't rely on someone else capturing it.

It all went too well. Mandelson turned up on time and was greeted by us like a fifth Beatle. He looked most confused and fled into the store. We tried to follow him in but were prevented by security. We then pressed ourselves up against the shop windows screaming our appreciation of him like maniacal teenybopper fans. When he eventually exited we threw black confetti at his feet and all tried to hug him. The money shot was the moment he got back into his chauffeur-driven Jag and he froze at the door surrounded by this chaos. The following morning the photograph was on the front page of the *Guardian* and the Paramount Comedy Channel was credited as being responsible.

We'd hit a rich seam with Mandelson as all the newspapers hated him and longed for anything to splash on him. I found out where he lived by going through every name in the Kensington & Chelsea electoral register. It took me ages and I couldn't find it until I eventually checked the Westminster roll and found him. The house itself was the one that would later get him into trouble because he purchased it using an interest-free loan from a political colleague. We arrived early one morning and planted a mock Millennium Dome in his front garden. This made the headlines again. We were on a roll. Next, I had a thirty-foot statue of Mandelson made and we erected it overnight on College Green in front of Parliament before twelve of us carried it through London's Trafalgar Square and then tried to donate it to Mandelson's Millennium Dome Exhibition.

The number of people who watched our little episodes was tiny but they were quite influential. I met Noel Gallagher a couple of years later and he told me that he and Liam used to avidly watch our stuff. We'd had a go at Liam. He'd been arrested after the Q Awards for possession of cocaine following a night out on the town. We hired a really good lookalike and took him round all the places Liam had been the night before.

We made him go in and apologise to confused receptionists and embarrassed owners for his behaviour. His final line was always: 'You didn't find any talcum powder here, did you? I left it somewhere . . .'

Liam had also challenged Mick Jagger to a fight in an interview and so we turned up at his North London house with thirty people wearing Mick Jagger masks and demanded that he come out and have a scrap. To our delight, he told us to 'foook off' on the intercom.

One day we came into work to find that the new leader of the Conservative Party, William Hague, was having his stag party at the Carlton Club in Mayfair. We quickly organised some strippers and got to the event in time to bum-rush Hague as he arrived. All we had to do was turn up at a news event and do something funny and the national news outlets would lap it up. It didn't matter if they knew why or what you were doing it for. I once chased Jeffrey Archer down the road dressed as a gorilla and throwing bananas at him. The redoubtable BBC (now *Channel 4 News*) reporter Michael Crick chased me, having filmed the incident. He demanded to know who we were in his rather pompous manner. I didn't reply and he got increasingly irritated.

'If you don't tell me, then I won't use the clip on my report.'

I continued to ignore him and hurled one last banana at a retreating Archer before hopping into the back of our vehicle and disappearing. The clip of our attack ran in full on *Newsnight* that evening with little explanation.

One day, Sam and I were walking down the Edgware Road in London when we saw a big display outside a mobile phone shop. One of the objects in the display was a two-and-a-half-foot plastic mobile phone. Larking about, I picked it up and told Sam that I should use this as my new mobile. He laughed and I walked off still holding it in my hands. The shop owner ran out and started chasing us, the thieves of his big plastic display phone. We both scarpered, running as fast as we could while carrying our stupidly heavy booty. Eventually we hopped on a bus and made good our escape.

We hopped off at the top of Soho Square. It was pub time but, as we walked down Oxford Street, we spotted the larger than life (media code for fat) Australian DJ Jono Coleman being interviewed by a camera crew. Coleman was jabbering on and I just acted instinctively. I got in the shot behind him, raised the big mobile to my ear and started shouting into it. 'HELLO!! WHAT?! I CAN'T HEAR YOU BECAUSE THAT ARSE JONO COLEMAN IS TALKING TOO LOUDLY ...'

It stopped traffic. Everyone on the pavement stopped and laughed. Jono Coleman stopped mid-flow and stared on in confusion, as did his camera crew. I continued: 'THAT'S BETTER. I CAN HEAR YOU NOW. THE ARSE HAS STOPPED TALKING ... NO, I'M ON THE MOBILE, IN OXFORD STREET ...'

I wandered away from Coleman down the street, with Sam hooting with laughter and following me. The Big Mobile was born, although we wouldn't actually use it again for a while.

As far as I remember we vaguely tried to theme every *War of the Flea* show.

- We had **Politics**: which mainly consisted of harassing Mandelson.
- We had **Music:** I went down to Piltdown Farm in Glastonbury and interviewed Michael Eavis while dressed as an idiot DJ. I kept namechecking classic Glastonbury sets by fictional bands – 'Loaded Manchobo ... what a performance ...' Poor old Michael Eavis could only nod and agree with my increasingly odd memories.
- We had **Food**: celebrity chefs were the new black. I gatecrashed Michelin restaurants dressed as a Michelin Man.

'You look after me, I'll look after you – you get my drift?'
I once said to an appalled Michel Roux while subtly
showing him a star hidden inside my jacket. It was
during an interview with Antony Worrall Thompson that
I started my habit of just running away in the middle of
celebrity interviews. Originally, it was just because I'd
had enough and wanted to escape. What I enjoyed was
listening to the tape of Sam pretending to be a freelance
and ringing a fictitious office to complain about my
behaviour. 'I don't know. I turned up and then he started
acting oddly. Then he went crazy and ran away. It's all
very embarrassing and incredibly unprofessional . . .'

- We had **Technology**: in which we set up gold email
  boxes next to real post boxes and rang Sir Clive Sinclair
  pretending to be Bill Gates, challenging him to a game of
  Tetris.
- We had **Art**: in which we got the artists Gilbert & George
  to autograph a plastic turd. We then travelled to Paris
  and placed said turd in the middle of their exhibition in
  the French capital. It caused quite the sensation and
  people gawped at it for a good couple of hours until the
  authorities removed it.

Everyone we showed the mini-series to seemed to like it. We
couldn't wait to show it to the powers-that-be at Paramount. A
new American guy had come over from the States and had
pretty much taken over the channel. He was the man we had to
present the series to. Confidence was high when he finally came
down to the edit for a viewing. Confidence drooped rapidly,
however. We screened show after show without even a hint of a
chuckle from the Yank. He just sat there looking bored and
pissed off. When it was over he said, 'Thanks, guys, good stuff,
we'll talk soon,' and left the edit.

We knew things hadn't gone well but couldn't guess just how badly. A couple of days later we got a call from someone else we knew at Paramount who called us into their office. The American, it turned out, had hated the whole thing, said it looked 'cheap' and was terrified about lawsuits and legal problems.

'You guys have got all the release forms and stuff you need for everybody in the series, right?' he asked, staring at us as you might at someone who had recently shat on your lawn.

We looked dumbfounded. This was the first time anybody had ever even mentioned release forms or needing any form of legal consent from anybody. We were comedy cowboys. We were punk comedians. We were … buggered.

It was announced the next day that *War of the Flea* would never be shown on Paramount … I can't remember what we did next. I know we smuggled all the tapes out of Paramount but it was then a downward spiral that involved me going to the pub a lot and Sam rearranging his entire CD collection into alphabetical order. I would now have to get a proper job that I hated, and life would return to hideous normality.

We'd had a friend of Myfanwy Moore, Gary Reich, nominally producing *War of the Flea* for us. I say nominally, because we mostly just buggered off and did our own thing without telling anybody. Gary was our grown-up link to everyone else.

Anyhow, Gary got us to write up a document pitching a full-length series of *War of the Flea.* He wanted to take it to Channel 4 along with the master tapes of the series that we had smuggled out of Paramount after the nasty American had tried to seize everything. We were shocked. Channel 4? That was a proper channel, with proper viewers … Gary was insistent. He told us about the *Comedy Lab,* in which they wanted new people to make sample shows for them. So off he went. I went back to the pub and Sam started reordering his CDs again, this time by album cover colour. Two weeks later we got a call from Channel 4. They wanted to see us.

We arrived at Channel 4 in Horseferry Road and were ushered into a room to meet a woman called Caroline Leddy. Caroline came straight to the point. She liked our stuff but was worried about taking on another programme that annoyed the establishment. She'd just finished dealing with the multifarious legal fall-outs from Chris Morris's *Brass Eye* and she couldn't face the idea of going through something like that all over again.

'Couldn't you do something simpler, just funny with no agenda?' she asked pleadingly.

I thought about this for a second. I could see no downside. The things that really made me laugh were pointless, stupid, silly, surreal . . . just what Caroline Leddy was asking for. So we agreed and she commissioned a *Comedy Lab*.

We walked out of Channel 4 trying to look cool. The moment we rounded the corner, however, we both went mental. We were going to be on the telly – proper telly, with actual viewers and everything. How the hell had we managed this? Whatever, we were off.

Chapter 2

Trigger Happy TV (Red)

We had a show to make, but nowhere to make it. I rang Alex Jackson-Long, who was now working at a production company called Absolutely, made up of all the ex-members of the surreal Scottish sketch show of the same name ('Stoneybridge!!') and it was immediately clear to me that:

They seemed a nice friendly bunch.

We had no other option.

We met the head of the company, Miles Bullough. We said: 'We've got a show commissioned at Channel 4, fancy making it with us?'

Unsurprisingly, he said yes and we were given an office on the eighth floor of their premises in Alhambra House on Charing Cross Road. It was built on the site of the old Alhambra Theatre, a place where the Marx Brothers had made their first UK appearance. I liked this fact a lot.

For the *Comedy Lab*, we tried to mix up all the different sorts of stuff we'd been filming at Paramount. The big mobile made its first proper appearance in the library of Imperial College

London. For some reason, I was wearing a really bad fake beard. I think I wanted him to be a 'character', but like anything else with a theme it was soon dropped. We started the *Comedy Lab* with me interviewing a bemused Irvine Welsh outside a night-club in Shoreditch, during which I proceeded to pretend to be suffering from an excessive intake of Ecstasy and collapsed mid-interview. I think, even then, we were keen to differentiate our hidden camera from the 'Beadle' model.

There was a great scene with me dressed as a Womble, wandering around Wimbledon Common, muttering to myself and chucking rubbish around. The idea of a Womble on the verge of a nervous breakdown really made me laugh. We used several fluffy costumes in the show and this became a bit of a trade-mark. Among these were the fighting dogs, a Dalmatian and a brown dog always beating each other up in public. In the edit I made these slo-mo and overlaid them with big, gorgeous, sad tunes.

The original idea was that there were so many CCTV cameras around London, and I wondered who actually monitored them? I thought it would be funny to set up these surreal scenes of vio-lence right under the camera. The idea of someone checking the screens and spotting the dog violence amused me. We'd start the shot on the CCTV camera and then pan down to the action but we cut this in the edit, as it wasn't relevant. Anything that was thematic or tried to make a point was soon jettisoned. There was only one intention in *Trigger Happy TV*: make it funny and occasionally beautiful.

With the *Comedy Lab* finished and edited, we handed it into Channel 4. A couple of months later we got an invite to attend the series press launch in Wardour Street. Sam and I went along nervously, not quite sure what to expect. Nobody paid any attention to us. Everybody was interested in this larger than life

Northerner called Peter Kay. He seemed rather full of himself and I've certainly never heard of him since . . .

Sam and I felt awkward and quickly slipped away into the night.

We only got one review. It was in the *NME* and it was rather good. The writer (a certain Mr Danny Wallace) was very nice and ended his review with the words:

'The church of *Trigger Happy TV* will grow and grow . . .' Sam and I were chuffed and bought several copies. Then . . . nothing. The show went out on, I think, a Wednesday night, and a couple of people I knew saw it, but it was not quite the great event I'd been anticipating.

Our main worry, I seem to remember, was that the elderly astronomer Sir Patrick Moore, whom I'd 'interviewed' at the end of the show, might die before it went out and we'd have to scrap the whole thing. We needn't have worried – it turned out that Moore was tougher than he looked and survived for many more years. Absolutely were making *The Jack Docherty Show* in a theatre just beside Trafalgar Square. We used to try and pinch their guests as they went in or out to use them for our nefarious purposes. We'd grabbed Sir Patrick and taken him into the square to interview him. I was asking him about the possibility of being hit by an asteroid whilst I kept looking up at the sky nervously. As he was in mid-answer I pretended to spot something, dropped the mike and sprinted away, before diving into one of the fountains as the credits rolled. Sir Patrick looked on bemused and befuddled. It was the *Trigger Happy TV* house style: if in doubt, run away . . . or fall down.

We were hoping that we might now get a full series. We made enquiries at Channel 4 but there didn't seem to be much of a hurry to make a decision. Channel 4 were putting together their attempt at a sort of *Saturday Night Live* show called *The 11 O'Clock Show* and Caroline Leddy told me that it would be very good 'politically' if we did something on it. I turned up for an ideas meeting – it was packed full of people like Sacha Baron Cohen, Marcus Brigstocke, Harry Thompson (legendary comedy producer), Francis Wheen, Ian Lee ... Everyone doing anything was there and as usual I felt very out of place – imposter syndrome again. The problem was that Sam and I were not very clubbable types. We didn't want to be in a gang. We wanted to be on our own, with no bosses and no hassle. We were realistic enough to realise that we had to play ball, however, so I suggested that with my political past, I go down to the party political conferences and take the piss. This was approved and we were put under the command of a strange, nerdy-looking bloke called Andrew Newman, who couldn't stop telling us that he'd worked with Chris Morris.

Off we went with a very young assistant producer called Damon Beesley (later to be a co-writer of *The Inbetweeners*). He had a list of jokes that Andrew Newman wanted us to do down at the conferences that I had no interest in doing whatsoever. We got to Brighton for the Tory conference. I was wearing my Westminster suit that I'd discarded after the interview for *The Mark Thomas Comedy Product*. It made me look the part of a political reporter. Damon Beesley wanted Sam to film me on the beach doing an intro piece to camera. We stood there and did a couple but they were a little boring and I could see that Sam felt the same. After the fourth attempt I stopped and had a chat with Sam.

'I'm just going to try something, Damon,' I shouted as I ran towards the sea.

'What are you doing?' he screamed but it was too late. I had dived into the cold waves and was swimming out to sea. Sam was still filming. I got to about fifty feet offshore and then started swimming back in. When I got to the pebbly beach I scrambled to my feet and approached the camera. I did a piece to camera announcing that I'd just swum to the conference:

'So ... Let's go see what's happening.' I walked out of shot and Sam cut.

Damon put his head in his hands but Sam couldn't stop laughing. I proceeded to try and interview ministers and MPs at the conference in a professional and serious manner but they couldn't concentrate with me, soaking wet, bedraggled and shivering.

'What on earth happened to you?' they'd ask.

'Don't worry about me. I fell off the pier, but I'm a professional. You're the important one here.'

It put them all off and made for some fabulously uncomfortable interviews. Sam and I even managed to get a chat with William Hague, the then Tory leader.

'Are you not worried that all Young Tories are ridiculously nerdy weirdos?' I asked Hague.

'You should be in bed with a cup of hot chocolate,' said Hague kindly.

'Don't worry about me, I'm a professional, you're the important one here ...' Hague looked horrified and was whisked away by a concerned-looking Sebastian Coe.

We overheard Damon on a phone call to Andrew Newman.

'They're just pissing about, he's soaking wet.' He then came up to us and said that Andrew Newman had an idea he wanted us to do. Damon was going to get hold of some hula hoops and we were to find out whether we could get MPs to jump through hoops. I told Damon that this was a terrible idea and not funny. He replied that this was what Andrew Newman wanted. I refused.

That was the end of our *11 O'Clock Show* work. At the back of my mind I worried that I had blown our chances with Channel 4 for a *Trigger Happy* series, but there was nothing we could do.

Then it all got worse when the show contacted Sam on his own to go and film something with Marcus Brigstocke. I was a bit jealous – I sort of considered us a team and didn't like the idea of him doing stuff with other people. Being British, Sam and I could never really communicate things like this so I sulked and he went off to film at a Test match. The idea was that Marcus was going to run onto the pitch dressed as a toucan. Marcus smuggled the suit in, plucked up both his feathers and his courage and stormed the pitch, flapping his wings, and promptly got ejected from the ground. To my secret joy and Sam's mortification, when they viewed the footage something had gone wrong and all they got was colour bars. He wasn't asked again. I was delighted. We were comedy outcasts together.

Neither Sam nor I had done comedy the 'normal' way, whatever that was – no stand-up, no Footlights, no writing jokes for others, no Radio 4 stuff. We just appeared out of nowhere and people didn't like it. We didn't care. As long as we had enough money to go out and muck about, everything was hunky-dory. The lure of a proper series on Channel 4, however, loomed at the back of our minds. We now both wanted it so badly but didn't dare think too hard about it.

Meanwhile, we needed some money. We got a call from an advertising agency. They were representing Peperami, the angry sausage snack. They'd seen our stuff on Paramount and wondered whether we would do some work with them. We couldn't resist. The 1998 World Cup was about to be held in France and seemed an obvious target. Both Sam and I loathed football but we knew that the demand for stories around the tournament would be perfect. We found out that Hoddle was to name his squad in a live press conference, from a plush five-star resort in Spain called La Manga, in three days' time. We decided to use an idea that we'd had for ages but never done. At press conferences there was always a cluster of microphones on the table in front of the speaker. These always had little boxes wrapped around them with the names of whatever news organisation they represented. We had an oversized box made, about three times the usual size, with the Peperami logo on it. We then hopped on a plane to Alicante and drove off in search of La Manga.

When we got there, it was certainly impressive but seemed to be mainly geared towards golf – most of the England team could be seen playing as we drove in. I knew and cared little about football but I was pretty sure that playing golf was not the best preparation for the game, but hey, who was I to argue with Hoddle? The press conference was scheduled to take place on the terrace overlooking one of the golf courses. We got there early and sat in the front row, right in front of the table where Hoddle was to sit. Two hours later and the place began to fill up with sports reporters. There was clearly a pecking order as to who sat where and we got some dirty looks from crusty old hacks who assumed we were locals. We sat firm in our prime position and didn't move. More and more microphones were placed on the table and it started to fill up. I didn't want to place ours too early in case it got moved, so I waited until Hoddle and David Davies, the then head of the FA, strode out onto the terrace. I then plonked the mike dead-centre on the table. It was a ludicrous size and stupidly prominent but nobody did anything. Suddenly we realised that we were live on every news channel with this curious box taking up much of the screen. We got a bonus when Hoddle announced that he wouldn't be picking Gazza for the team. This made international headlines and got much more exposure for our box than we had anticipated. I got another bonus when David Davies pointed at me during the Q&A session and said:

'The gentleman from Peperami TV?'

I busked it and suggested that Gazza had been dropped because of one too many kebabs? If he had kept to a strict diet of Peperami he would be fighting fit?

Everyone laughed but you could see in Davies's panicky eyes that he had marked us out as ne'er-do-wells. We legged it out after the press conference. On the drive back to Alicante we got a call from the ad agency back in London. They were over the moon.

Two weeks later we broke into Bisham Abbey, the England team training ground, and barged our way through a practice session dressed as the Peperami sausage. It was all over the papers next day:

Angry Sausage Breaches England Security . . .

The ad agency later won advertising campaign of the year but we weren't invited to the ceremony. This was probably for the best as, experience would later show, ceremonies and me didn't mix too well.

We finally heard from Channel 4. *Trigger Happy TV* was a go. We had a full series: six half-hours of telly to make. For the second time in a year, Sam and I walked out of Channel 4 trying to look cool and were once again unsuccessful. After the euphoria came the reality. What the hell were we going to fill six half-hours of telly with? It all felt rather terrifying so we went to the pub, a place where many a good idea often appeared. It was a long night in the Cock and Bottle in Notting Hill Gate.

The following week, we turned up at Absolutely ready to start work. A normal comedy show would allocate a certain amount of time within which to film – essentially, however much time you could afford to hire professional camera and sound people for. Whatever you filmed in that period was what you then made into the final show. We had the luxury of being cheap. We bought two cameras and leased them back to the production along with a couple of radio mikes. We could pretty much keep filming until we had what we needed. This was a dangerous thing to happen, especially for someone as naturally lazy as myself. A normal production might look at the coming month and block out what was needed to film on every day. This would give everyone time to plan the shoot, clear and recce locations, get props, costumes ... We were naive idiots and didn't do anything like that. We were very disorganised. Maybe that was why it worked?

An average day in the *Trigger Happy TV* office would be: Sam and I would arrive on our Vespas (urban twats) and sit around in the office for half an hour, having coffee and laughing about stuff we'd done the night before. Then we'd start thinking about what we were going to do that day. I might have an idea about doing something as a traffic warden. We'd then call a couple of costume places. The largest, Angels and Bermans, were always a bit full of themselves. They wanted us to book in an appointment with a 'fitter'. We were too impatient for this type of thing. We didn't want a 'costume', we just wanted something that looked official. It didn't even matter if it looked a bit crap. We eventually found this little place in Camden High Street called Escapade. It did costumes and fancy dress for parties. It was perfect and we got pretty much everything from there, which sometimes gave us problems. We used their two dog costumes for the fighting dog sketches. In hindsight we should have bought them but we didn't. So often, when we needed them they were rented out. Even worse, sometimes we would get them only to find that the last renter had drunk too much the night before and clearly thrown up into the head ...

Anyway, we would drive up to Escapade in our Toyota Previa, the most essential component in our team. It had tinted windows and we would use it as a mobile film hide. Having selected the costume we would then argue about where to film. Normally it would be somewhere in West London where Sam and I lived, or somewhere in Soho near the office. By the time we had decided and got to the location it was usually lunchtime so we would all decamp for an hour. One of the big rules of filming was not to have lunch, as you really didn't feel like doing much in the afternoon.

We did a lot of the first series near the office. I hated traffic wardens. To me, the sign of a decent country was one where you could park anywhere you liked without finding yourself the main source of revenue for the local council. I loathed the way they wielded their silly powers with such intensity and seriousness. It was a hilarious dynamic to watch: people sucking up to them to avoid a ticket but then turning mental if this didn't work.

We rented a decent uniform but it came with an antiquated ticket machine that looked like it was from the 1920s, so we made our own one. It looked more like a toaster than a ticket machine but just turning it on would terrify motorists and grant us total command of a street. I'd step out of the office onto Charing Cross Road and I became the Terminator. We hadn't even decided where we were going to film yet. We were just going to wander off into Soho and get started, but I simply wasn't prepared for the hellish life that is being a London traffic warden. About ten seconds onto the street two different drivers had run up to me and pointed to their cars, saying they were just there for twenty seconds and that it was a medical emergency. Even they knew this was a weak excuse, but I just smiled and said:

'Sure, park as long as you like, it sounds really important ...' The look of confusion and uncertainty on their faces was a picture. I walked on, smiling.

Passers-by didn't like a traffic warden smiling. I quickly became aware of an undercurrent of abuse floating around me like a foul cloud as I walked:

'Wanker, get a proper job, you fucker, lowlife, shitface, arsehole ...' It was non-stop and from all walks of life. One very well-dressed old man stopped as I walked by and said: 'You really are a fucking horrible human specimen, aren't you? If I had a gun I'd kill you here and now ...', all in a gloriously posh voice.

I was starting to fear for the mental health situation of traffic wardens. I hadn't realised that things were that bad. I'd discovered that their headquarters was through an anonymous-looking door in Lexington Street, and Sam and I had toyed with the idea of supergluing their locks and blocking them in their office. Now this just seemed mean. I was now ahead of Sam and the others and walked onto Old Compton Street. There was a fire engine in the middle of the road and firemen were unravelling a long hose and running into a nearby building. I didn't hesitate. I pulled out a fake ticket and slapped it onto the windscreen of the fire engine. Passers-by and firemen looked on in disbelief. Finally the lead fireman came up to me:

'What the hell do you think you're doing?' he asked.

'You are parked illegally, so I have issued you with a ticket,' I replied in a monotone.

'This is a bloody fire engine, we're putting out a fire ...' gasped the stupefied fireman.

'There's always an excuse ...' I said, wandering off, '... and if you're still here when I come back I'll get the clampers in ...' I was half-expecting to be hit hard on the back of the head with a fireman's axe but he was too astonished to do anything.

As per usual with *Trigger Happy TV* we hadn't filmed this moment. It had been off the cuff and unplanned – Sam and I called these moments: *for the beauty*. They were just for our delectation and amusement. It had certainly proved that we had a winning character on our hands, though. I spent the rest of the day giving tickets to people waiting at traffic lights, cars stuck in traffic jams and buses at bus stops. The reactions of most motorists were genius. They hated traffic wardens so much, and for once were so certain that they were in the right, that they argued in a most un-British manner and were not going to stop until the matter went to the European Supreme Court. My last hit of the day was hailing a black cab and then giving him a ticket when he stopped to pick me up. I thought the cabbie was going to have a seizure.

On my way back to the office I was summoned over to a large Bentley. The driver told me that he had Sir John Mills in the back and that he was waiting to go into a meeting so could he stay where he was for five minutes? I asked for verification that it was Sir John Mills. The back window rolled down and the old thespian himself smiled at me. I saluted and thanked Sir John for all he had done for his country against the 'filthy Nazis' and told him that he had special dispensation to stay here all day should he have nowhere to go. Sir John looked a little puzzled but smiled benignly back and rolled up his window. I was glad to have been of service.

Another successful character was the spy. This was myself dressed up in a trench coat and a hat, carrying a briefcase and looking not unlike Inspector Gadget, approaching people as though to make some prearranged exchange. I would sidle up to someone feeding the ducks at the Round Pond in Hyde Park and whisper: 'The cows fly backwards over my house ... you have the package?' At first they would be startled and then terrified as they realised what they were implicated in. They would stammer that I had the wrong person and I would get all apologetic and hurry away while they stood staring after me.

We were always on the lookout for new places to film and I'd spotted a little park off the Embankment. As usual, the Previa parked up on the road behind a row of benches just inside the park. Sam then snuck inside and took up his camera position. When we were ready, I wandered in and chose a bench on which sat a man in a suit, eating a sandwich. I waited for a moment before sliding the briefcase along the bench to him. He looked at me quizzically. I indicated that he should take the briefcase. He looked utterly terrified.

'The wind on the tundra is cold at this time of year, yes?' I looked at him but he was up and gone in an instant. I shrugged my shoulders at Sam and we prepared to go again. I exited the park and waited for someone else to sit on one of the benches. Five minutes later, I was on my way in for another hit when two men grabbed me and pinned me to the ground. I couldn't understand what was happening? All was soon revealed.

The park we had chosen was right behind the Ministry of Defence. Most of the people in the park were employees of said ministry having their lunch. The sudden arrival of an unsubtle Soviet spy in their midst had caused quite some kerfuffle and the gentlemen pinning me to the ground were special security from the ministry who had been alerted by the first guy I had spoken to, a senior official who thought he was being 'turned'. It took a lot of explaining to get out of that situation. We were lucky not to have been arrested, but the situation was so ludicrous that in the end we were given a stern ticking-off and sent on our way.

As we were so inexpensive we just filmed and filmed. Days ran into weeks, and weeks ran into months. I started to get tired, very tired. I think it was partly from the unusual adrenaline peaks and troughs of this sort of filming. I really enjoyed doing it, but it takes nerve to approach strangers on the street and interact while trying to comedically control the situation. Often it just wasn't funny, or the radio mike would break or someone wouldn't sign the consent form (we always had to get consent from people involved in a hit). This would be the most frustrating part – you got an incredible moment and then the person involved wouldn't sign. I didn't blame them – I don't think I would ever sign a consent form – but it was heartbreaking, as you knew that you wouldn't get another one that good ever again.

Things were also getting a bit rocky at home. I had split up with my girlfriend Izzy after two years together and she'd moved out of my flat in Notting Hill. The one thing I've learned in show business in the last fifteen years is that there are two important parts of your life: work and home. It is very difficult to do one if the other is up in the air. I wasn't aware of this then. I was young and stupid, and things were falling apart fast.

We had taken a week's break in filming and I had gone off to Morocco for a road trip. It was supposed to have been with Izzy but I was now driving through Morocco for hours and hours just thinking about stuff, and this was not good for me. I came back home early. I'd lent my flat out to an old friend, Johnny, who was very surprised to see me back. He had taken the opportunity of having my flat for a week to organise a series of dinner parties. He rapidly tried to cancel these but people were constantly ringing the doorbell. Johnny rang me up the next day when I was in the bath. He could hear I was in a bad way and urged me to join him at an Italian restaurant in Notting Hill Gate, where he had rescheduled one of his dinner parties. I said no, I wasn't up to it, but he persisted and I eventually agreed. I sat next to a rather gorgeous Canadian girl, who made me feel a lot better about things. I thought I'd played it quite cool but, according to her, I ruined things by driving away on an old blue Vespa that 'made you look ridiculous'.

I saw Johnny the following night and the Canadian was there again. We all ended up going to the Cobden Club in Notting Hill. There were too many people about so I asked the Canadian whether she wanted to go for a drink with me somewhere else. She agreed, and I said I'd wait outside for her. Half an hour later and she hadn't come out. I was about to head home when I plucked up some courage and went back in. This time she came out with me and we ended up in the bar of the Hilton at the end of Holland Park Avenue. The only other person in the bar was ex-footballer Ally McCoist, who sat and stared at us disconcertingly. The Canadian said that she was going off on a day trip the following day. She asked me whether I'd like to join her. I drunkenly agreed, but then forgot all about it. The following morning, I got a phone call from her: was I coming?

I tried to shake off my hangover and met her at a train station. It turned out that we had a ticket to Rye. Now, I had no idea whether Rye was a dump or a nice place? She worked at the *Sunday Times* and had asked some of the 'boys' on the sports desk where she should go in the UK. They'd suggested Rye. I groaned inwardly. If I'd been one of those 'boys' and a trusting Canadian blonde had asked me where to go, I'd have sent her to the ugliest place I knew for a laugh. I was now convinced that Rye was going to be a nightmare. As it turned out, Rye was OK – the 'boys' weren't as nasty as I was. The place was a little odd in that it had all the trappings of a seaside town except that the sea had decided to retreat about three hundred years ago, leaving the town high and dry. We spent the whole day there, wandering around aimlessly with me wondering how to make a move without being rebuffed. I still hadn't when we returned to London and went out for dinner.

I must have finally plucked up the courage, as the Canadian was called Stacey and, six months later to the day, I asked her to marry me. It was the best decision I ever made.

So, I was now in a new relationship with my beautiful Canadian, but I still wasn't in the best mental state. I was worried that this new relationship wouldn't work out and I was back at work with the break having done me no good whatsoever. If anything it had stressed me out more. I was a mess. Things finally came to a head just round the corner from Sloane Square tube station. I was filming stuff while dressed as a ludicrous

Dutch tourist. I was wearing shorts, a red mac and a tall Union Jack hat. The joke involved me just approaching people and asking nonsensical questions using a dodgy phrase book. Weirdly, it was a funny one and plenty of it made it to the final series. I stopped a black cab and confused him with my questions, before hopping into the back seat despite his protestations and announcing in a thick Dutch accent: 'My egg must be boiled ...'

When I got out, my brain was boiled ... I walked over to Sam in a panicky daze. I was having a massive anxiety attack. I'd had them before in my year off after school and a couple of times since in my twenties, but I couldn't believe that it was happening to me now. It was a difficult experience to describe, a sort of floaty feeling, almost a disassociation with reality, an out-of-body experience. It was like having a really bad, paranoid trip but without having taken any drugs. Mental illness is a country so hard to describe to those who haven't travelled there.

It was frightening and I just wanted to get away, to run away and hide in my flat where I felt safe. I told Sam that I had to go. He looked at me as though I was mad. We were on a roll, getting funny stuff and, whereas I was inherently lazy, Sam was a borderline OCD workaholic and wanted to crack on.

'I have to go, Sam ... Sorry ...' And go I did.

I went home and didn't get out of bed for days. I couldn't talk to anyone. Everything was spinning out of control. I was waging a vicious personal battle for domination of my head – all this in the middle of production.

Soon, Absolutely knew that something was amiss and that I wasn't just ill. I was dispatched to a Harley Street doctor with a clinic that looked more like a Renaissance brothel than somewhere medical. I tried to explain what I was going through. I told him about my previous panic attacks and used very inadequate descriptions like: 'It's like this invisible band is tightening around my head ...' I was trying desperately to hang onto something – sanity, control, whatever – but it felt like if I were to let go then I would fall into some bottomless abyss from which I'd never return. It was utterly terrifying. The doctor listened to my ramblings, asked me some questions about my state of mind and then announced confidently that I was suffering from clinical depression and that I should be immediately hospitalised.

Trust me, there is nothing guaranteed to depress you more than being diagnosed as having clinical depression. The doctor wanted me to check into his special hospital, but the very idea of it freaked me out more – I just wanted to go home and hide from the world, not check into the cuckoo's nest. Eventually he stopped trying to insist that I enter hospital and prescribed me some pills, something called paroxetine (Seroxat), a cousin of the new wonder drug Prozac and a member of the SSRI family. In simplistic terms, they increase the extracellular level of the neurotransmitter serotonin by inhibiting its reuptake into the presynaptic cell, thereby increasing the level of serotonin in the synaptic cleft available to bind to the postsynaptic receptor. More scientifically speaking: I had low serotonin levels and these pills upped said levels and should make me feel better.

I really didn't want to take any pills, but having looked at the list of possible side effects ...

- nausea/vomiting
- drowsiness or somnolence
- headache (very common as a short-term side effect)
- bruxism (teeth grinding)
- extremely vivid or strange dreams
- dizziness
- mydriasis (pupil dilation)
- changes in appetite
- insomnia and/or changes in sleep

- excessive diarrhoea
- weight loss/gain (measured by a change in body weight of 7 pounds)
- increased risk of bone fractures by 1.7 fold
- changes in sexual behaviour
- increased feelings of depression and anxiety (may provoke panic attacks)
- mania
- tremors
- autonomic dysfunction including orthostatic hypotension, increased or reduced sweating
- akathisia (agitation or distress)
- suicidal ideation (thoughts of suicide)
- photosensitivity
- paraesthesia (pins and needles)
- cognitive disorders

... there seemed little to worry about. Even the faint hope that some wonder pill could make me feel better was enough for me to give it a go. Not only that, but *Trigger Happy TV* production had ground to a halt while people were still being paid. The insurance company had been informed and they certainly weren't going to keep this unknown quantity of a production in limbo forever. This panicked me even more. Had I got this far, got my own TV show, only to have some bloody anxiety disorder screw it all up? I couldn't sleep and this in turn got me more and more worried. I'd go through every possible outcome in my head and each ended badly. The doctor had said that the paroxetine would take a bit of time to kick in – I wasn't sure if I had the time. I was also very doubtful it would work at all.

Two weeks passed and I was getting worse, as was the news from the production office, who said that they had been given a deadline: one more week and then the entire production would have to be cancelled. To make matters worse, I could see that Stacey, my new girlfriend and a woman who very much worked on the 'pull your socks up' life philosophy, was also starting to wonder just what the hell she had got herself into. I started to imagine Sam and everyone else on the team sitting around, gossiping about me and all agreeing that they'd always known I was a freak, a nutter, unstable, homicidal: 'Always something not quite right about him . . .' Mental illness leaves you not only paranoid but ashamed. This is ludicrous, but it's how it is. I hope it changes.

As it turned out, I found out later from Sam that they had spent the 'down time' filming a music video for some indie band on Camber Sands and then did somebody's wedding video. Apparently they'd had a brilliant time. It was heartening to know that my mental breakdown had provided positive opportunities for someone.

Then, just as all seemed lost, I woke up one morning feeling a tiny, little bit better. I couldn't put my finger on it. I don't know if it was the paroxetine or not. I don't know if I would have got better anyway. All I knew was that things seemed a little brighter, there was a tiny chink of light at the end of a long, scary tunnel. I had four days until the insurance deadline. The following day and things improved again slightly. The day after that, I felt almost normal. On the insurance decision day . . . I went into work. I still felt different but I could just about cope.

It had been a seriously tight-run thing. I dread to think what would have happened had I not got better. I never talked about it at the time, because the press instantly labels you under the 'mental health nutter' banner and it comes up in every interview you do and starts to define you. It's criminal that the stigma around the issue prevents so many people from talking about it, especially as it's rare to meet anyone in showbiz who hasn't suffered from it. I read about Matt Johnson, the lead singer of The The, when I was having anxiety attacks in my youth. He talked about having the same sort of thing and it really helped me to know this. I thought, if he could make an album like *Infected* then all was not lost, I could do something too. Having something like this *is* a weakness, just as is a heart condition or a dodgy hip. It's an Achilles heel that hits you when you least expect it. But I think it makes me stronger. If I can defeat stuff going on in my own head then I can take on anything that the big, bad world throws at me. I strongly believe that a touch of madness is necessary for good comedy. I've stayed on paroxetine ever since. I've not wanted to wean myself off it as there appear to be very few downsides and I haven't had any serious issues since. Three days after I was back at work, we started shooting again. Nobody ever mentioned anything about it – it was all very British.

We decided to try and blag a couple of trips out of the show budget. I don't think that we imagined there would be a second series so we wanted to make the most of what we had. The first trip was to New York. I had no particular ideas of what to do out there but both Sam and I were obsessed with America and so a trip to New York just seemed to make sense. This was pre-9/11, and the crazy airport security that took over American airports had not yet happened, but there was still much suspicion of my big mobile. They couldn't understand the concept of it and kept asking me to turn it on. I kept reiterating that this was impossible as it was a prop and non-functional. There would then be a long silence followed by someone else asking me to turn it on. Some things never change.

Once through and in New York, the plan was to do some of the characters we'd been doing in London just with a Manhattan backdrop. It wasn't as easy as we assumed. Americans were very different to Brits in their public reactions. If I pulled the big mobile out somewhere in the UK and started shouting into it, the British public would freeze in embarrassment and just hope that I would go away. Americans, certainly in New York, were very different – faced with me screaming into my 'big cell' they would either shout at me, 'Hey, buddy, you want to shut the hell up?' or, as in one case, just punch me hard in the face. Fortunately, the New York gun laws were reasonably restrictive, otherwise things might have got a lot worse. I could imagine the headline:

Trigger Happy Comedian Gunned Down By Unhappy Trigger Happy Passer-by

We took the spy character up onto the Empire State Building. I thought that there could be no better backdrop for an illicit bag drop. There were four of us: Sam and me and two runners, Paul Young and Matt Gilbe. I was dressed as the spy and, once on the outdoor observation platform, I started scoping for targets. Sam was hanging around, pretending to be a tourist filming.

Most of the people up there were tourists and therefore often not English-speakers but I managed to get a couple of decent reactions. About ten minutes in, and I was just approaching a British-looking couple when I felt a firm hand grab my shoulder. I turned round and was immediately put into an armlock by an undercover security guard with clear desires to be in SWAT.

'I've seen what you are doing, you and your friend are going to jail, son . . .'

I panicked. I wasn't sure if he thought I was a real spy or knew we were filming. Either way we had no permission of any sort. I saw a guy chasing Sam who bolted round the terrace. It turned out later that Sam had thought fast. He'd ejected the tape from the camera and passed it to Paul Young, who had hotfooted it into the lift with Matt and got out of the building.

Sam and I were taken to a room where we were interrogated for an hour or so. The guy wanted to put us into this weird cell that they had, an Empire State Prison. Fortunately, he got on the phone to someone and we took the opportunity to bolt. We ran down loads of stairs until we grabbed a lift at about the eightieth floor. The security guards on the ground floor tried to stop us but we got past them and disappeared into the Manhattan crowds. We went for a drink at the Soho Grand to celebrate our freedom. U2 were in the bar with Naomi Campbell – all in all, it was a very New York day.

I decided that it would be good to film in a ski resort. Unlike our New York trip, I had some specific snow jokes that we could film. I opted for Zermatt, a ski resort that I loved (before the Russians came) – it had the required chocolate-box look with the added bonus of not allowing cars. We packed the trusty Previa with costumes and props and set off from Charing Cross Road, bound for Switzerland. It was a *Trigger Happy European Vacation*. We stayed at a Bond-like hotel in Zermatt that you accessed by way of a long underground tunnel and then a lift up into the lobby. Much schnapps was drunk upon arrival, and the first day's filming was cancelled due to extreme hangovers. Ever-resourceful, we turned it into a 'recce' day. I've had a lot of 'recce' days over the years.

When we eventually started filming, things went well. I spent four hours standing in a snowdrift dressed as a snowman, throwing snowballs at passers-by. This was funny but I nearly lost two toes to frostbite as my shoes were not insulated. I wandered around town, carrying an ordinary plank of wood in lieu of a snowboard and trying to 'get down' with other boarders before advertising for my 'Shki Shkool' while covered in bandages and plasters.

The following day, we hit the slopes only to find out that Paul Young had 'forgotten' to tell us that he couldn't ski. We were

44

forced to improvise and found him a toboggan so that he could follow us down. Halfway down the slope, we stopped and set up a sign that read:

DANGER YETI

The joke was not a complicated one. I was dressed as a big hairy yeti and would jump out at unsuspecting skiers about ten metres past the warning sign. I terrified a couple of Japanese groups until the ski patrol turned up. They were not best amused and I was arrested, still dressed as a yeti, and taken down to the town, where I was locked up in what appeared to be the only prison cell in town. Sharing my cell was a Swiss burglar who looked very freaked out to be in a small room with a big hairy beast. I was in there for two hours and he didn't once look at me directly. He just stayed in the far corner, muttering to himself until my release was negotiated from London.

On the way back to the UK we stopped in Bruges, the 'Venice of the North'. For some reason we had a British policeman's uniform in the back, so I put it on and started wandering around town, trying to think of a joke. In the end what made us laugh was my chatting up a couple of Belgian policewomen. The joke evolved into me being both incredulous and jealous that they had handguns. We were halfway through this patter when a van pulled up next to me and I was arrested by some very aggressive Belgian gendarmes. Filming abroad was definitely turning into a bit of a chore. They rounded us all up and we were all interrogated separately back at the police station. The gist of the charges seemed to be that we were impersonating a policeman and that this was illegal in Belgium. Fortunately our production manager back in the UK, Sarah Banwell, was very efficient and had got some basic filming permit to do stuff in Bruges. She faxed it over and this seemed to placate the police.

We were eventually released on the condition that we no longer wandered around dressed as a policeman.

We'd seen locals take tourists for a trip round old Bruges on horse-drawn carriages. We paid one of them to let me sit next to him and be the guide. Once we had a couple of Americans on board we were off. We went round and round the central square for about twenty minutes as I made up rubbish about the old 'windowsh' you could see. The Americans were perfect, very annoyed but just too timid to demand that we stop. I ran the whole, uncut scene on the end of the first *Trigger Happy* DVD.

There was one joke that I am still determined to film in Bruges but never have. It is a city of many bicycles, and there are several places where you can rent them. All the bikes look almost identical, black with no handlebar brakes and a little brown basket on the front. My idea was to make an exact miniature reproduction of one of the bikes, complete with tiny corporate signage. I would then rent a real bike, return the next day with my tiny copy and complain that it had shrunk in the rain. Sadly, every time I have visited since, the weather has been perfect with not a drop of rain. One day, however ...

Another idea I'd had was to hide a celebrity in each show and then run a competition at the end for anybody who could spot them all. We rang around but nobody was interested apart from Carol Decker, the ex-lead singer of T'Pau. I'd already come up with the concept of sending two people in a bull costume into a china shop. Suddenly it hit me: we could put Carol into the shop pretending to be a customer and she could have ... wait for it ... *drumroll* *China in her hands.*

Carol was charming and very up for doing it. On the way to the shoot, in the van, she asked what other celebrities we were using. I panicked before namechecking Malcolm McLaren, Plastic Bertrand, Tony Hadley, Yazoo and ... Prince.

'Prince?' gasped Carol. 'As in "Purple Rain", superstar, Prince?'

I nodded.

'Well that's cool.' Carol looked seriously impressed and not a little chuffed to be in that kind of company.

I kept quiet and we never went any further with the celebrity cameo idea. There never was a competition. Despite this, Carol came back to work for us in the Christmas Specials when I'd knock on random doors, introduce her to old ladies and then try to flog them washing-up cloths. It was all very random.

The little weird moments made me laugh more than anything. One day, we were filming in a street in Brook Green. I was dressed as the Grim Reaper and the joke was simple. I would ring a doorbell and someone would answer. I would then pronounce, in a deep voice: 'Mr Jones, it is time . . .'

Whoever answered the door would invariably say something like: 'I'm not Mr Jones, you must have the wrong door.'

I would then answer: 'Are you not Mr Jones of number 38 ***** Road?'

The confused person would say: 'No, this is number 40, you have the wrong house.'

I would then immediately drop the menacing voice into a normal one and politely whisper: 'Oh, I'm so sorry,' and then they would watch out of their door as I went next door.

I rang on one door and an elderly gentleman answered. As he opened the door I realised that he was blind. Obviously he didn't see the Grim Reaper but just asked who was there? I didn't want to freak him out so I put on my poshest voice, apologised and told him that I had the wrong address and not to worry. He was fine about it and shut the door as I walked away. It was then that I spotted the small CCTV camera in the corner of the porch. I imagined the man's son or daughter popping round and checking the footage, only to see their father talking to the Grim Reaper at the door with no sound to explain what it was all about ...

Once we'd finished filming, we then started the mammoth task of editing our months and months of footage into six shows. It was a long and often torturous process, but I loved being in an edit. It was where you took all the random puzzle pieces and fitted them painstakingly together to make the big picture. Music played an enormous part in the success of *Trigger Happy TV*. I'd always longed to be musical, but lacked much ability. I was the singer in a band called Hang David in the late Eighties, but we never got anywhere, save a mini tour of the USA where we supported the Tom Tom Club at CBGBs and played a twenty-two-minute version of The Cure's 'A Forest' to twenty drunk rednecks in Binghampton.

I may not have had much talent as an actual musician, but as a listener I definitely had more form. Most importantly, I was not a music snob. If I heard a song – on the radio, in a film, at someone's house – and got that wonderful, addictive feeling of needing to hear it again and again, then that's what I'd do. It didn't matter if it was Napalm Death or Men Without Hats. Music could and still can touch me like nothing else – it made a massive connection with me on the inside. It made me alive.

I despised people who would dislike a song because it wasn't 'cool'. That was bollocks. Music was music and I loved a perfect pop song as much as any angsty indie opus. I could never really understand other people who didn't 'feel' a song the way I did. I'm terrible on other people's music systems – I play one song and people like it, and then I can't switch off – I have to keep playing another and another and get really annoyed if everyone in the room doesn't stop what they're doing and demand to know what each and every song is ... I guess I should have been a DJ, but they are invariably awful people.

So when it came to making *Trigger Happy TV*, it just made

total sense to me that I should put beautiful, haunting tracks over almost every sketch. It was the closest I'd get to linking the music that I loved with me. It was almost like remaking pop videos for my favourite songs, except with me blagging as the star. I'd grown up with a fairly mainstream taste, mostly drawn from my elder brother and sisters – The Beatles, Supertramp, Queen, David Bowie, Jacques Brel, Pink Floyd, Dylan, The Stones, Neil Young and Simon & Garfunkel. Once I started making my own choices, the list just grew and grew. Huge infatuations included – Pixies, House of Love, Prince, James, The Cure, Mercury Rev, Psychedelic Furs, Spear of Destiny, The Sound, JJ72, Grandaddy, Grant Lee Buffalo, Babybird, Tricky, The Church, Suede, PJ Harvey … the list goes on. I still fall in love with a new album practically every week. One day, however, I could put it all on the screen.

I cut *Trigger Happy TV* to the music. Often I'd leave things to go for longer than they should – comedically – so that they would fit a tune. This was a problem when the show was sold abroad as, due to cost constraints of licensing the original soundtrack, people just plonked random soundalike soundtracks on top. The show needed to be listened to with the original music as I'd spent weeks and weeks getting it exactly right. It helped that our editor was my old friend Dave Frisby, the drummer from Hang David. Unlike our time in the band, in the edit we were in total synch.

But my music choices started to become a big problem. I would choose a track only to find that permission to use it had been refused – this was always so frustrating. We had some very weird moments, like when we waited on the phone while someone called Paul McCartney for permission to use a song (he said yes) or persuading Gordon Lightfoot to let us use the 'most requested' song on the soundtrack – 'If You Could Read My Mind' – on the DVD. I was unaware that Gordon was a seriously big cheese in Canada and when permission was initially refused, I sent his management a copy of the show so that they could see how brilliant it was. I imagined Gordon was living in some hut in the middle of nowhere and he would be thrilled when a local delivery boy ran up his dirt drive shouting, 'Gordo, Gordo, they love you in England!' I even started thinking about getting him to rerelease the song with us doing the video, a possible Christmas Number One? We waited and waited and there was no reply from Canada. Finally I rang his people myself. They said no. I persisted and asked why? Had they not shown the show to Gordon? They said yes, Gordon had watched the show and he thought 'it was a bunch of crap'. That was very much that.

The worst moment was around the title sequence. I was obsessed with Elastica and their debut album, and I wanted to use the track 'Connection' for the titles. I'd already commissioned someone to make the titles to correspond exactly to that tune when news came in that permission had been refused. Once you had a track in mind, it was difficult to think of anything else. I rang Sam and we both decided to drive into the edit to try other music. As we drove up Portobello Road I spotted Justine Frischmann, the lead singer of Elastica, standing at a cash-point. It was so weird and fluky. I didn't hesitate. I jumped out of the cab and approached her. She looked nervous of me.

'Hi, you don't know me but I'm making a comedy show and I want to use your track for the titles and your record company said no and I'm asking you to rethink ...'

I was panting and must have looked a bit weird but she wrote down her address and told me to drop a copy of the show off and she'd have a look. We made a copy and popped it through her letterbox with an explanatory note. The next day the track was cleared. It taught me to be persistent – often people at record companies just couldn't be bothered and said no without thinking simply because it was too much work for them.

The soundtrack would become an integral part of *Trigger Happy TV* – we released three soundtrack CDs and they sold like hot cakes. I was so chuffed about that. In a sense, I was more interested in music than comedy. The music gave the show an indie soul, an outsider attitude. It was probably the thing I'm most proud of.

Remarkably, nobody from Channel 4 interfered with us in the edit at all. We were left alone until we eventually had six shiny new programmes ready to hand over. Sam's OCD brain had nearly exploded after he had itemised every clip we had onto bits of coloured card that indicated whether something was *Talky* or *Music* or *Both* or *Bitty*. He also had sub-genres like *Running Gags* and *Strands*. It made sense to nobody else but us. When we'd finished, we handed the shows in to Channel 4 and waited.

When the news came back, it was insane. The show was going to air in the New Year on Friday nights, between *Friends* and *Frasier*. This was crazy stuff. This was prime time, and we hadn't expected anything like this. I became stupidly nervous and disappeared off to Toronto with Stacey, where I spent a very weird Millennium night eating Chinese takeaway and watching the world explode into fireworks. I didn't know what to expect. I watched *Scarface* on New Year's Day, that scene where Pacino looks up into the sky and sees the blimp with the words 'The World Is Yours'. Was it? Or would it all screw up as usual?

Back in England, I woke up and looked out of the window of my All Saints Road flat to see a wall of posters with my face on them. I'd come up with the idea for a teaser-type ad campaign where we just had photos of me with phrases like 'Don't Trust This Man' and 'This Man Is A Liar' emblazoned underneath. They were very effective, especially as Channel 4 had 'arranged' for them to be flyposted so they looked all edgy and under-ground. I spent the day driving around London taking photos of the posters – very uncool. In my office at home, I have a photo-graph of my flat and the people in it watching the first moments of the first show going out. The photo caption reads:

9.03pm – 14 January 2000

Sam and I were a bit ignorant as to just how lucky we were when the show took off. We had nothing to compare it to and just didn't realise how unusual the show's level of success was.

As usual I nearly screwed everything up. On the morning that the first show aired on Channel 4, I broke into *The Big Breakfast* garden and launched a full-frontal attack on the window behind which Johnny Vaughan and Denise van Outen were presenting the live show. I was dressed as a sausage and being chased by a carrot. Viewers saw the presenters jump before a burly security man sent me flying out of shot. This was part of a further Peperami guerrilla marketing campaign Sam and I had agreed to without much forethought. I was arrested and marched out of *The Big Breakfast,* and put in a cell in Limehouse police station, still dressed as an angry sausage. For the second time in less than a year, I had to share a small cell with a criminal who looked very worried about his strangely dressed cellmate. I was eventually released, only to enter a shit-storm as the powers-that-be at Channel 4 wanted to know why they were broadcasting the show of a moron who spent his time attacking their flagship breakfast show? It was a good question, and one that I should possibly have asked myself before embarking on the stunt.

There was no immediate realisation that things were going well – we had some amazing reviews including one from Victor Lewis-Smith, who said that I had 'turned the practical joke into an art form'. Which was nice … He also called us the 'greatest comedy of this century so far', which was flattering but, as we were only fourteen days into it, not quite as good as it sounded. Nevertheless, I used the quote for years afterwards.

My two strongest memories of things changing were with the public. Firstly, there was the time I was on a train and THAT ringtone (originally 'Grande Valse', but then changed to the default Nokia ringtone) went off and three separate people shouted, 'HELLO, I'M ON THE TRAIN . . .' They didn't know I was on board. Two days later, I was in a restaurant on Westbourne Grove and a guy came up to my table to ask for my autograph. I'd imagined what this moment might be like for years, but tried to act all cool, like it was no big deal. Stacey, who – being Canadian – is both nice and overly chatty to strangers, ruined my silly act. 'Oh you have just made his day – this is his first autograph request ever. He is so excited.'

Stacey smiled at the guy, who smiled back. I tried to remain looking cool, but it was impossible – the guy now knew that, like everyone else, I was a gibbering idiot. Stacey was very good for me in that way.

Invitations started arriving for me – to premieres, events, parties – it was all a bit overwhelming. I wasn't really interested in any of them except for the music-related ones. I got an invite to come and be on The Brits, not just attend The Brits (which would have been exciting enough), but to actually be on the show. They wanted me to interrupt the host, Davina McCall, halfway through one of her monologues. This seemed easy enough. I got my Artist Access All Areas laminate and duly turned up at the side entrance to find myself in a queue and standing in front of Lou Reed. I was a massive Lou Reed fan, and tried to appear unruffled and not bring too much attention to the big mobile in my large black duffel bag. Sadly, I was searched at the door while Lou Reed waited. He observed proceedings with a withering mixture of pity and confusion as the security guy brought out my big mobile. I wasn't assigned a dressing room, so I sat on the floor between the Spice Girls and Macy Gray and pretended to be busy. When my time came, I wandered onto the stage and bellowed something into the phone while Davina tried to look puzzled. I felt a bit uncomfortable doing it as an act as opposed to for real. As I walked off, there was a noisy commotion that I didn't understand. It turned out that a drunk DJ called Brandon Block had thought his name had been called out and he had stormed the stage before being evicted by security. I walked into the backstage area – Robbie Williams high-fived me, and Baby Spice winked at me. My life was now officially very weird.

Chapter 3

Trigger Happy TV (Purple & Green)

W e worried that things might be harder with the second series, as I'd now be recognised more and people might be savvier. As it turned out, it worked to our advantage, as members of the public seemed far happier to sign consent forms when they found out that it was for *Trigger Happy TV*. The only problem was that the success of the first series kept throwing up exciting temptations that were serious distractions. For instance, we got a call out of the blue from Ian Brown's manager.

Mr Brown, it turned out, was a big fan of the show and wondered whether we would be interested in directing his next video? Ian Brown, King Monkey, the ex-lead singer of the Stone Roses? We would have paid him to make the thing but, as usual, we tried to play it cool and agreed in a nonchalant manner. We'd never made a pop video before so we had an emergency think about what we wanted to do. Everyone always went on about that Massive Attack video of 'Unfinished Sympathy', in which the singer was filmed wandering around LA. The whole video was one single uninterrupted take and this appeared to be quite a big deal. We decided to do our own one-take video – in the end we had one cut – as:

a) This didn't seem too tricky.
b) We were quite lazy.

We did a storyboard. Ian Brown would leave our offices, wander through Leicester Square, be attacked by a gorilla, frogmen and a bunch of ninjas before disappearing into the Prince Charles Theatre, where he'd watch a film with a motley bunch of *Trigger Happy TV* characters. We were slightly nervous to meet the great man, as we'd heard things about his temper and he had recently been released from Her Majesty's Pleasure for an air-rage incident in which he'd threatened to cut an airhostess's hands off. When he turned up, however, he was delightful. I'm not sure if he'd been badly represented in the press or just that this was the first example of prison changing a man for the better, but he was then and remains now the single nicest man I've met in show business. Many years later, when the Stone Roses got back together, he sent me a text telling me that there were tickets ready for any show I wanted to go to – a total dude.

After some (but not much) pre-production, Series Two went into production and we found ourselves back on the hidden camera treadmill. I'd had three giant squirrel costumes made, and we turned them into a weird street gang who beat up actors playing the parts of cyclists, fishermen, picnickers, while bemused onlookers stared on in confusion. In my favourite scene, they raided a local corner shop, keeping appalled shoppers at bay while shouting:

'Everybody relax, we're only here for the nuts . . .'

Years later, I was living in the Cotswolds and my home got flooded. The loss adjuster turned up to assess the damage, only to find three sodden and slowly rotting squirrel costumes in the courtyard alongside several other curious costumes, including a six-foot turd. The loss adjuster was American and unaware of my profession, but showed impressive nonchalance in her dealing with the matter.

We used to use a particular phone box outside Sam's flat in Ladbroke Grove, as you could see it from his side window. We had the number of the phone and we'd installed radio mikes in the box. We'd ring the phone until a passer-by answered and then warn them that there was a dangerous gang of squirrels about. As we did this, the squirrels would turn up, pull an actor out of the next-door box and beat him up. This eventually worked, but not before some serious complications. We'd just set up and started filming from Sam's flat when a Rasta walked into the box and picked up the phone before we could ring it. We could hear the whole conversation and it turned out to be related to a very serious drug deal. Sam was terrified that the guy might spot the cameras and assume that he was some kind of undercover cop. He had paranoid visions of his house being burnt down or him being stabbed in the streets. We all had to lie on the floor and gingerly take the cameras away from the windows until the deal was done. In hindsight we should probably have sent in the squirrels, but something terrible would undoubtedly have happened.

Another costume we had made was the giant snail. This was for what turned out to be, to my mind, the best-ever *Trigger Happy TV* sketch: the snail crossing the road. I had the idea in the Cock and Bottle, the last pub in Notting Hill Gate not to have been turned into some trustafarian gastro nonsense. Most people have silly, funny ideas when they are drunk in a pub. We had now got to the wonderful stage where, instead of ordering another pint and forgetting about it, we'd get up the next day and go do it. The snail wasn't exactly the next day, as we had to get the costume made, but it was pretty soon after.

When it arrived, it was magnificent: an enormous shell, a set of horns with a chinstrap for my head and a tight brown body stocking to finish off the look. It was one of those jokes that I knew would work before we did it. We filmed it on a zebra crossing on Redcliffe Gardens in Chelsea. When I was younger, as a confused Goth, I used to cross the very same zebra crossing to get to a nightclub called Café des Artistes, where I would unsuccessfully try to snog Sloanes. Now I was back dressed as a snail, and once again ready for action.

Sam hid himself in a garden and I approached the zebra crossing. This being Britain, the traffic acquiesced for the seven-foot brown snail waiting to cross the road. I'd approached the crossing standing up but the moment the traffic stopped I got down onto my belly and started inching my way across the road reeeeaaaalllllyyyy slowly. As I approached the middle of the road I did speed up a tad as there was a gap between the two front cars and I envisioned a motorbike, unaware of my presence, speeding through and ending my short comedy career in another of my fantasy headlines:

Comedian Dressed As Snail Crushed To Death In Bizarre Road Accident . . .

Once safely past the gap I slowed down again and continued my slow progress across the road. Rather wonderfully, all the traffic just waited patiently until I'd got to the other side, stood up and walked off normally. Had this been the States a couple of rednecks would have hopped out of a large monster truck, sauntered up to me and announced, 'Weeell, looks like we've got us a Mexican snail . . .', before beating me to a pulp with a baseball bat. Sam came over laughing, and we both knew we'd got something special. That should have been that. We'd got it on the first take. We were both so adrenalised, though, that we wanted another go. Sam went back into his garden hide and I prepared to cross the road again.

It all went to plan. The cars stopped and I started to inch across the road. This time, however, I noticed two pairs of feet hit the tarmac as the occupants of the lead car disembarked and started approaching me. I wondered whether they might be red-necks on vacation and braced myself for violence. I couldn't really look up because of the snail horns but I could see that both pairs of feet had now stopped right by me. There was a pregnant pause, a Mexican snail standoff. The feet belonged to two plain-clothed policemen who were understandably per-plexed by the situation they had encountered. It reminded me of the great Paul Merton sketch about a policeman who had taken acid:

I observed the suspect, dressed as a large gastropod, inch his way across the public highway . . .

Finally one of them spoke as he politely lowered his badge almost to street level for me to peruse.

'Morning, sir, would you mind explaining just what it is you are up to?'

I tried to sound as dignified as I could under the circum-stances.

'Certainly, officer. I am filming a sketch for a television comedy series. If you have a word with my cameraman over there in the garden, I'm sure he will clarify everything for you.'

The officer looked over to where Sam had been hidden. There was nobody there. Sam had finally got his own back and scarpered. I was on my own.

'There doesn't appear to be a camera crew there, sir. Maybe you were mistaken?'

The copper's tone was laced with sarcasm.

I tried to explain further but realised that, to these officers, I just looked like someone who had taken a cupboard full of mushrooms and was having a full-blown meltdown. Any explanation was futile.

The other officer, who had said very little up until now, chipped in.

'Listen, mate. I don't know what the fuck it is you're up to. And I don't give a fuck. But if you don't fucking get up and fuck off in the next five seconds, you're fucking nicked.'

All thoughts of dignity now abandoned, I stood up awkwardly and sprinted over the road, away from the sweary policeman and off down the Fulham Road. Unable to take the costume off myself, I was forced to wander around as a snail for a good three-quarters of an hour as cars hooted before I found Sam, who had retreated to a nearby pub.

I have a vivid memory of visiting Longleat Safari Park as a kid. Opened by the Marquess of Bath in the grounds of Longleat House, it was the first stately home to try and pay its way by stuffing the grounds full of exotic creatures and allowing the public to pay money to come and see them. To say that the current Marquess of Bath was odd would not be an exaggeration. He liked to paint erotic murals in the house and has a series of 'wifelets' to whom he gave cottages on the estate. We eventually ended up doing three separate shoots there. We started off by driving a car out of the monkey enclosure with two people dressed as gorillas sitting on the roof, hammering at the vehicle with baseball bats. Cars exiting the enclosure went straight past the long line of vehicles waiting to go in. Despite the gorillas obviously being fake there were some very anxious looks from drivers who suddenly wondered whether they'd misunderstood what they'd signed up for. They were mentally prepared to lose a car aerial but this was way over the top . . .

Longleat were so accommodating that we decided to chance

our arm and get an interview with the Marquess for the part of the show when I interviewed a 'celeb' and then did something weird. The Marquess was duly booked and he seemed to have no idea that we'd already filmed a comedy sketch on his premises. We pretended to be a serious show interested in his arboretum. As I interviewed him about his trees, I made out that I was having major bowel problems which eventually led to me running into the bushes and 'emptying my bottom' while shouting, 'I'm sorry, Your Majesty ...' The Marquess looked most bemused by events. A year later, we would return to Longleat to film a scene in the maze where two mobile sections of green hedge would slowly block in a confused visitor. Thank you, Your Holiness ...

I went to SOAS (School of Oriental and African Studies) as a student. This was a place full of strange people learning strange languages. Unsurprisingly, it was also a major spot for recruitment by the intelligence services. Everyone was told that someone would approach you at the bar, buy you a drink and ask you whether you'd thought about what you might do when you finished university. A strange-looking man finally approached me in my last term. I was a full-blown Goth, and so possibly an unlikely spy, and I very much got the feeling that this was a sympathy fuck.

'Hello, can I buy you a drink?' asked the intelligence services man.

'Yes, please, a pint of cider and black?' I replied, sweeping my crimped fringe out of my guy-linered face.

'So ... Have you considered what you might do when you leave university?' asked the man upon his return with my cider and black.

'No,' I replied truthfully.

'Right ... Well ... Nice talking to you.' The man got up and wandered off. I think he'd made a decision that I was not the right stuff. It's possible, of course, that he was just a man chatting me up. I like to think it was the former.

I decided to revisit my old university and do a bit of recruiting myself.

Sam had cut a hole in a 'man bag' and shoved a camera into it. This way he could stand around trying to look inconspicuous and film me. I was dressed in a pink shirt and blazer with slicked-back hair, and stood in the corridor leading from the bar to the entrance hall of SOAS. I spotted a pretty-looking Asian girl approaching. I asked her whether she'd thought about what she'd do when she left uni? She said something about the diplomatic corps. I told her that I worked for the intelligence services and was looking for recruits. She informed me that she had already thought about this area. I told her that she might have to sleep with people for information and even sometimes … (I pulled my hand across my throat in an indication that murder would be part of the job). Not only did she not baulk at the thought, but she informed me that she was very 'sporty' and very up for that sort of thing. I gave her a number to ring with the instruction that she leave the password 'Mugwuffin'. Over the next week she left no fewer than nine messages. God only knows what she's doing now, but be careful out there …

Sam's parents lived in Coggeshall in Essex, and we decided to use their house for one particular set-up. The idea was that we would call a series of chimney sweeps to come to the house as we had a 'blockage'. Once they started poking around the chimney, Sam, dressed as Father Christmas and perched on a little ledge inside, would fall down into the hearth and then leg it. I can't remember the exact logic for the Father Christmas costume. It was either that he'd got stuck there at Christmas or that he was a drunken burglar. Both were funny, and we were pretty sure that this would be a slam-dunk. The only worry I had was that, being in Essex, we might come across a have-a-go hero with a criminal past, who might assault Sam instead of looking scared. As a precaution we removed all potential weapons, like pokers and brushes. It was best to be careful – this was Crim Central after all. We made the calls and waited for the chimney sweeps.

The first guy to turn up was not quite what we expected. I'd assumed that chimney sweeps were tiny little men, not unlike jockeys – tough, strong and lithe. The first guy was about eighty and looked pretty close to death. As he slowly got out of his van and started inching his way unsteadily towards the front door we had to make an executive decision. Either we came out and stopped him, paid him for his time and sent him on his way, or we let things unfold and crossed our fingers that the shock of Sam falling out of the chimney would not provoke a terminal heart attack. In the end, we intervened and sent him on his way. Afterwards we decided that, had we allowed him to continue and he'd suffered the feared heart attack, we would have had to wipe the tapes clean, carry him out to his van, drive it about two miles away and dump it before claiming that he'd never arrived. Essex criminal culture was starting to rub off on us.

I had a 'burglar' character who was very honest about his chosen career. He would lean out of windows and ask people to hold his ladder while he climbed down with a bag of swag or announce to passers-by that he was about to steal a dog. We actually had quite a problem finding a *Beano*-esque striped robber's top. In the end we used a white polo neck and made black stripes by sticking strips of black gaffer tape round it. This just made the burglar look even stranger to anybody he spoke to.

We drove down to the Cotswolds and ended up in a little village called Blockley. It had loads of big houses owned by people from London who only came down at the weekends.

My burglar stopped a local woman in the middle of the village and started asking her which houses were empty in the week. He claimed to be only interested in this information because he was a keen student of architecture. The woman was very forthcoming and pointed out several empty houses including one belonging to the editor of the *Guardian*. She appeared very calm and completely unflustered by my curious line of questioning. When we'd finished, one of our runners approached her and told her what was going on. She happily signed a consent form and we moved on to another village with a nice bit of footage in the can. About two hours later we finally got to an area with mobile phone reception and we noticed that we had about five messages from the office. We rang them and there was audible panic in our production manager's voice.

'Some woman has rung the police to say that Channel 4 have paid a black man to wander around her village waving a shotgun and boasting that he was going to rob the post office ...'

It appeared that the Blockley lady was neither ethnically aware, nor had she understood any of the explanation that our runner had given her. According to the office, the equivalent of Cotswold SWAT had been dispatched to find us but ... they'd so far drawn a blank. This was curious since we were driving a blacked-out Toyota Previa with three large squirrel costumes attached to the roof. We weren't exactly inconspicuous. We eventually handed ourselves in to a confused policeman at Moreton-in-Marsh police station, where we were held for questioning for three hours before being released with a caution and a severe ticking-off.

Once the second series was in the can and edited, Channel 4 went to town with the publicity. Suddenly there were enormous billboards advertising the show popping up all over the country. This was incredibly flattering, but I did start to wonder whether it was the best thing to do with someone supposedly making a hidden camera show? I had a feeling that, were we to make any more shows, we might need a bigger disguise budget.

Meanwhile, things had changed up a gear at home with the arrival of our gorgeous daughter Parker. I was now dealing with two wonderful but very life-destabilising events: massive success and a new baby daughter. It was obviously far more difficult for Stacey, who was doing the hard, mother–baby work, but it meant that both areas of my life were now in flux. Experience was teaching me that this was never a good thing. Like a stool, I needed at least one leg firmly on the ground.

Series Two was an enormous hit, and things really took off. Ironically, this was just when Sam and I were thinking about knocking it on the head. Sam was always keen to move on and do new stuff. He was a very restless individual. For my part, I hadn't yet learned a valuable lesson. Never make any decision on your future immediately after finishing something. Making *Trigger Happy TV* was an all-consuming experience that left me drained and empty and this, plus our lovely new family arrival, made it not the time to decide on anything. I should have disappeared for three months and done nothing but a load of strong cocktails and beach time. Sadly, I didn't have the experience, nor did anybody advise me otherwise, and so we launched ourselves into conversation with Channel 4 about 'other projects'.

I wanted to make a series of different ideas: a spoof documentary, a travel show called *Breakfast with the President*, an offbeat chat show. I wanted to present all these new disparate projects under one umbrella, called *Trigger Happy TV Presents* – this would allow us to make weird stuff while still letting *Trigger Happy TV* fans know that, if they liked that show, then they might like this. Channel 4 didn't like the idea. Eventually we carved out a deal where we could make a spoof doc about my life and a pilot for the chat show as long as we made two *Trigger Happy TV Christmas Specials*. In hindsight, I should have just made a deal to produce three more series of *Trigger Happy TV* with a two-year gap in between each series, in which we could pursue our more 'experimental' projects. Hindsight, however, is a wonderful thing ...

So we kicked off with the final two *Trigger Happys*. We wanted to start the first one with a big stunt, and we asked fans to turn up for a shoot at a location in London. We had about two hundred people turn up at a church where they were all given multifarious animal costumes to wear. At the last minute we gave out some signs, all with random lyrics from Lionel Richie songs on them. Then we herded everybody behind two corners at the end of a long, thin lane and waited for somebody to walk up it. At our signal, the animal crowd leapt into action and poured down the lane and started running towards the man like some surreal riot in Disneyland. Unsurprisingly the man pegged it, closely followed by our motley riot. When it was all over, we had a turkey with a broken leg and severe grazing to a rhino.

I had an art gallery guard character who sat, bored, on a chair in Dulwich Picture Gallery. I love art galleries – they are awkward places, like lifts, where normal rules don't apply and everybody feels a little unsettled ... My guard would sit and stare at people staring at the Old Masters before approaching them to enquire as to whether they'd like to buy a pack of Bic razors or some combs? In another scene, my guard quietly slipped off his chair and started to crawl very slowly out of the room as a silver-haired gentleman watched in utter confusion, undoubtedly wondering if this was really what he had fought a war for.

I never, ever accepted jokes from members of the public. Mostly this was because they were spectacularly awful, but also

I was warned that people would claim that I'd stolen ideas from them, so it was just easier not to take any. We had professional writers who'd come in and brainstorm, people like David Quantick, Jane Bussman, Andy Riley and Kevin Cecil, Bert Tyler-Moore and George Jeffries. Sometimes they would have a great, fully formed idea and sometimes they would spark stuff off one another. I would always know a great one when it surfaced.

Members of the public would come up to me in the street, tell me how much they loved the show and then hit me with their 'totally hilarious' idea. One suggestion (a serious one) was: 'So you run into a supermarket, naked, pretend to staple your head to the floor and shout, "Help, I'm stapled to the floor ..."'

It was as though they had been watching a different show. One exception to this 'no public' rule, however, was the gang of giant cats. I was on Kiss FM's annoying breakfast show, and rather wishing that I wasn't, when somebody rang in with a 'great' idea for the show. I braced myself but, to my surprise, it was a cracker. Six days later, it was dawn in North London as three giant cats started stealing milk from a bemused milkman and people in the close awoke to find their bins being ransacked. Thank you, whoever you were.

There was a hideous urban canal that ran behind my flat in Westbourne Park in London. There was always something horrible floating in it, and I'd lost count of the number of shopping trolleys I'd seen tossed in. The concept that there would be anything living in there was ridiculous. So we filmed the urban fisherman sketch.

The idea was simple: I'd wait for someone to walk past before hooking the biggest fish you'd ever seen. To do the joke was more complicated than we thought. The first attempt was using a hollow shell of a seven-foot fish but it filled with water, sank and was impossible to reel out of the canal. We went back to the drawing board and the props department produced a much more realistic fish made of some kind of slimy, dense foam. The problem with this one, however, was that it wouldn't sink. Undeterred, we hired a frogman to come and hold it down underwater on the canal floor until I jerked the line. The frogman was unable to hold it down and eventually we needed three frogmen, submerged, to hold the bloody thing down. By now this had become a seriously expensive joke but it made the cut, so I guess it was technically worth the expense ...

I tried not to film anywhere that either Sam or I frequented but we made one exception when it came to a little Italian restaurant in Notting Hill Gate called Bertorelli La Toscana. 'You know we are not a- the famous Bertorelli's?' would be how they would endearingly answer any telephone request for a reservation. Both Sam and I ate there a lot. I used to have awkward meals with my dad in there. It was where my divorcing mum and dad took me for a terribly stilted meal. It was also where I'd first set eyes on my wife and the first restaurant that Stacey and I took our tiny daughter Parker to just after she was born (she slept). On the walls were multifarious signed photos to the owners from people like Chris de Burgh, China Crisis, Duran Duran and, in pride of place, Sophia Loren. The front onto the street was a big glass window that gave the diners inside an almost Edward Hopper-type look at night. We both decided to film something in there for memory's sake and also because it looked so good. The idea we came up with was the Mafia Hit.

I was dressed in an all-white suit, seated at a central table and surrounded by tables of real diners, like some lonely Mafia don on solo date night. As I tucked into a vast bowl of spaghetti an assassin, dressed all in black, walked in, produced a silenced pistol and shot me. I fell headfirst into the bowl of spaghetti and the assassin walked calmly out of the restaurant. What I hadn't anticipated was that the pasta would be scalding hot.

The moment my face hit the bowl my skin started to melt. I knew that we only had one shot at the scene and so had to keep my face immobile until I was certain that the assassin had cleared the frame. These laughs came with a price: a trip to the hospital and second-degree burns to my face. The looks on the diners' faces were priceless as, first the assassin killed me, and then, after about twenty seconds, I jumped out of my seat clutching my face and screaming blue murder. Bertorelli La Toscana, like so many good things, is gone now. In its place is a faceless Tex-Mex bar. How I miss it.

With the two *Christmas Specials* in the bag, Sam and I embarked on a couple of what, in hindsight, were clearly vanity projects. I was finding the whole situation of being a 'celeb' rather stressful. It was undoubtedly fun, but it came with a very weird set of rules that nobody ever explained to me. My way of coping was to make a spoof documentary of my life. I thought it would be funny to send up the life that people assumed I was now living. Looking back at it now, it was hideously self-indulgent and should never have been made. It must have meant very little to anybody not privy to the in-jokes of the *Trigger Happy TV* production team. It was an attempt to show that I wasn't some dumb prankster but that I had a sensitive, artistic side ... Whatever, it was a mess and I apologise wholeheartedly for it.

The doc started off with me recreating a *Trigger Happy TV* shoot: the tortured portrait artist in Trafalgar Square. We'd got Hugh Cornwell, the ex-lead singer of The Stranglers, to pretend to be the sitter who got angry with me taking the piss and threw me into a fountain. It went downhill from there. The premise was to satirise the ludicrous things that people assumed that I did as a celebrity. If anything, it just turned out to be eerily prescient. We got Ronnie Corbett to come and do a cameo with me on a golf course. The joke was that I was very into the world of charity golf. I now do like golf and have taken part in the occasional charity event. Similarly we filmed a cheesy ad for Joly Finance, a dig at celebs doing ads for loan companies. Seven years later, I would find myself in Israel in a swimming costume, making a TV advert for on-line poker. Life imitates art.

We filmed a real signing in HMV in London. Actual punters were queuing up to get a photo and an autograph and we put up a large sign with rules like:

Don't look at Mr Joly. Don't attempt to shake hands. No beards.

while I sat guarded by a giant squirrel and wearing one of those Michael Jackson surgical masks. It was a dig at those celebs who had gotten too big for their boots. Ten years later and I caught myself having a huff about being described as a 'prankster' by Jonathan Ross in the intro of his chat show.

If I think back to what was happening on that day in HMV, however, it was madness. I'd flown in from a quick holiday at La Mamounia in Marrakesh. On the flight, I'd read a review of the new *Trigger Happy TV* in the *Sun* that described it as 'the funniest TV show since *The Simpsons*'. Upon arrival at Heathrow, I was picked up by taxi bike and driven straight to HMV in Oxford Street, where people were queuing up for the signing. I was trying to spoof my whole situation but I think I was suffering from Ricky Gervais Syndrome. A basically decent person tries to stay normal and balanced by constantly taking the piss out of their success, by being ironic and pretending to be a cocky wanker. In the end, people just see a cocky wanker.

We definitely had fun making these shows. The problem is that there is a reliable formula that suggests the more you have fun making something, the less fun it is to watch. This was when I first met Robert Smith from The Cure (see next chapter for hideous details). I also met Damien Hirst. I'd bumped into his American wife, who told me that Damien adored *Trigger Happy TV*. So I wrote in a confused cameo for him in *Being Dom Joly*.

He insisted on meeting me for lunch before agreeing to do the scene. We met at J Sheekey, a very plush fish restaurant in Central London. When he arrived, the *enfant terrible* of British art was very, very, very pissed. He ordered a stupidly expensive bottle of wine and then, after ten minutes or so of awkward chat, went a bit … mental. Without warning, he stood up and shouted: 'Who wants to see my stomach cancer?' before whipping out his scrotum sack for the entire packed restaurant to admire. There was a stunned hush around the room but you could see that everybody was thinking: 'I can't wait to tell everyone about this!'

When he eventually settled down I took the opportunity of getting Damien to draw something on a matchbox. He drew two rabbits shagging with the words, 'I love Trigger Happy TV' and signed it. I'm pretty sure that will just about pay for the bottle of wine one day …

About a month later, and Hirst arrived at the shoot with a horrible entourage. They had all just flown in from the Monaco Grand Prix and once again were utterly slaughtered. The shoot was an unpleasant nightmare, with one of the Hirst entourage swearing and being really rude in front of a couple of very young extras. I thought I was bad, but there was still clearly far, far to travel …

In one scene from the documentary, I went to open a school event. My dry-cleaner's in Notting Hill Gate were fans and had asked me whether I would open the fete at the school that their kids attended. I agreed on the proviso that I could film it for the spoof doc. On the day, I turned up with an actor who was going to play the part of the headmaster. The idea was that we would film me refusing to open the fete until I'd been given a large cash payment. This we would film separately in a corner of the school playground. Unfortunately, a local reporter who was covering the 'story' overheard this discussion and didn't realise that it was for the documentary. She splashed with the story the next day:

Trigger Happy Comedian Demands Cash Payment Before Opening Junior School Fete.

It was funny, but obviously people thought it was real. I was starting to tread a very thin line.

Channel 4 seemed a little wary of the documentary when we'd finished editing it. They eventually slipped it out at about 11pm one night. It got some decent reviews but the warning signs were there. Things were falling apart. Next up we went into the studio and recorded a pilot of *Dead Air*, my surreal attempt at a chat show on acid. I describe a little of what it was about in the next chapter. Suffice to say that it was as unplanned and ill-thought-through as the documentary had been. There were occasional moments of greatness, but overall it was a mess and I could see Channel 4 starting to panic.

Just as this was unravelling, I got a call. The BBC wanted to meet. The King of the BBC, Alan Yentob, had summoned me to the River Café. Things were getting interesting. At the lunch, it quickly became apparent that the BBC wanted to sign me up for a big deal. I couldn't believe my luck but I tried to look like I needed persuading. Yentob is well known for name-dropping but I was astonished at the sheer Olympian level at which he operated. One minute there was a story about Mick Jagger in the loo at Tom Stoppard's and then we were onto him being responsible for the Everly Brothers getting back together. I hadn't realised that Yentob had been responsible for directing one of my favourite documentaries, *Cracked Actor*, which followed a coke-fuelled David Bowie on a *Ziggy Stardust* comedown tour of the USA. I happened to mention how much I loved said doc and, to my surprise, received a box-lot of Yentob's documentaries sent to my home the following day. It was a valuable lesson in how not to be shy in promoting your genius.

After some, but not overly protracted, negotiations the deal was done and Sam and I were off to the BBC for a three-series deal. I would imagine Channel 4 was relieved. We, however, were no longer the punk outsiders playing around on the fringes of comedy. We'd now joined the establishment.

Chapter 4

No More Heroes

They say you shouldn't meet your heroes, they can only disappoint. This is not entirely true but it's never an easy thing to do – trust me, I've been there.

The very first event that I was ever invited to as a 'celebrity' was the Orange book awards at the V&A. Now, I have no interest whatsoever in the Orange book awards (unless this tome gets selected, in which case they are a highly valuable contribution to literature) but the invitation looked glossy and expensive, and my wife Stacey was up for a night out on the town as we'd just had our first baby.

So we got all dressed up and set off on our first adventure in ligger-land. Soon we were in the bowels of the imposing V&A amidst the great and not-so-great of London literati, plus a handful of random famous faces not much linked to literature but tucking into the free champagne and adulation. Not for the last time in the past fifteen years, Stacey and I felt out of place. We wandered around like small-town folk, nudging each other whenever we saw someone famous. There was very little reason for us to be there and we knew it.

We went out into the garden, where fire-eaters and men on stilts meandered aimlessly through the guests. It was then that I spotted Charlie Higson. He was one of the brains behind *The Fast Show*, one of my all-time favourite programmes. More importantly he played Ralph to Paul Whitehouse's Ted in the pathos-strewn Ted and Ralph sketches in which Ralph, the nice but dim country squire, desperately tried to establish a relationship with Ted, the monosyllabic estate worker. It was a series of sketches that nailed so much about Britain and the class relationships that still tether it to the eighteenth century. Best of all, it was pant-wettingly funny and I could quote every one verbatim.

'It's Charlie Higson . . .' I mumbled to Stacey.

'Who?' she replied.

'Charlie Higson . . . Ralph from *The Fast Show*.' She looked mystified but was pleased to see me so enthused.

'Well go and say hello then,' she urged.

'I can't, I'm embarrassed.' I was pathetic.

'Oh, come on. Tell him you like his stuff, say hello. What's the worst that could happen? Imagine if someone did that to you. You'd love it.' Stacey, being Canadian, is not only sensible and kind but never really gets the British fear of public interaction. Nevertheless, spurred on by her enthusiasm, I gingerly approached Charlie Higson.

He was in the middle of telling a story to two people and so I half-joined their group and laughed along a little too hard at what I soon realised wasn't a funny story, but something about someone whose wife was leaving them. Higson finished the story but nobody paid me the slightest bit of attention, and I was left hanging like a lemon as they started talking about something else. It was crunch time – I had to either slip away in shame or say something. I made the wrong choice.

'Mr Higson . . . Excuse me, Mr Higson . . .'

Charlie Higson turned to look at me but in a way that implied he didn't really want to.

'I just wanted to say that I'm a fan. I even have a single by The Higsons.' My nerves had forced me to start making things up. I knew that Charlie Higson had been in an indie band called The Higsons at university and so, rather than just say hello, I was trying to impress him with my knowledge of his work. I was lying, I'd never heard a song by the band but I was desperate to separate myself from the common hordes that must normally harass him in public.

He looked at me as though dealing with a simple relative. His tone was not appreciative, as I'd assumed it would be. It was not even that friendly.

'Oh really, which one do you have?'

I could feel the blood rushing to my cheeks. I was speechless with ignorance. There was a long, awkward silence. To me it felt like a minute but was probably only a couple of seconds. Finally I said something.

'All of them ... I've got all of them ... Really good ...' I longed for a hole to open up and swallow the entire V&A. Admittedly it would have been a blow to the London literary scene but it would have made my life a lot more comfortable at that moment.

Higson looked at me for a second as though checking for a concealed weapon. He then turned and resumed talking to the two people, and I was cut adrift. I stood listening for a couple of seconds before pretending that I saw someone I knew and slinking off. They didn't even notice.

'How did it go?' asked Stacey.

'I need more drink,' I replied with a distant look in my eyes.

That was pretty much it for my first night out as a 'celebrity'. I dimly remember trying and failing to say something intelligent and funny to a rather gorgeous Zadie Smith before Stacey hinted that it was time for us to go. I went for a pee on the way out and found myself standing at the urinal next to Dave Gilmour from Pink Floyd. I spent the entire Seventies being weaned on Pink Floyd through my elder brother and sisters. I'd listened to *Wish You Were Here* driving through the Syrian desert. I'd gone to sleep every night of boarding school listening to *Dark Side of the Moon*. I even loved 'Several Species of Small Furry Animals Gathered Together in a Cave and Grooving with a Pict'. I loved Pink Floyd and wanted to tell Mr Gilmour but I had already learned a valuable fame lesson from Charlie Higson. Play it cool ... Maybe Dave Gilmour was a *Trigger Happy TV* fan? Maybe he'd say hello to me? Maybe we'd become friends and hang out together and he'd teach me to play guitar? I could be his new Roger Waters? I was thinking so hard that I was unable to pee and the more I worried about this, the less likely it was to happen. It was male stage fright. There I was standing next to Dave Gilmour, with him peeing away and me just holding my penis and staring at him. It was quite a traumatic night. Years later I would embarrass myself in front of another member of Pink Floyd. I was invited to Jeremy Clarkson's fiftieth birthday party at his house, a party so over the top that I assumed somebody had spiked my drink. Everywhere I looked there were famous people – Bryan Ferry, Steve Coogan, Harry Enfield, Jemima Khan, oh ... and Richard Littlejohn.

There were tributes from Simon Cowell, the prime minister and Ozzy Osbourne before a wall was lowered to reveal the entertainment for the evening, Squeeze supporting The Who. It was insane. As I stood, quite pissed, watching The Who, I noticed a Sloaney-looking man standing next to me. It was Nick Mason, the drummer of Pink Floyd. Again I was tongue-tied but finally managed to stammer:

'Are ... you not playing then?'

Nick Mason looked at me like you would a simpleton.

'Clearly not . . .' He walked off. I really was rubbish at talking to Pink Floyd.

The Higson incident (as it came to be known in my household) was quite an oddity for me. Most of my heroes tended to be musicians and not comedians. History had shown me that meeting comedians was rarely a pleasure.

Shortly after *Trigger Happy TV* was out I was asked to perform at the *Secret Policeman's Ball* in aid of Amnesty International. A big honour. I'd seen the earlier ones with people like John Cleese and Python performing alongside Sting doing a stunning acoustic version of 'Message in a Bottle'. This was the big time and I didn't spend too much time worrying about what I'd actually 'perform' or that I'd never, ever done anything live in my life.

The list of performers sent to me was impressive – U2, Radiohead and Woody Allen were a few of the names mooted. I was too green to check whether these names were confirmed, however, as when I eventually got to Wembley Arena, the headliners were Tom Jones, Stereophonics and the host was Eddie Izzard. Not to take away from these good people but it was not quite what had been originally promised.

I got there very early and wandered round the empty arena marvelling that I was going to have my very first live performance here. As I was trying to find my dressing room I spotted Harry Enfield talking to Paul Whitehouse. Harry and I shared an agent. He was very pleasant, said hello and I hung out with the two of them as they chatted. Harry was obsessed with my DVD sales and kept telling me I was a 'lucky bastard'. I couldn't argue. Eddie Izzard arrived and greeted Harry and Paul warmly. He nodded vaguely in my direction. He invited us (well, them) into his dressing room and we entered a suitably vast space, where I sat quietly while the three established comedians swapped banter. I couldn't believe that I was there. How the hell had this happened? A man came in and told Harry and Paul that they should sound-check. They left and I felt that I should go with them but, like an idiot, I didn't. I sat in Eddie Izzard's cavernous dressing room while he put on a particularly garish, shiny costume and studiously ignored me. I finally spoke to break the awkward silence.

'Thank you so much for having me on the bill ...'

Izzard looked up at me dismissively.

'Oh ... I had nothing to do with that, you're not my choice ...' There was another long period of awkward silence before I mumbled something about finding my dressing room and I slunk out. Suffice to say that I shall not be voting for him for London Mayor.

Come the actual show and I'd decided to go ahead with a drunken idea I'd had about doing a *Stars in their Eyes* pastiche in which the joke was, 'Tonight, Matthew, I'm going to be Black Box.' I would disappear into smoke and reappear stumbling around dressed as a big black box to the sound of 'Ride on Time'.

I asked Harry Hill (whom I loved) to be Matthew Kelly for me. Despite him going on to present a revamped version of the show in 2015 he was clearly not keen on the idea back then as he declined. I then asked Jonathan Ross, who said yes immediately before killing any vestiges of humour in the thing by overegging his role. This was the first of many random showbiz meetings with Ross. The one common factor of all these meetings was that he would always ask if I played tennis? I would invariably reply in the affirmative and he would tell me that I should come and play doubles at his house with David Baddiel and Les Dennis. I would accept, thinking that this was a weird experience too good to miss. I would then never hear from him again. I heard Jimmy Carr telling the same story about Ross on the radio (although I think he actually played there) so this is clearly his default showbiz conversation starter.

I like Jonathan Ross. Like Piers Morgan and Simon Cowell he is peculiarly un-British in his pursuit of showbiz hegemony. He's certainly a veteran – I used to leave messages on the answering machine of his first chat show, *The Last Resort*, when I was still at school. When we were filming stuff in the days before *Trigger Happy TV*, we found his distinctive Union Jack-painted Vespa parked in Hampstead. I left a note under the seat. It read:

> To the owner of this bike. By chance you have painted it exactly the same colour as the television presenter Jonathan Ross. We want to drive it into a shop window, take a picture and then try to sell a false story to the tabloids about Ross being drunk and indulging in some ram raiding. If you are interested then call this number.

I rather hoped Ross would take the bait and ring us himself but he never did. Ironically, when I came to try and insure my own Vespa for the first time as a 'performer' the premium tripled. When I asked the broker why it was so expensive the reply was that in my line of work I could be riding around with Jonathan Ross on the back and, should I then crash, the insurer would be liable for him as well as me. I didn't really follow the logic and asked if I could negotiate a clause that rendered me liable should I have any crash in which I had a celebrity pillion passenger. They weren't interested.

Years later, when the first series of *Fool Britannia* aired, I was a guest on *The Jonathan Ross Show*. There was a very curious moment when I was on the set but we were off-air as they showed a VT of *Fool Britannia*. Ross took the opportunity to lean forward and whisper to me in a really creepy voice: 'You'we on fire, you weally want it, don't you? I can smell it ...' Now, an innocent observer might think that he was hitting on me. Not at all. I'm pretty sure that the 'it' he was referring to was success, fame, showbiz status … He was asserting his own showbiz status and letting me know that this was my chance to return from the entertainment wilderness. At least I think this was what he meant? Maybe he *was* hitting on me? I've never been good on signals. Whatever, for the first time there was no mention of tennis but he did tell me about his up-coming Halloween party and that 'you must come'. Predictably, the promised invitation never came.

I didn't mind what happened in my encounter with other comedians. As far as I could make out, no comedian could ever really be friends with any another. Comedians being friends with each other is a bit like an open marriage – it's doomed to failure, as inevitably one will be getting more action than the other and it will start to tell. The exception to this rule for me is Jenny Eclair, whom I adore.

With musical heroes, however, it was a different matter. As a teenager I had two: David Bowie and Robert Smith, lead singer of The Cure and the 'Gothfather' to slightly chubby, depressed teenagers around the globe. I have met both with varying results.

The very first thing I did when I got to London was to find Heddon Street and have my photograph taken recreating the cover photo of *The Rise and Fall of Ziggy Stardust and the Spiders from Mars*. Unfortunately I was wearing black and white spandex trousers and sporting a badly bleached ponytail. It would be fair to say that it's not a great photo. I had every Bowie album, knew every lyric, had a collection of his appearances on much-watched VHSs … I really liked David Bowie, OK?

So, when I spotted him sitting at the bar of a little place in Geneva airport, I couldn't believe my eyes. I walked past him about three times, trying to look inconspicuous, but he spotted me and looked almost amused by my incompetent stalking. On the fourth pass I swooped. I walked up to him and proffered my hand. He shook it. My mind went blank. I should have left it at that but I couldn't. For what seemed like an interminable period of time we stared at each other. I took in his distinctive odd-coloured eyes, the result of a childhood knife incident. I looked at his teeth, once the principal exhibit in an American trial of the state of British dentistry but now almost too white, too shiny, not rock 'n' roll enough. Bowie continued staring at me with an amused smile appearing at the corner of his mouth. Finally I was ready ... but as I opened my mouth to speak, David Bowie got up, said, 'Excuse me,' and walked away ... fast. It took me five or six years to be able to tell this story without weeping at my social incompetence.

Robert Smith on the other hand, well that's another story ... and quite a long one.

While filming *Being Dom Joly* for Channel 4, I'd faked a back story in which I was a war reporter in Bosnia, had a nervous breakdown under fire, was hospitalised and subsequently married my Bosnian psychiatric nurse – following this so far? We wanted to fake footage from my marriage to said nurse at Marylebone Register Office, the place where I got married for real. While we were discussing the scene, I suggested that we should have a cameo role for a best man figure. Who could we get? I jokingly said, 'How about Robert Smith?'

So someone placed a call to The Cure headquarters. It turned out that Robert Smith was a *Trigger Happy TV* fan and agreed to take part in a day's filming. This was insane. As the big day approached, however, I had a nagging concern. I hadn't seen The Cure for a while. What if Robert Smith had grown old gracefully and cut off all his backcombed bird's nest of hair and removed the badly applied make-up? What if he turned up and was unrecognisable? What if he now looked like an accountant?

Then I had a brainwave. We contacted The Cure HQ again and asked whether Robert Smith needed a make-up person on the day.

'No,' was the message that came back. 'He'll do his own.'

We were all relieved. He was still the Gothfather.

The designated day came and I arrived at our offices on the Charing Cross Road very early. I was nervous and buzzing – life was good. I sat at my desk and tried to think of things to do while I waited for the great man's arrival. Before I knew it, he was there. A runner came in and said the words: 'Robert Smith's in reception for you.' I took a deep breath and walked out. There he was, it was bloody crazy – Robert Smith had come to see me. I tried to keep calm but this was so out there. I made what passed for polite chat and briefly ran through what we were going to do. He played it just right. He was cool, a touch aloof in a rock star way, but also very polite and friendly. You don't want your heroes to be too normal – they lose their mystique.

The crew was ready and we were going to set off to the location. Robert Smith had a large, comfortable, chauffeur-driven limousine and he suggested that I ride with him so we could chat. I nodded like this was normal but inside I was like a 19-year-old girl being given the key to John Taylor's hotel room (for younger readers, please substitute sixteen for nineteen and Harry Styles for John Taylor). I slipped into the back seat alongside Smith and we were whizzed through Central London inside our tinted showbiz cocoon. I can't remember what we chatted about but I think I managed the journey without too much embarrassment. I remember Smith telling me that he and his long-term partner Mary divided people on the telly into two camps – Ronnie Barker and Ronnie Corbett. One category was the good guys and the others were the wankers. Sadly, I can't remember which Ronnie signified which category.

Back in the Cure limo we were now cruising down the Marylebone Road and I could see the register office just up ahead. Right outside the building was a little slipway off the main road, clearly designed for cars to stop and deposit or pick up soon-to-be or recently wedded folk. The chauffeur turned into the little spot and stopped. I was so relieved that I hadn't behaved like an idiot. For once I'd played it cool – maybe I'd turned a corner? I opened the heavy door of the limo and there was an immediate, earth-shattering impact. I was hurled back into the lap of a very confused and startled Robert Smith. I got up as quickly as possible to see what had happened. I had opened the passenger door on the street side of the car, and in my excitement had not looked to see if anything was coming. A white builder's truck had been coming ... and fast. The truck had sheared off the whole passenger door of the limo before coming to a stop against the traffic lights ahead. The limo driver was out and staring at his vehicle in a state of some agitation. The builders were clambering out of the truck and had begun swearing at me. Robert Smith was sitting in the limo just staring at me in disbelief.

'Is this a hidden camera joke?' he asked in a tone that indicated that, if it was, it was not tickling his funny bones. I assured him that it was a genuine mistake on my part but I could see that he was not convinced. Once the angry builders had been calmed and the limo driver reassured that we had production insurance, we eventually commenced filming. I could see that Robert Smith was not quite the same with me after that incident and, frankly, who could blame him?

I was not to be put off. About six months later I was filming an experimental pilot for what would eventually end up as my fake chat show, *This Is Dom Joly*, on BBC Three. This pilot was shot for Channel 4 and was far stranger and more experimental than the watered-down version that eventually crawled out and died on the BBC 'Yoof' channel. I called it *Dead Air*, and the show started with me coming on stage singing the song 'Sympathy', an old classic by the band Rare Bird. Halfway through the first verse a fake light crashed down from the roof and knocked me unconscious. The rest of the pilot was my hosting a chat show with a profusely bleeding head and clearly very concussed. It was no holds barred and, thinking back, should have been the way forward.

I needed a band to play live on the show. There was no discussion. I rang Robert Smith and asked him whether The Cure might play. He agreed. Hurrah! We were back on course for a beautiful friendship.

The filming went pretty well. I had the gorgeous Melanie Blatt from All Saints and the equally gorgeous and funny Ronni Ancona on as guests. Nobody really seemed to know what was going on, and to say that the show was not fully formed would be an understatement, but The Cure played us out and everything was good in the world. As I was winding down in the green room, Robert Smith knocked on the door and asked me whether I'd like to go for a drink. He'd come up from the south coast where he lived and was up for a bit of a night out. I told everyone I could see that I was off for a drink with Robert Smith and we then headed out into Carnaby Street where we had been filming. There was a pub on the corner, and we went in and downed quite a few drinks or ten. Soon, however, it was closing time, but Robert Smith wanted to carry on.

'Where shall we go?' enquired the Gothfather. Robert Smith was asking *me* where to go?

I racked my brains for a cool suggestion but eventually all I could come up with was a feeble: 'Well, we could go back to my place?'

'Fine,' said Robert Smith, 'my guy will take us there. Where is it?'

'Notting Hill Gate,' I replied.

We clambered into his car and the same chauffeur as he'd had the last time stared at me with trepidation. I smiled at him and gave him my address. Off we sped through the darkened streets of London again, just me, Robert Smith and the driver who hated me, in our tinted rock 'n' roll limousine.

If somebody had told me this would happen when I was a teenage Robert Smith lookalike, I'd have laughed in their faces. I'd been to see The Cure at Wembley Arena on the *Kiss Me, Kiss Me, Kiss Me* tour. I had great tickets ... not. We were in the very back row of the whole arena. I was so pissed off. I wandered around the place bumping into other Goths and drinking way too much cider and black. I later read an article in *NME* in which Robert Smith said he'd wandered around the arena himself before the gig and nobody had recognised him. 'I saw at least twelve people who looked more like me than me,' he told the magazine wryly.

And now here I was in the back of his limo taking him back to my flat for a drink, and I'd just played Wembley Arena myself. Things were pretty good. Then I remembered that my flat was full of photographs of me looking just like Robert Smith. I panicked. This was going to be like when Alan Partridge went back to his fan's house and there was a room just full of Partridge photos. The limo stopped in my road and I jumped out very quickly, much to the anger of the driver who assumed I was going for the 'double'. I rushed up my stairs ahead of Smith and entered the flat, ripping down evidence of my Goth past as fast as I could. I managed to get rid of the worst examples, and soon Robert Smith and I were in my sitting room listening to Babybird's sublime album *There's Something Going On* and getting rather drunk.

All went well for a while until I got so smashed that I thought it would be a good idea to secretly film Robert Smith in my sitting room, as otherwise nobody would believe me. In my drunken state 'secret filming' meant getting my video camera and holding it by my knee and pointing it at Robert Smith while I carried on chatting nonsense. He noticed it immediately and I could see him staring at it for quite a while before he finally asked me why I was filming him? I was too embarrassed to reply and just dropped the camera and carried on like nothing had ever happened.

We kept on drinking until finally, at around four in the morning, I had a surreal transition from 'Oh my God, Robert Smith is in my sitting room,' to 'Oh my God, is Robert Smith going to go home or is he going to stay the night? I've got to be at work tomorrow morning early.' Eventually he left at about five in the morning and I passed out on the sofa. Life was getting really, really odd. I might have dreamed the whole thing except that I have a photo of him in my kitchen.

I did have some great moments with Robert (he's my mate, I can call him Robert, can't I?). There was the time when my BBC Three chat show had wrapped (he played on it twice), and they kept the audience in and The Cure called me out so that Robert could say thank you and dedicate 'Lullaby' to me. He played a version that brought me to tears. I could have died fairly happy.

Then he was up for a 'legend' thing at the Q Awards and he invited me along. I was very nervous, and got seriously drunk and pissed off Edith Bowman, who gate-crashed our table. I didn't care, though, because I sat next to the legendary video director Tim Pope and chatted to Tricky, who was decidedly not tricky. The last time I saw Robert was at an incredible Cure *Greatest Hits* show in Islington. I got very drunk at the after-show party and think I was very rude to Chris Martin while I was trying to tell him how much I liked Coldplay. Robert seems to bring that out in me.

It's the weird thing about being famous – it's a bit like being a dad. You know that certain tiny people call you 'Dad' and you answer to this moniker but, deep down, you wonder whom they are really talking to. You can't be 'Dad'; you're the same nervous, stupid idiot that you were when you were sixteen, or at least you feel that way. Being famous is sort of the same thing. After a while, you accept that some people see you in that light, but you can never quite believe you actually are on the inside. There is a constant sense of being a fraud. This often leads you to behave badly because you're uncomfortable playing the role of 'celeb'. The moment you are comfortable with being famous is the moment you become Ronnie Corbett as opposed to Ronnie Barker (or vice versa).

You don't stop being a dribbling fan the moment you end up on the telly. When I was living in Notting Hill Gate, my nearest supermarket was a Tesco Metro that was often more like an episode of *Stella Street*. On an average day you could spot Chris Evans, Nick Cave, Jason Donovan, Damon Albarn . . .

One day, however, I had a five-star spot. There, in my local Tesco Metro, looking at the yoghurts, was Mick Jones from The Clash, the quintessential Notting Hill band. Having little else to do, I decided to follow Mick Jones and see what he got up to. In my mind I suppose I imagined he might bump into some fellow musos, jam under the Westway, buy some 'erb and head back to some cool pad to chill.

As it was, I followed him out of Tesco Metro, keeping what I thought was a safe distance. If I'm honest, Mr Jones cut a slightly shabby figure – pallid skin, bad teeth, losing some hair and wearing a long, dirty coat – but this was the guitarist from The Clash for Christ's sake! I followed him all the way up the Portobello Road. He stopped at a greengrocer's and I watched him through the window as he bought some carrots. He exited, carried on, and I followed him until he disappeared into an Oxfam shop. I entered the shop and pretended to browse as I observed what he was up to. He was standing by a revolving rack of old paperbacks, mainly the works of Wilbur Smith. He rotated the books with little enthusiasm and looked around several times before shuffling out of the store and on down Notting Hill Gate. By now I was bored of following the ex-lead guitarist of the greatest punk band ever. I was expecting a slightly more exciting stalk. He'd let me down.

A couple of years later and I was upstairs at The Electric, a poncey drinking hole in the Portobello Road. Through Harry Enfield, I had befriended the bassist of The Clash, Paul Simonon (a truly lovely man) and his now ex-wife, Trish. That night I bumped into Trish and she told me that she was at a private party upstairs, and that I should come on up. I walked in to find a curious group watching a Chelsea game on television. There was Bobby Gillespie from Primal Scream, Paul Simonon, Trish, Sadie Frost, a man who was introduced to me as Stephen Fry's boyfriend and a girl who introduced herself as, 'Hi, I'm Kate.' It was Kate Moss. I tried to look relaxed, as though my normal night out was hanging out in a *Grazia* cover story. Kate Moss was busy lusting after 'The Special One', José Mourinho, and I was busy pretending that I had the remotest interest in football. After half an hour of this, the party moved on. Everybody dived into cabs and I jumped in too, despite Sadie Frost glowering at me in a 'you don't belong here' sort of way. The taxis stopped at a familiar place on Holland Park Avenue. In fact, right next door to my old family home. When I'd lived there, the author P. D. James had been my neighbour. Now, there was clearly a new celebrity on the block and it looked like we were about to go late-night drinking in his pad. The front door opened and there stood . . . Mick Jones. I couldn't believe it, the night was just getting better and better. I'd popped out for a pint and I was now in a rock 'n' roll lock-in with half of The Clash and Kate Moss. I wanted to tell someone about what was going on but thought it might be a tad uncool to use the house phone. After about half an hour Mick Jones and I ended up chatting. He seemed to know who I was and was very chatty. Suddenly out of the blue, just as I was relaxing, he hit me square between the eyes: 'Why did you follow me all the way from Tesco Metro in Portobello to my home a couple of years ago?'

The room went quiet and everyone turned to hear my answer. I was mortified. To my horror Mick Jones continued: 'I spotted you and thought you was gonna do a hidden camera thing on me. I tried to hide in a charity shop . . .'

I wanted to die right there and then. My powers of speech deserted me. I had nowhere to go. I had broken the tricky, unspoken rules of celebrity/civilian interaction and Sadie Frost knew it. She was now staring at me with utter contempt. I can't really remember much more, it was all too hideous. I spent the next half an hour waiting for my moment to escape. It came when Stephen Fry's boyfriend appeared to get angry about something and started stripping down to his Y-fronts. Like all great queens, from Marie Antoinette onwards, Kate Moss had a sycophantic entourage who fought for the scraps of her attention like rabid dogs. One of them had angered the man in Y-fronts. I wish I could explain more, but I honestly have no idea what was going on, both because it was crazy and because I was now dangerously off my face. Whatever, everyone turned to watch the Y-fronts man and I took my moment and slipped out of the front door and headed home, slightly less keen to tell everyone about my night out.

And then there was Michael Winner. Now, to clarify, Michael Winner was never one of my heroes, although I did share his love of La Mamounia Hotel in Marrakesh and stayed there several times when he was in residence. He would always take an entire corner of the pool and wallow in the shallows, barking orders at staff like some perma-tanned walrus. He was pretty loathsome but somehow I was rather fond of him and his fuck-you attitude to the world. But this story is not about Michael Winner, it's about his neighbour.

As I was filming a fake video diary for my BBC Three chat show I decided that a good running joke would be that Michael Winner was my celebrity neighbour. We proposed the idea to him and he was very up for it. He would, however, only film the segment at his own rather splendid mansion in Melbury Road in Holland Park (since bought by Robbie Williams after Winner's demise). We told him that this would be fine but we would need to film from his neighbour's garden as that would technically be my house.

'That's fine, Jimmy will be fine about that. Goodbye,' said Winner grandiosely before hanging up.

So we turned up on the appointed day to film the sequences. I was looking forward to poking around Winner's house but it was not to be. We were told by his assistant to set up in the garden next door and he would be along soon. This we did and we waited and waited for Winner to come down, but he didn't show and we started to get a little bored. Suddenly a man wandered down to say hello. He introduced himself as Binky and said that he worked in the house whose garden we were in.

'I look after stuff for Jimmy,' he said.

'Who is Jimmy?' I asked.

'Jimmy? Jimmy Page from Led Zeppelin? Do you want to look round the house?'

Suddenly nobody was interested in waiting for Michael Winner, and we all followed Binky into the mansion behind us. I asked Binky if Jimmy was about and was told that no, he had a bad back and was off seeing his chiropractor. You couldn't make it up. I assumed that this was what happened when you lumbered about stage carrying two-headed twelve-string guitars.

Binky showed us an amazing dining room with a large round table designed as an enormous Ouija board. It appeared that Jimmy still dabbled with dark forces from time to time. My favourite part of the house was in the basement, where Jimmy's climate-controlled guitar room was situated. Binky told us that he used to be a guitar roadie and that his main job now was to make sure that any of the multitude of guitars was tuned and ready to go at any time of day or night when his master beckoned. I loved the image of Page reclining on a set of devil horns and shouting: 'Binky, bring me my '72 Stratocaster . . .'

There were some letters on the chest in the hall addressed to James Page, and I couldn't resist. One of my strangest souvenirs from the last fifteen years is Jimmy Page's council tax bill. Years later, I was covering the Olympics in Beijing for the *Independent* and blagged my way into the closing ceremony after-show party, the place where Boris made his famous ping-pong/wiff-waff speech. It was a good blag as the other guests were David Beckham, Leona Lewis, Gordon Brown . . . and Jimmy Page. I chatted to Page and tried to apologise for stealing his council tax bill but his mind was still somewhere on top of a London bus, playing a guitar solo to an audience of billions, so he wasn't very interested and I can't say I blamed him.

Back in London, when we finally exited the Page house Winner was waiting for us and in a very bad mood because we'd kept *him* waiting. I wrote about it in my *Indy* column and it began a long and rather enjoyable feud with the old rogue. If I had any spare time I'd always enjoy going into his Wikipedia page and adding extra films to his canon. My favourite one was:

Trellis, a Polish art-house flick that Winner directed as a palate cleanser following the arduous *Death Wish* series (he insisted on directing all at once over a period of six days, with no breaks – four films in six days). *Trellis* was inspired both by Winner's childhood as a Latvian coal miner and his inexplicable love of the sea. The film's central storyline is based around three naked sailors who wrestle in olive oil for seven hours.

Winner's page was eventually locked and a very useful boredom-breaker facility sadly became off limits to me. The last time we met was on an edition of *Celebrity Mastermind*. Winner waltzed in, ignoring everyone in the green room, especially me. He then proceeded to crash and burn on the show, getting an embarrassingly awful score – one of the lowest ever. Most people would run and hide at this moment – Michael Winner took to the *Daily Mail* to announce that we were all stupid and, when it came to me, he had not forgotten our feud:

> One was a burly, lower-league version of Jonathan Ross called Dom Joly. He'd come to my house to film a minor sketch in my garden with me in it for his TV show once. He forgot his lines endlessly and then wrote, quite untruthfully, that I'd kept him waiting for half an hour.

RIP Michael – hope the dinners are winners down there.

Not content with these individual encounters with heroes, the bar was really raised when I found myself to be an unlikely guest at the GQ Man of the Year Awards. My friend Simon Kelner, then editor of both the *Independent* and *i*, was up for editor of the year or some such nonsense (all awards are nonsense unless you win one). Simon had got a table for the evening and invited some friends to join him. Weirdly he chose two 'celeb' friends who were both currently in the showbiz wilderness. The first was Alex James, the bassist from Blur. At the time, Damon Albarn had headed off with Gorillaz and other solo projects, leaving Alex and the rest of Blur a little high and dry. Alex had put on weight and grown a nervous-breakdown beard – I knew how he felt.

The event was being held at the National Opera House in Covent Garden and I turned up pretty early, as I do for everything. Outside, there was a scary red carpet entrance with a wall of paparazzi shouting and jostling for photos of the great and good. I hadn't done a TV show for three years and was seriously out of the loop. I hated red carpets at the best of times but this one was freaky. I stepped onto the carpet, showed my invite and kept walking with my head down. The cameras were deathly silent, not a click to be heard. It was like a bloody monastery. I kept walking faster and faster until I was in the relative safety of the lobby. I got into the lift and was joined by a group of three blonde women who were still heady from the excitement outside.

'Wow ...' said blonde one.

'That was crazy,' said blonde two.

'Can you imagine being a famous name and doing that walk and nobody taking your photo? It would kill you ... So stressy ... Nightmare ...'

I looked up to see if blonde three was taking the piss. She wasn't. None of them had noticed me. They were just expressing the awful truth. I felt lower than low. I didn't want to be here, didn't want the 'celebrity' life. Having it then flick two fingers at you was even worse.

I got into the main room and it was Insaneville. There were so many famous people milling about, chatting to each other like some exclusive club that I was definitely not a member of – there was Ozzy and Sharon Osbourne, David Beckham, oh look Robert Downey Jr ...

I escaped to the terrace where I downed about nine glasses of fizzy courage. To my left stood Ant and Dec chatting away to each other, inseparable as ever. Didn't they ever get bored of each other? Surely there must be *one* moment when Ant or Dec turned to Ant or Dec and said: '*Oh*, piss off, you're so clingy ...' It seemed not. Ant howled with laughter at something that Dec said. It was probably: 'Hey, isn't that the bloke with the big phone? Wosssiisssname? You know ... Dim Jelly. What the hell is he doing here?'

I had another couple of champagnes for good measure and then braved the melee inside. I found Simon, who was already at the table, and I plonked myself in my allocated chair. Alex James sat down and, because I was nervous as well as a serious Blur fan, I made some comment about him looking like Jim Morrison days before his demise. It didn't go down well with either Alex or his wife, although Simon howled with laughter. I've never been the greatest polite conversationalist. The more nervous I get, the ruder I become. It's nearly always funny but at someone else's expense. I've always been good at that and it's not something I'm proud of.

A waiter poured me a large glass of white wine and I downed it. Simon Kelner was still laughing at my comments. This was bad news, as it only encouraged me. I can remember very little of the rest of the evening. I know I behaved very badly because I received a letter the following day informing me that I was banned from the event for life. I can dimly remember shouting things at anyone who received an award. I remember people on the next-door table telling me to be quiet. I remember Stacey with her head in her hands. The two things I really remember are so embarrassing that I often hope they are mere hallucinations.

First there was me shouting: 'Oi oi, lads, backs to the wall, wiggy man is here ...' as Elton John came up to say hello to Alex.

And then there was me throwing a large table decoration at

Jonny Wilkinson while shouting: 'Oi, Jonny, catch this, you boring bastard ...'

I was shouting 'oi' a lot that night, but that was the least of my worries. A combination, I think, of mild depression, alcohol and nerves had turned me into a posh Danny Dyer. Oh, the shame. Although, to be fair, Wilkinson has to be one of the dullest men on the planet, but he had done nothing to offend me. I was, and am, a big Elton John fan (apart from *The Lion King*, which is music to kill yourself to) and can't believe I behaved like that in front of him. In the very unlikely event that either of them are reading this, I would like to apologise unreservedly.

F. Scott Fitzgerald wrote: 'Show me a hero and I'll write you a tragedy.' I'm not sure that he was specifically referring to my situation, but when it comes to heroes and me, I think they're best kept at arm's length. I'm just not very good with them.

Chapter 5

BBC

I think I knew that things weren't going to go very well at the BBC from the very first day. I'd been given a parking permit, something I later found out was a highly prized object at the Beeb. I arrived at the car park on Wood Lane and drove in. It was quite a tight squeeze as spaces were like gold dust. I finally managed to navigate the car halfway into a space before realising that I wasn't going to make it. I reversed and slammed straight into a car that had been trying to slip past me. I'm not sure whose fault it was, most probably mine – it normally is – but I think I was more nervous than I realised and my stress levels were high. I got out of the car and gave the driver of the other vehicle a volley of abuse along the lines of needing glasses, questionable birthright and general fuckwittery. Twenty minutes later and I was in my new office in Television Centre and having a chat with Myfanwy Moore, my old boss at Paramount who now had the unlucky task of trying to make things work for me at the Beeb.

'Did you have an incident in the car park?' she asked.

'Yes, I reversed into some moron who shouldn't be allowed to drive.' I was astonished at how quickly news travelled in these parts.

'That "moron" was the Head of Light Entertainment . . .' said Myf.

I gulped. I had a bad feeling already: this wasn't going to end well. That afternoon, a man turned up in my office and asked me what colour I'd like the room painted. I hadn't given this much thought; in fact I was quite surprised at having the option. I had a think for a moment before going for a deep red. Some say that red on the walls drives you mad – possibly this had something to do with the next couple of years? Two days later, I realised that being at the BBC was going to be very different from Channel 4 when someone sent me a snippet from the *Daily Mirror*. It was a piece about me that read: 'Trigger Happy Star Sees Red – Dom Joly has refused to start work at the BBC until everything in his new suite of offices is painted red.'

I laughed, but I knew that I was headed for trouble. I got myself into enough scrapes without having newspapers start to make stuff up about me. There was a definite feeling that, as you were at the BBC being paid for by the licence fee, you were public property. This was not a good place to be for someone like me.

I was very keen to do something different at the Beeb. I'd started to pitch a show called *100 Things to Do Before You Die* at Channel 4 just before I left. It was going to be like someone had given the show to the wrong person – no skydiving and seeing Niagara Falls, this was going to be offbeat and very weird. Channel 4 had liked it so much that they'd set up a website for people to send in suggestions. I pitched the show to Jane Root at BBC Two and, although I could see that she wasn't that keen on it, the lesson here was: when you're hot you can get anything through. She commissioned the show and we were off.

I think the first thing we did was: *Shoot fish in a barrel*, which involved my standing on a chair in a field firing a shotgun into a barrel full of water (no fish).

Then we did: *Go see your favourite old teacher.* This had me meeting an elderly actress (playing the teacher) in her home in a very awkward encounter where clearly she had no memory of me whatsoever. The rushes were looking very strange but interesting – there was definite promise in the thing.

We'd been filming for about a month when I happened to open the *Guardian* and see that Channel 5 had announced their new schedule. Prominent among their shows was *100 Things to Do Before You Die*. I couldn't believe it. The people in charge of Channel 4 comedy had just moved to Channel 5 and they appeared to have nicked my idea. Normally you can't really prove this sort of thing, but the fact that Channel 4 had actually made a website based on the idea was pretty conclusive. I was so angry I ended up blabbing to someone at the *Evening Standard* and the story went public. This was not the best way to keep friends in television but I'd never been good at keeping my mouth shut. Channel 5 vehemently denied the whole thing and claimed it was a 'coincidence'. Yeah right. In the end Channel 5 changed the name to *99 Things to Do Before You're 30*, so that was OK then ...

Their show was scheduled to come out before us and would steal any thunder mine might possess. I reached what I thought was a sensible conclusion and decided to stop making my show and try something else. I genuinely thought this was the sensible and most responsible thing to do. I wanted to make the best, funniest show I could, which was now not going to be this one. I hadn't understood the way the BBC worked, however, and my decision had the same effect as a dirty bomb going off in White City tube station. The BBC, I soon discovered, was a giant lumbering monolith that did not take kindly to disorganised, 'punk' programme-makers like Sam and me. It was quickly made clear to us that our cards were marked. My decision to stop making the BBC Two show had complicated budget ramifications that were still plaguing me when I left two years later and they asked for money back. I should have just ploughed on – it seemed that nobody actually cared what a show was like; it just needed to not mess up the Kafkaesque entanglements that constituted the BBC system.

Meanwhile, I got an offer from America. I had agreed to the sale of *Trigger Happy TV* all over the world with a substituted (soundalike) soundtrack created by some guy in a basement on a Yamaha – it was awful, but the music was prohibitively expensive to clear worldwide and I had little choice. Curiously, Germany was the only country to pay for the entire soundtrack as it was. I'd held out in America, however. MTV wanted to buy the series and I'd said no, hoping that someone would manage to show the thing with the proper soundtrack. When nothing else seemed to be on offer, I eventually agreed for Comedy Central to show the butchered version.

The show did very well in the States and they asked me to come over and do a US version. I had mentally moved on from *Trigger Happy TV* and didn't really fancy upping sticks to the States. Looking back now, I can't believe I made that decision. I should have been all over it and moved to the States and made a proper, controlled version of the show. As it was, Comedy Central came back and asked whether they could make their own version. They offered some serious money, and Sam and I agreed. The deal was that we would go out to the States, film a couple of sketches for the series and that we would executive produce. Comedy Central handed over the production to a company that immediately started making the series. The show was being made before we'd even realised it had started.

We flew out and met a couple of the people who were to be 'me' in the show. They were young and keen, but something about the whole thing was already not feeling right. Sam and I filmed some scenes in Miami and New York that were OK – not classic, but a good start. I was then taken into the Comedy Central HQ in New York to do some interviews. While I was there they asked whether I'd like to see the first show. I was very surprised – we hadn't even finished filming our bits yet, let alone looked at anybody else's. What did they mean by the 'first show'? I was told that the first one was going out that week. I was gobsmacked. I assumed that Sam and I would be in the edit as usual, making decisions, guiding the thing. They sat me down and showed me the first show. It was so awful that I actually assumed it was a joke at the beginning. It was like somebody had spoofed *Trigger Happy TV*. Random bad costumes along with appalling, soulless indie music haphazardly slapped onto scenes that occasionally went into slo-mo for no reason. It was horrific. It was a car crash. It was a valuable lesson about keeping control when dealing with America.

I remember staggering back to our hotel, the Soho Grand. I was incredibly depressed. I got into my room and looked out of the window to see a twelve-storey billboard with Sacha Baron Cohen as Ali G on it, staring down at me. We'd started off together at Paramount but he knew exactly what he wanted and had moved to the States to single-mindedly pursue it. We'd been half-arsed and didn't really know what we wanted and we had paid the price. Bugger.

Sam and I flew home and asked for our names to be taken off the series. We were mortified. The US version tanked, as it should have done, since it was so awful. Only in hindsight do I now look back and think about all the things we should have done differently. People still come up and say things like: 'I loved *Trigger Happy* but not the American version ...' Trust me, I know ...

If I thought about it too much it could drive me mad.

I think I have thought about it too much . . .

The BBC was about to launch their new 'youth' channel, BBC Three, and I was introduced to the energetic head of it, Stuart Murphy. He was very keen for Sam and me to do a show for his channel. We talked about *Dead Air*, the pilot we'd made at Channel 4 before we left. We wanted to make a show like that: weird, offbeat and silly. Stuart green-lit it, and Sam and I went off to try and work out what it might be. This was when I made another giant mistake. Instead of making the show as a spoof character with a fake name (à la Alan Partridge) I opted to be a spoof character but use my real name. Thus *This Is Dom Joly* was born. The joke to me was obvious. This clearly *wasn't* Dom Joly, but I think I expected everyone to know this. They didn't. All they knew was that the bloke from *Trigger Happy TV*, who had been in every scene but you never really got to know, now had his own chat show and appeared to be a monumental wanker. To be fair, I probably am a bit of a wanker, but the wanker I played on *This Is Dom Joly* was not me – different wanker. I should have just called the show *This Is Jom Doly* and it would have all made sense. But I didn't.

I was an idiot.

The concept of the show was that I, like everyone who achieved overnight success, had been offered a stupendous deal by the BBC and decided that I should have my own bloated, egotistical chat show. I made yet another mistake when trying to explain this concept in press interviews by using Johnny Vaughan as an example. I thought Johnny Vaughan was an amazing TV presenter and he'd been very supportive of *Trigger Happy TV* when he was on *The Big Breakfast*, but I'd heard terrible stories about him at the Beeb from people who'd worked on his show. I made my usual mistake of opening my big mouth about it. It got very bad – on the launch night of BBC Three he refused to do any links with me despite my show being one of the centrepieces of the new channel. This was all ahead of me, however ...

Personally, I'd never had any real interest in having a chat show or interviewing people. My specialty was mucking about. We split the thing into two parts. There was the studio element in which I 'interviewed' guests and hosted a real band. Then there were the VT elements in which we filmed a fake video diary of my life. The VTs were like filming a spoof version of *The Osbournes*, and I used it to get loads of cameos. I set up the premise that I lived in a house with a Cato-like manservant who would constantly attack me and that Michael Winner was my neighbour.

We filmed scenes in which I knocked a clown unconscious at a children's party (with Suggs from Madness), tried to sell my house to real punters adding a 'celebrity' surcharge to the price, got furious at 'papped' photos of me and Vanessa Feltz on a date, and embarked on a stag party dressed as Ali G with Mark Owen from Take That as a confused guest.

My enduring memory of the video diaries was a day we spent filming at Paradise Wildlife Park in Hertfordshire. The joke was that I'd adopted some animals and had turned up with my 'entourage', demanding to see them. The wildlife park was in on it but none of the real punters had a clue what was going on. We'd booked Lemmy from Motörhead to be part of my entourage. He agreed on the rock 'n' roll condition that he be picked up in a chauffeur-driven limo and that there be a bottle of Jack Daniel's in the back. It must be very tiring, being Lemmy.

On the day there was a mix-up and one of the extras for a later scene turned up beaming and a bit pissed in a chauffeur-driven limo. Half an hour later, a very, very angry Lemmy arrived sober, in a beaten-up minicab. We had to spend a long time placating him.

Later that afternoon I was filming a scene with the actor playing my dad. We were chatting by the tiger enclosure with a large beast just on the other side of the fence from us. I was in mid-sentence when the tiger lifted its tail and a powerful stream of hot tiger piss hit my face with considerable force. I was temporarily blinded, stank to high heaven and remain astonished that this clip has never found its way to one of those *TV Blooper* shows.

The studio element was very different. I wanted bands on to play live. This was great, because I could get some of my favourites on. The problem was that I then had to interview them and behave like a total wanker. Not all the bands, like the public, understood that this was an act. The Cure really got it. I'd met Robert Smith before, of course, and they eventually played twice on the show. Nevertheless, each time they came on I would do some awkward interview with Robert Smith, and I would get a barrage of online abuse from Cure fans who thought I was doing it for real.

Over the two series of the show we had Suede, The Waterboys, Ian Brown, The Cure, Gomez, Gary Numan, Grandaddy, Mercury Rev. I found myself doing surreal things like duetting with Marianne Faithfull on 'The Ballad of Lucy Jordan'. I adored the song and I'd organised for a false floor on the stage to collapse halfway through when I stepped on it. Unbeknownst to me, a roadie had unwittingly walked onto it and the thing had collapsed just before the show. The entire studio audience knew about the joke but I wasn't told this by production. I was therefore very surprised when there was total silence when it happened during the show.

The green room for *This Is Dom Joly* was always fun. After the show I would get gloriously drunk as I was so ripped on nervous adrenaline. I particularly embarrassed myself with the band Gomez. I was happily drunk-chatting to them when the guy who sounded like he should have been eighty years old but appeared to be only sixteen said: 'You're on fire . . .'

I thanked him profusely for his kind words and told him that I thought their new stuff was very good as well.

'No, I mean you're actually on fire ... Your jacket ...'

I think someone had passed around a joint and I'd taken an extra-large toke on the thing. This had left me a little confused, as dope tended to do, and I'd put my lit, normal cigarette into the top pocket of my suit jacket where it proceeded to smoulder quite dramatically. I was incredibly embarrassed but took the cig out and smoked it like nothing had happened. I could see in Gomez's eyes that they weren't sure if I was mad or stupid.

One night the sound man came up to me and made me listen to a very amusing sequence in which Marianne Faithfull, who had forgotten she was still wearing a radio mike, had wandered off to the bathroom to 'powder her nose'. She'd ended up dropping the mike down the loo. This was a two-grand mistake but made for some very funny listening back in the office.

Guests were random and hard to come by. We pretty much took who we could.

David Dickinson was all perma-tan, signet rings and packets of B&H, and suddenly dropped his cheeky chappy persona just before the show and snarled threateningly: 'We won't be mentioning anything about me and prison, right?' Up to that moment I had been unaware he had ever 'done time' but of course all I then wanted to do was ask him about it.

When Eamonn Holmes came on I spent the whole interview asking him anodyne questions like, 'What time do you get up?' and 'Do you use an alarm clock?' The next day the *Mirror* printed a whole page asking whether these were the worst, dullest questions in chat show history. They were. They were meant to be.

I also seem to remember that we had Nicholas Parsons sitting in a glass case with the words 'Break Glass In Case Of Guest Emergency' on it, but I might be making that up (I'm not).

In hindsight, I think I was suffering from Radioheaditis: make something very popular and then get freaked out by success and wilfully implode by making stuff that nobody really understands or likes. I should have got Coldplayitis: much simpler – repeat but bigger.

I'd set out to make a show where twenty per cent of the viewers believed it was real while the rest understood it was a spoof. The reality was flipped round and eighty per cent believed it was real and that I was a massive wanker. I am, unfortunately, rather good at playing being a wanker. I could tell that things were not going well at the BBC as Alan Yentob stopped popping in – success garners many friends but nobody hangs around to watch you die. There was the stench of death about me and people were starting to distance themselves at a fast trot.

I went onto the Radio 4 show *Front Row* to be interviewed by Mark Lawson. I was rather thrilled to be asked onto it. Three minutes in and I was not quite so thrilled. The general gist of the interview was: 'What has gone wrong?' He ended by telling me that he knew loads of people who had loved *Trigger Happy TV* but were now loathing the shouty person on the chat show. I checked again that he knew this was a spoof character and not actually me? He just looked back blankly at me. The studio smelt of failure and farts. I pushed open the heavy soundproofed door and escaped. Just to reinforce how badly things had got: John Leslie, the former *Blue Peter* presenter who was fighting off rape allegations in Ulrika Jonsson's autobiography, then harangued me in a bar. He leant over and asked me how I'd screwed up so badly: 'You were top of your game and then ... nothing.' It was bad enough having someone confirm your status in public, but when it was John Leslie then you knew you were in trouble.

Then, another hammer blow: Sam announced that he was getting out. He wanted to break our three-series deal with the

BBC and leave. I sort of knew this was coming as he had a lot less to do on the studio show and he wanted to start doing his own things but ... I felt very abandoned and really let down. We'd signed up to do this together and to me he was jumping a sinking ship. I'd gone fifty–fifty with Sam on everything we'd done together and it had worked well. There was something indefinable about the tension between us that created great stuff. He went off to direct adverts. I'm sure the pay was good but I knew that he'd never have as much fun as we'd had.

There was to be no third series of *This Is Dom Joly*. This left me with one series left to make for the Beeb as part of my dying deal. I decided that, much as I'd been loath to make another hidden camera show, I needed to give them a 'banker', something that I could be fairly confident would work and be a success. So I made a show called *World Shut Your Mouth*.

The basic premise was that we would do jokes all around the world. I was just blagging free trips abroad again. It's a problem that I've always suffered from: wanderlust. If someone is prepared to pay for my habit, I binge. It seemed that, having half-done BBC Two and conclusively done BBC Three, it was time for me to be handed over to BBC One like some increasingly toxic pass-the-parcel.

I dimly remember having a meeting with Jon Plowman and Lorraine Heggessey, the then head of BBC One, in which they said that they wanted some family-friendly type of show. They even gave me an example of the sort of thing that they wanted: outside a cinema showing a pirate film would be ... a big queue of pirates. I stared at them and nodded in a non-committal sort of way, and then wandered off to make the show I wanted to make.

To be fair, they probably could have guessed that I was not making the show they wanted early on when I asked for permission to visit the Seven Wonders of the World in one trip, to film the six opening scenes. I would travel to the Taj Mahal, stand in front of it for ten seconds or so before declaring, 'Now that . . . is shit . . .' and walk off. That was it. To make it worse, I decided that we should film nothing else on that trip so that the whole point of the journey was solely these scenes. I felt it was comedically pure. I was approaching maximum self-indulgence.

Nobody at the BBC stopped me. Three of us flew to Beijing, did a *that is shit* on the Great Wall of China, followed by the Taj Mahal, the Pyramids, the Grand Canyon, the Colosseum and (I'm not sure why) the Guggenheim Museum in Bilbao. The last one let the side down a little but it was a seriously out-there start to every show.

Another trip I made was to Newfoundland, the lonely island off the east coast of Canada. I'd had a Post-it note stuck to my desk for ages that just had the words 'Frighten an Eskimo' on it. Without doing a vast amount of research, I hopped onto a plane headed for Newfoundland. The immigration guy at St John's airport asked me my reason for visiting Canada?

'I'm here to frighten an Eskimo,' I replied cheerfully.

'We don't have any Eskimos in Newfoundland, sir . . .' replied the baffled immigration guy.

'Oh . . .' I said less cheerfully.

I decided that the joke could still be done with a non-Eskimo. I just needed to find someone ice-fishing in the middle of nowhere. We drove out of St John's and drove and drove out into the tundra without much idea of where we were headed. We just wanted to get somewhere remote. We had to stop in the town of Dildo. The inhabitants seemed blissfully unaware of the comedic value of their town name.

After about four hours' drive we finally came over a hill to see an enormous frozen lake in front of us with, joy of joys, an Eskimo-looking-type fellow ice-fishing right in the middle.

We parked the car and the cameraman set up in his position.

When he was ready he gave me the signal and I crept slowly towards him across the frozen lake. As the distance shortened between us, the camera slowly zoomed in and you could see that I was holding a large pair of cymbals. Finally, I got right behind the fisherman, who had not heard me approach. I lifted the cymbals and smashed them together. The Eskimo/fisherman jumped out of his skin, and I turned and legged it back to the van. I jumped in, the crew jumped in, and we all sped back to St John's and flew home. The footage revealed the fisherman to have just stood and watched in stupefaction as I ran away. I long to know what was going on in his mind. Were he an Eskimo he would have had over fifty words for snow, but possibly only one for me: 'Asshole!'

Another idea that I'd long wanted to do was to pretend to fly over the Grand Canyon with a big rocket strapped to my back. As a kid, I had always been a touch obsessed with people like Evel Knievel. They were always jumping the Grand Canyon in elaborate motorbikes or machines. Hidden camera jokes work best when there is plausibility to them. People hate traffic wardens and so, when they are faced with one trying to give them a ticket for something that they know is one hundred per cent wrong, this makes for good telly. Similarly, people associate the Grand Canyon with stupid stunts and so I knew that they would most likely accept the premise of a man wandering about with a rocket attached to his back.

First, though, we had to get a rocket. This involved one of our researchers having to organise the construction of said rocket somewhere in Las Vegas. This being Nevada, with very permissive gun laws, he had some problem explaining that no, he didn't want a real rocket, just a prop. Eventually someone was found who would make us a seven-foot rocket, with a red nose cone and the word ACME (it stands for *A Company that Makes Everything*, in case you wondered) down the side.

We needed a helicopter to film some of the scenes, so we rented one in Vegas that took us up to the canyon. Nothing brings out the inner child more than hopping into a chopper, especially when the pilot buzzes you down the Vegas Strip before heading out towards the desert. Once there, we got set up and waited for the rocket to arrive. A runner in a rental van was driving it to the canyon from Las Vegas. We waited and waited ... all rather conscious of the ticking clock on the helicopter rental meter. After a couple of hours we were starting to get worried. There was no sign of the rocket. Finally we managed to get hold of the runner. He was under arrest at a police roadblock by the Hoover Dam. In this post-9/11 America, there was much security around 'target sites' and the Hoover Dam was an important one. When the policeman had stopped our van and asked the young runner what he was carrying in the back, he was astonished to be told that it was a large rocket. Despite him showing said rocket and its clear non-functionality, the poor kid was arrested and we eventually had to send the production manager down to rescue him.

Our next problem was that the only part of the Grand Canyon that we could film in was on Injun' territory. The rest of the canyon was National Parks and they would not let us film there. Despite having fully explained what we were up to on the phone from London, the Native American official sent to deal with us just couldn't understand that we were not doing this for real. He kept going on about insurance and police involvement in assisted murder. By the time we had explained it all, it was getting late and we needed to get a serious move on. It worked brilliantly. The moment my character, British Bob, stood on the edge of the canyon with the rocket strapped to his back we attracted a sizeable crowd of tourists seemingly eager to watch a man crash and burn – we even got one of them to light the fuse.

For the TV joke we needed a second act and so we flew down to the floor of the canyon, smashed up the rocket, slashed my clothing and I then lay on the ground, supposedly unconscious, by the remains of the rocket, waiting for a hiking group to come upon us. As it so happened there weren't too many people wandering past. To get to the bottom of the canyon was quite a struggle and had taken some serious doing. We were starting to panic – light was fading – the helicopter meter was ticking ... Then fortune favoured us. Out of nowhere appeared this lovely old couple from the UK who looked as though they had just popped out for a walk on the village common rather than appear on the floor of the Grand Canyon. They fully believed my story, offered me a cup of tea and tried very hard to stop me climbing back up to the top and '... have another go'. God bless them.

When I returned from the US trip I took a couple of weeks off. Stacey was heavily pregnant with our second child and he/she was due any day. Six days later, our son Jackson was born in the John Radcliffe in Oxford. Stacey had to have a caesarean section and I followed her nervously into the operating theatre, trying my best to hold it together while someone cut her stomach open. It all got a bit surreal. As the operation proceeded, a nurse suddenly asked me whether I was Dom Joly. Slightly distracted, I replied in the affirmative.

'I went to the Dragon School with you,' said the nurse.

I stared at her for a moment and then recognised her.

'Oh yes ...' I said. 'How are you?'

'You went to the Dragon School?' asked the surgeon, looking up from my wife's innards.

'My boy goes there ... It's a good school,' he continued.

'Fooorrr fuccckkk's ssssake,' screamed Stacey weakly. She really had had enough of the UK's old boy/girl network.

To finish things off, our insurance company later informed us

113

that they had no record of the anaesthetist who worked on Stacey that day.

'According to our records he doesn't exist ...'

Sometimes real life got a bit too close to hidden camera ...

We brought Jackson home, but I couldn't hang around for too long. We were still mid-production and, although the budget apparently wouldn't stretch to non-stop foreign holidays, I had to be back filming in the UK.

I wanted to film outside London and chose to do quite a bit in the Exmoor area. My mum grew up there and not only did I know it quite well but there was a superb mix of topography to film in. Within an hour's drive you had moorland, thick woods, picturesque villages and seaside towns. We based ourselves at the Luttrell Arms in the quaint village of Dunster. This was a mistake, as the place had a lovely secret garden at the back, it was sunny and they served a very potent local brew called Cheddar. We spent a lot of the time down there 'totally ched-dared'. We did get some stuff done.

I'd already filmed here for *Trigger Happy TV* – it was where I'd done the strange sea captain who wandered around, randomly lying to old ladies about losing his wife and dog to the sea. For *World Shut Your Mouth* we filmed a lot in Horner Wood, just up from Porlock Weir. There was something primeval about the place and it had a strange atmosphere to it. In *Trigger Happy TV* we'd filmed things like the Troll Bridge there, but this time we positively carpet-bombed the place. For a brief period, anyone wandering through the woods could have been accosted by me as a very happy/depressed Goth, a lonely druid who needed to chat, having a fight to the death with a life-sized badger, as the world's fattest ninja rolling down the hill to land in a heap in front of them, a lonesome squeegee merchant who had set up traffic lights in the middle of nowhere ... There was something about the area that really clicked with hidden camera.

The weirdest thing we filmed there was my random Scotsman. I had an idea for a Scotsman approaching people and enquiring as to whether they were wondering what was under his kilt? My disguise was great: violent ginger hair and a full beard plus kilt kit. For some reason that escapes me now I decided to hang an uncooked chicken from my belt to dangle under the kilt (over pants). There then followed a frankly uncomfortable hour or so of filming in which I would approach ramblers and ask them (in a quite awful Scottish accent): 'I bet yoo're wooonderring what's oonder me kilt?'

What they were actually wooonderring was whether I was about to expose my genitalia to them. So, when I lifted the kilt to show the uncooked chicken, there was a reaction of confusion mixed with relief. 'It's a chicken that ay'lll be cooking tonight for my suupper ...' I proclaimed in an accent that was rapidly drifting towards Ireland.

I was astonished that anybody ever signed a consent form. My accents were always the subject of much mirth to the crew on shoots. Truth be told, they are mostly pretty awful. I do a passable West Country, a dodgy Cockney, a very good Dutch but the rest tend to wander all over the continents, starting in Belgium and sometimes travelling as far as South Africa by the end of a sketch. It never really bothered me too much – most Brits class people as 'foreign' and don't normally bother to work out which part of 'foreign' they're actually from.

After three months of filming, we were finished. I retired into the edit suite with Dave Frisby to put the series together. It was less bitty than *Trigger Happy TV* – the sketches were longer and so editing it all was a slightly easier process. When I'd finished I sent the shows over to the BBC and waited ...

I heard nothing for quite a long time and, as the show had been scheduled to air fairly soon, I was getting worried. Finally the call came and I went to see Jon Plowman, the head of comedy. I could sense something was wrong the moment I entered his office. I sat down, made the usual small talk and waited for the blow. When it came it was worse than I'd expected.

'Well, we've seen the show and ... to be blunt, it's really not a BBC One show. It's too dark, too weird, it's got terribly depressing music on it. Lorraine doesn't like it. In short, it's not going to be shown on the channel in the foreseeable future ...'

I sat there, absolutely stunned. After my inept handling of *100 Things* and then the failure of the chat show, this was the final nail in the coffin. I could hardly have screwed up at the BBC more if I'd staggered around the building drunk, naked and randomly firing an AK47 at people.

Back in Jon Plowman's office, however, there was a long awkward silence before I made my excuses.

'I'm sorry about this, Dom. I'll let you know what happens next,' said Plowman. He never did. Like the rest of the BBC suits, the stench of death about me was now so overpowering that it was the most they could do not to hold handkerchiefs over their faces as they spoke to me. So nobody did speak to me.

I can't remember much of that period. It's all a bit of a blur (a title, for the record, that I gave Alex James from Blur, a fellow *Indy* writer, for his autobiography). I know that I was really unhappy. I think I just came into the BBC and sat in my office in a funk every day for about two months with nothing to do. Finally, I found out from a newspaper that *World Shut Your Mouth* was to go out on BBC One, but there was very little publicity about it. The show was being buried and me with it, and there was nothing I could do. *World Shut Your Mouth* went out, got respectable ratings but made very little noise.

I remember being told on the phone, after about the third episode had aired, that the BBC had confirmed there would be no second series. This hardly came as a surprise but still nobody broached the subject of my future and what would happen next. I had a three-series deal. I had made three series, so now what? The answer came in a very BBC fashion when one day my pass simply didn't work at the gates and I couldn't get in. I had been electronically terminated.

I gained access to the building by signing in as a guest and parked my car in the horseshoe next to Jonathan Ross's special parking place. I took the lift up to my office, got a box and put everything into it. There were photos, some knick-knacks and the big mobile phone from *Trigger Happy TV*. I wandered downstairs and back into the horseshoe, where I opened the boot and put all my belongings in it. It would have made a fabulous pap shot, an ignominious end to an ignominious period. I drove out of the BBC gates and out of mainstream show business. I wondered what on earth I was going to do now. In four years, I had come from nowhere to the precarious top of my game and now I had tumbled back down into the abyss and I had no idea what lay at the bottom.

Chapter 6

Excellent Adventures

In the words of my new best friend, Jimmy Page, I was a little dazed and confused. I had no job. I had no idea what to do next. So I sold my flat in Notting Hill Gate to Salman Rushdie, moved to the country and went on holiday to Iceland.

Selling a flat to Salman Rushdie is a curious thing. Firstly, you become very paranoid at how lowbrow your bookshelves look. Admittedly this is probably not as paranoid as Salman Rushdie must have felt every time he saw a burka waddle towards him down the street, but I have to admit to binning Jilly Cooper's *Polo* and a couple of Wilbur Smiths before his first visit.

How I now regret not proceeding with the joke I told everyone I was going to do when I heard that it was Salman Rushdie, notorious recluse and hider from mad jihadis, buying my flat. I announced that I was going to re-tile my roof terrace before moving out. The new tiles would contain a pattern that you would only be able to make out from the air. It would have a voluminous target and the words 'Salman Rushdie Lives Here' in five-metre-high letters. The next time Google Earth swooped over London, the joke would be revealed to the world. I was very tempted and even got a quote for the thing to be done but in the end I thought it might just be going too far. He did, after all, still have a death threat over his head. It could have all gone spectacularly wrong. I'm not a complete wanker.

The idea for moving to the country was so that we could get cats and dogs and allow our children to roam the lush, golden fields in some idyllic, Albion childhood scenario that UKIP could have filmed and used for publicity purposes. The reality was that kids get very bored and most are hooked on hard cider and glue by the age of fourteen, when they hang out in bus stops wishing that something/anything would happen. We liked it, though. It was perfect for my writing.

I moved into a house in Quenington, in the Coln Valley, that I subsequently found out had been Anne Robinson's. She had moved out into a new enormo-dome that she had built with her *Weakest Link* earnings. (Later she and Joanna Trollope announced that they were moving back to London because of interlopers like Alex James and me ruining the Cotswolds. I was rather proud of this.) The house had a very curious and large red stain in the corner of the main living room. We were never sure whether there had been some sort of murder or it was just that Robinson had had an accident while topping up the ginger in her hair ...

I became the new 'village celeb' and started to learn the rules: Liz Hurley ran the next village, Kate Moss was mistress of another, Gwyneth Paltrow was rumoured to be house-hunting in the area. It was crazy – this was what I'd left London to get away from. Things came to a head when some entrepreneurial fellow set up a 'Tour of the Cotswolds Stars' Homes' in a coach. It only lasted a couple of months or so as it started by parking up outside Hurley and Winslet's pads but quickly nose-dived by the time it reached me and Gary Kemp. I used to go out and throw stones at the coach until I realised that this was fast becoming a highlight of the trip.

People in the area were pretty nice to us, but a bit bemused by my lifestyle. Several of them used to look at my wife with a pitying stare and I couldn't work out why until I found out that they used to regularly walk past the window of the room in which I would play online *Call of Duty*. These games would get quite intense and the language I used on my headset when dealing with a cowardly Frenchman or a racist US redneck was particularly colourful. I make no excuses for this; these things happen in war. Unfortunately, my neighbours assumed that I was having regular arguments with my wife and were about to take action when all was finally revealed.

My nearest big town was Cirencester which I frequented regularly, occasionally performing local celeb duties like turning on the Christmas lights. Things were good. Then, one morning, I drove into town to find it strangely quiet. People spotted me and would walk the other way and nobody would make eye contact. I couldn't understand what had happened. Then I spotted a photograph in a shop window. It was of the bemused owner shaking hands with the TV designer fop, Laurence Llewelyn-Bowen. Slowly I realised that every window of every shop in town had a similar photograph. It seemed that overnight a coup d'état had taken place and he had conquered the town. I could do little but retire to my village and lick my wounds.

I had started writing a column for the *Independent on Sunday* and this had brought me to the attention of publishers. A woman from Bloomsbury took me out for lunch and asked me whether I'd thought about writing an autobiography? I told her that I'd spent the last three years slagging off people who wrote their autobiographies when they were about twenty-five years old. It was stupid and pointless and greedy. There was no way I could write an autobiography at my age. She told me that there would be a hundred-grand advance. I asked her when she might need it by?

I flew to Harbour Island in the Bahamas to write the book. Looking back, I'm not quite sure why I did this as my study at home would have been fine. I think I thought it would be quite a literary thing to do. Actually, I just got very sunburnt and was so badly bitten by mosquitos that I found it hard to type. I also came to the conclusion that I didn't want to write an autobiography, despite having banked the money. So, instead, I wrote a pastiche book that, like my chat show, veered violently in and out of reality. To me it was clearly a work of fiction (the talking dog in the first chapter was a bit of a giveaway), but readers seemed confused. I was clearly having real problems equating my 'Dom Joly' character with the real me. I think that I can now see that I was trying to create some sort of division between the two. This is presumably why people like David Bowie become Ziggy Stardust and comedians become characters like Mr Bean or Ali G. This becomes a costume that you can put on and take off at will. I had no costume, or maybe I was wearing it all the time? I don't think I could tell.

I found it very difficult to divide the showbiz me from the one at home. My 4-year-old daughter, Parker, came back from school one day and asked me whether I was 'Dom Joly' as other kids had said that she was 'Dom Joly's daughter'. To Parker, 'Dom Joly' was what I went off to be in London. At home I was just 'Dad' and I felt a lot more comfortable with that. At least with 'Dad' I vaguely understood the rules – but my lives were very intertwined and this was a problem.

I was a bit lost. I'd had my fill of comedy for the time being and I had a long think about what I wanted to do next. As I'd proved with my endless travel blags on the comedy shows, I definitely had a bad case of wanderlust. I think, analysing it now, I saw travel as an escape – an escape from the insecurity of fame and scary family responsibilities that I didn't think I'd be up to. When I was abroad I could forget everything, be selfish, be anonymous. It was a temporary detachment from my life.

I was running away and I was to become rather addicted to it for some years to come.

I decided that I should concentrate on travel, both in television and writing. I started to think about what kind of show I wanted to make. I was an obsessive watcher of travel shows but felt strongly that they were very dishonest. Whereas most of the rest of TV had grown up and broken the fourth wall in terms of not patronising the viewer and being honest about stuff, travel TV was still in a little bubble. For instance, I'd watch Michael Palin travelling *Around the World in 80 Days*. There'd be much tension (telly loves tension) over whether he'd make a train in Egypt. He made the train at the last minute but then there was a glorious shot of the train leaving. Who took that shot? Again, in a Palin show I remember him being in Ethiopia and the voice-over telling us that this was a very dangerous area and they couldn't get out of the car – all this while we watched his car wind its way through hills in a shot taken by a distant cameraman who had clearly got out of his car.

Travel telly even lies about meeting a local fixer when you arrived in a city. Normally you meet them in the reception of your hotel but the director will always make Paul Merton randomly bump into a strangely helpful local at an exotic market. This chance encounter will then decide to help him for the rest of the show. I wanted to make a travel show that spoofed these ludicrous practices while also taking me to places that I wanted to go to. As I was wondering just how I'd go about doing this, fate intervened. Firstly, I got a call from the editor of the *Sunday Times* travel section asking me if I'd like to become a writer for them? I asked her what sort of things she wanted me to write about. She told me that she wanted me to go and 'do the things that everyone wants to do but never gets round to'. I didn't need much urging.

In the very same week I got another call: Sky 1 were making a 'celebrity' travel series called *Excellent Adventures*, in which they wanted people to head off on ... well ... an excellent adventure. So far, the list wasn't that exciting. Minnie Driver was off to swim with sperm whales and Vinnie Jones was off to Mongolia to fish. I saw both these shows and they struggled to make an hour of telly. Minnie Driver flew somewhere, got in a bikini, got on a boat and then fell off said boat next to some sperm whales ... Meanwhile, Vinnie Jones just wanted to fish but his director decided that he had to drive for days over flat, monotonous country to get there. Vinnie Jones was not happy. I had been asked as Macaulay Culkin had pulled out of his *excellent adventure* for personal reasons. Did I have an excellent adventure that I wanted to do? As it so happened, I did.

I grew up in Lebanon, and every year we'd drive off into neighbouring Syria on great expeditions. We'd take tents and camp in the desert, explore Roman ruins, swim in ancient dams ... I adored Syria – a truly magical country. I hadn't been back for twenty or so years. This would be my adventure. I would head off from Beirut into Syria and end up in Palmyra, a little town in the middle of the Syrian desert. I wanted to try and find a set of caves that we used to camp under. Somewhere, I'd scratched my name in one as a kid. I wanted to find it. Television loves tension, but it loves 'quests' even more. Sky said yes.

They wanted every celeb to travel with a friend. *Long Way Round* with Ewan McGregor and Charley Boorman had just been a hit and telly likes nothing better than to slowly milk and dilute a successful format to death. So they asked me whether I had a friend who could drop everything and head off on this trip with me? I certainly did. One of my oldest friends, Pete had married a girl from Newfoundland (the island with no Eskimos) and was now living out there amidst the icebergs with his wife and four daughters. Pete was an 'artist' but things artistic at the time were not going that well. He was free and, I think, longing for an excuse to head off somewhere hot. I called him – he was in. We were off.

Two weeks later, Pete and I landed in Beirut. The plane flew in low over the shattered city but nobody took a shot at us, as they would have done in the bad old days. Everyone clapped when we landed. The Lebanese are always appreciative of arriving somewhere safely. Someone had finally mended the sign over the terminal that used to read 'Welcome to Leb . . .' with the rest of the letters shot off. I was glad they had mended it – it was never the most reassuring welcome to a country. We picked up our rental car and headed into Beirut along the airport road that used to be such a sweet spot for kidnappers. We spent the night in the Commodore, one of the world's great war hotels. You used to pay less if your room faced the mountains, as that was where the shelling came from. There was a parrot in the bar that had a microphone in its cage. The parrot had been trained by some wag to make the sound of incoming shells. Many a rookie correspondent had found themselves diving for cover on their first night in town while the old hacks howled with laughter and downed pints of Black Label.

The following morning we drove into the hills above Beirut, where I'd grown up in a curious cocktail of paradise and war. I wanted to start our 'adventure' from where we used to set off when I was a kid, my family home. At the last minute, I thought twice about filming with my rather tricky family and so we headed off to Brummana High School, an English Quaker school that I attended before being sent off to boarding school in the UK. It was as I was wandering around this school filming that I discovered that I had been at school there with Osama bin Laden for a year back in the 1970s. This was quite a discovery, but I wrote about it at length in my first travel book, *The Dark*

Tourist (now, according to Hatchards, a Travel Classic), so I won't bore you with the story again here but you could always buy the book and read it for yourself.

We set off over the mountains of the Metn, headed for the Bekaa Valley, where in prime Hezbollah land we were going to visit the Kefraya vineyard, a place that had been making wine since Roman times. We filmed a scene where a very pretty Lebanese sommelier gave us glass after glass to sample. Playing it for laughs, I downed every one until I was so drunk that I had to retire outside and pass out under a pine tree to the incessant, reproachful wail of the muezzin in the town below. We spent the night in Baalbeck at the Hotel Palmyra, where my family always used to stay on our way to Syria. The hotel, once so elegant, was on its last legs. Baalbeck, so beautiful, had been starved of tourists and we found only one lone Japanese man wandering among the ruins when Pete and I checked them out.

We drove from Baalbeck to the tiny northern frontier post that I remembered from when I was a kid. Back then we would always have to wait for hours and hours while the documentation was sorted. Very little had changed. There was a little shaded river nearby and I used to swim in there until I spotted the water snakes darting about in the shallows. This was Syria all over, darkness lurking beneath a beautiful surface.

Things were fine on the Lebanese side of the border but we were given the full going-over on the Syrian side. They got us to empty the entire van and went through every case. There was a wonderfully embarrassing moment when a soldier opened one of Jamie the cameraman's cases. It was packed with tiny bottles of spirits stolen from the Commodore's minibar. I think that Jamie had assumed that Syria would be a 'dry' country. Far from it – although suffering under a horrible regime, the Ba'athists were a secular movement and alcohol was freely available. Syrian beer was surprisingly good.

there. We didn't inform our spy of the plan, as he would have definitely said no.

The following morning we drove out into the desert and I was astonished to find that, despite not having been there since I was a 9-year-old kid, I recognised things and managed to guide us for an hour to the base of the cliffs. There was no need for any fake excitement for the purposes of telly. I shouted at the top of my lungs and my words echoed around the cliffs just like they had back in 1977 (although possibly a couple of octaves lower). The director, Matt Reid, decided that we should make the climb up to the caves for the big reveal the following day. So we started to set up camp. Our spy went absolutely berserk. There was no way we could stay out here. We had to return to Palmyra. We asked him why we couldn't camp there? He lost all pretence of being a tourist guide and started going on about secret military bases. We all looked around the vast, arid expanse that surrounded us. We saw no bases. He insisted that he was not going to camp out in the desert and that, because he wasn't going to, we couldn't. I'd had enough of this bastard by now and I lost it. We had a violent slanging match that went on and on, with Pete giggling nervously nearby. Eventually I told him that we were going to camp here whether he liked it or not. He caved in and said that he would stay at the Zenobia but drive out to check up on us. I promised him that we would not do any looking for any secret bases and hinted that, thanks to progress in satellite surveillance, there were actually no secret bases in his country that the US and Britain were not intimately familiar with. He looked puzzled by this statement while also seemingly becoming more convinced that we were up to no good. He eventually disappeared back off to Palmyra and possibly another naked bath lady. For the first time, we were properly alone in Syria.

I still have dreams about that night. In this, the desert valley of my youth, we sat by our campfire and consumed copious amounts of Kefraya wine that we had bought at the vineyard back in Lebanon. At about midnight I put on Pink Floyd's *Wish You Were Here*. Back in the Seventies, we'd had an eight-track player in our early Range Rover and, apart from opera, *Wish You Were Here* was the only cassette we'd had. I opened the car doors so that the speakers were facing out and pressed Play. The music droned out over the desert. There was a full moon, which waltzed in and out of the low night cloud. At one moment, as we were all singing, a great swathe of moonlight marched across the desert plain until it hit us and lit up the cliffs that loomed high above us. I wish this had happened to me earlier – I could have found the right words at that urinal in the V&A . . .

Life didn't get much better than this.

There was no sign of our spy all night but he turned up the next day just as Pete and I were clambering up the steep, rocky slope towards the little caves at the base of the cliffs. He ordered us all to come down but everyone just ignored him and carried on upwards. After fifteen minutes of scrambling we got to the caves. Pete ducked into one and I went into another. They were small and had clearly been used overnight by hunters, as there were spent shotgun shells on the dusty floor. I headed to the back of my cave where I peered at the wall. There it was: still pretty visible, the word 'Dominic' carved into it by my 9-year-old self. This was as close to a result as travel television ever gets. I was unexpectedly moved and took a moment to reflect before exiting and starting a sarcastic chat with Pete about how we could now cash the cheque and get home. Eight years later I would be back on the border of Jordan and Syria to visit a vast refugee camp full of innocent civilians who had fled their homes and the chaos that had enveloped that beautiful, magical country.

Chapter 7

Happy Hours

I've had a long and steamy love affair with America. Growing up in Lebanon, the civil war was Levantine, my education and family were British, but my home entertainment was all-American. Lebanese TV broadcast almost nothing but American shows, and there was an early pirate video library in the nearby town of Brummana called Cineteque that contained almost every American movie ever made. Fortunately, they also had no truck with things like age restrictions and so I had a particularly broad education in every aspect of Americana from a young age.

My first actual experience of America was in 1987. My train pulled into Grand Central station early on a crystal-clear-skied New York morning. I dragged my little black suitcase through the breathtaking central hall of the station. It was like stepping onto the set of a thousand familiar movies. There was an energy in the air that you could almost touch. All around me, an ethnic kaleidoscope of New Yorkers rushed from destination to destination as though their lives depended on it. It was the *Wall Street* movie era – greed was good. Lunch was for wimps. I felt out of place, the only living boy in New York without a purpose.

I drifted out of the station into the sprawling expanse of the Manhattan jungle. It was a world of vast shadows, the sun blanked out by the sheer enormity of the Manhattan skyline. I rode the Staten Island Ferry, conquered the Empire State Building, explored Central Park. It was like meeting one of your childhood heroes and finding out that not only did they not disappoint, but that they were far cooler than you'd ever dared hope.

One of the most common insults thrown at Americans is that they are insular, disconnected from the rest of the world, with only twenty per cent of the population in possession of a passport. To us this seems unthinkable. When you travel in America it all makes sense. Why travel abroad when it would take you a lifetime to discover your own country?

To begin with, I only really flirted with the place, skirting the periphery, visiting the oh-so-cosmopolitan cities around her edges: New York, Miami, New Orleans, Los Angeles, San Francisco. Each with its own individual character, and complicated identity – enough to keep you busy for years.

I first went to Miami by chance. I had to film some American *Trigger Happy TV* clips there. I wasn't really looking forward to it. To me, Florida was all about neon tackiness, *Miami Vice* and hideous theme parks. In a way, I was right. There was a kind of gloriously confident kitsch to Miami. That was part of its appeal. This, after all, is the only city in the world where a yellow Ferrari makes sense.

The combination of fabulous climate, art deco architecture and a mellow Cuban-Hispanic influence instantly made Miami one of my favourite cities in the world. Nothing quite beats sitting on the terrace of the Tides hotel, mojito in hand, watching a perfectly toned world glide by. One breakfast, the rapper Ja Rule and his pet lion sat at the next-door table to me for breakfast. Moments later, Mike Tyson and an entourage of twelve took the table on the other side. Only in America ...

People warned me about Los Angeles: 'No one walks anywhere, it's not a real city, it's all so fake, so artificial.'

They were right. It was all those things and you needed to embrace them to enjoy the place. When the wheels of my plane first touched down at LAX, I got the same weird feeling in my stomach that I'd had way back in 1987. Such familiar places, yet I'd never been before. It was 3D déjà vu. I'd just stepped through the screen.

My first time in LA, I did the place the way it should be done. I was there for meetings at Comedy Central and they really pushed the boat out. I got sent a stretch limo to the airport that whisked me in air-conditioned splendour to my suite at the Chateau Marmont, the Sunset hotel that's borne witness to the very worst of Hollywood excess. Whilst unpacking I was unable to keep my eyes off the smoggy LA skyline through my French windows. I wandered into the Chateau's small courtyard garden to find Johnny Depp nursing a Tom Collins. It was a celluloid fairyland. Even the urinals, for some unexplained reason, had crushed ice in them instead of the usual, oh-so-common blue cubes. I'd never be content peeing anywhere else again. Every sharp-suited executive at every meeting promised me the earth was mine – it was a merry-go-round of broad smiles and green lights. It all went pear-shaped, but my God, it was fun. I was living the cliché: the American Dream.

All of this and nothing ... I'd only dipped my toes in some of the coastal outlets of this enormous entity. Politically, America is two countries – one, the big coastal cosmopolitan cities that encircle the second, the more insular and, to our eyes, more unsophisticated heartland: the Republic of Middle America.

It was into Middle America – Jesus Land – that Pete and I flew for the first episode of *Dom Joly's Happy Hour*, possibly the greatest blag in TV history. It came about like this.

Back in the UK after the *Excellent Adventure*, we edited the show together and gave it to Sky. It made quite an impact. Sky came back and said that they'd like to make a travel series with me. I went into a meeting with the bosses at Princess Productions, who had made the *Excellent Adventures* series. Henrietta Conrad and Sebastian Scott were proper telly professionals and it was certainly quite the experience to see the medium stripped to the bare essentials.

Sky were very keen to do a series with Pete and myself – did I have any ideas for a theme? I wanted to continue the Lebanon/Syria idea and go to dodgy, *Dark Tourist*-type places and try to get underneath the headlines to find some fun. They felt it was a bit too close to Ross Kemp's territory. He was already making his *Gangs* series for Sky. We batted about various ideas until Sebastian brought out the *Guinness Book of Records* and flicked through it. *World's most dangerous cities? Most extreme weather zones? Most remote destinations ...* So this was how telly was made? Find a peg, pick a presenter and off you go ... Kerching. I wasn't that interested in any of these ideas, and we chucked some more about until someone finally said, 'Don't you have any hobbies?'

I thought about this for a moment and then jokingly replied, 'Well, I like a drink ...' It was as though I'd invented electricity. Everyone lit up and started nodding.

'That's the one – very Sky. That drinking scene in Lebanon worked.'

And that was pretty much that. Suddenly we were commissioned to make a show about drinking all around the world. I still maintain it was indeed the greatest blag in the history of television (apart from when Chris Evans went round the world playing the eighteen greatest holes in golf). I rang Pete in Newfoundland and someone in his village went to get him off the whaling boat, and I told him the good news. 'Tiger ... You remember all that drinking we did when we were younger?

Me and Sam in the first *Trigger Happy TV* photo shoot.

Trigger Happy hitchhiker.

'Hello, is that Rentokil?
I have a large rat in my
flat . . .' – *Trigger Happy TV*.

Transmission card for
the second series of
Trigger Happy TV.

Robert Smith in my
kitchen, Notting Hill.

'Now that . . . is shit . . .' Cairo
– *World Shut Your Mouth*.

British Bob at the bottom of the Grand
Canyon – *World Shut Your Mouth*.

Celebrating the end of shooting
Ian Brown's 'Golden Gaze' video
on the roof of Absolutely, London.

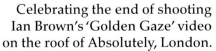

Shit Fingers, Mexico –
Dom Joly's Happy Hour.

Pete and I join an
armed biker gang in
Australia – *Dom Joly's
Happy Hour.*

Miami Nice. Me and Pete on South Beach –
Dom Joly's Happy Hour.

Les Boys do cabaret . . . Me
and Pete in Munich – *Dom
Joly's Happy Hour.*

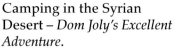

Camping in the Syrian
Desert – *Dom Joly's Excellent
Adventure.*

Me and Gordon Brown on a seriously hot night in Beijing – photo taken by Sarah Brown.

About to dance live in front of the nation for Comic Relief with my underwhelming baggy pants.

About to sneak into Liz Hurley's grounds – *Deadline*.

A rare moment with Tom Daley – *Splash!*

Me and Stacey, Mexico.

Coming out of the jungle to find that Shaun Ryder had adopted my son, Jackson – *I'm A Celebrity . . . Get Me Out Of Here!*

Parker and Stacey Solomon in the hideous Versace Hotel, Australia – *I'm A Celebrity . . . Get Me Out Of Here!*

Me in heaven, diving off cliffs on Lake Joseph, Muskoka, Ontario.

The ASBO Vicar – *Fool Britannia*.

'Wot you looking at?'
Watermelon, Glasgow
– *Fool Britannia*.

Stupidly sunburnt
man and Paul Young,
Benidorm – *Fool
Britannia*.

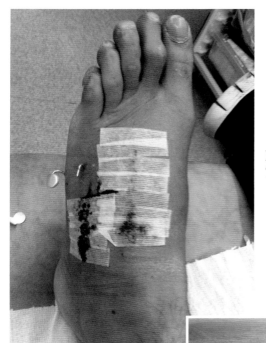

Reason you don't go on *Total Wipeout*, Buenos Aires.

About to ski down a live volcano in a show Channel 5 never bothered to air – *Rough Guide to Nicaragua*.

The hopeful moments before the fall – *Who Wants To Be A Millionaire?*

The kebab to give you nightmares forever – *Fool Britannia*.

That is now considered research – we're off round the world drinking ...' He was predictably amazed, although even more so when Princess announced that they weren't going to pay him to make the show.

'Oh, come on, the travel itself is a treat for him,' said Henrietta Conrad, a multi-millionaire.

I eventually managed to get them to buy Pete four shirts from Paul Smith as payment for the series. I still can't quite believe this happened, but Princess were not ones to treat their staff with much love ... It was to become an issue throughout the series and I grumbled about it – a lot. This got me a reputation as being 'difficult'. If being 'difficult' means that you think people should be paid for their work and that a show should be something you put your heart and soul into so that it doesn't become some formulaic piece of crap then, yes, I'm very 'difficult'.

We started filming in Miami, easing our way into the danger zone. We drove down Ocean Boulevard, marvelling that this was the run-down location for the violent drug deal gone wrong at the beginning of *Scarface*. Now it was the funkiest strip in America and packed to the rim with the beautiful people ... and us.

We quickly learnt that people in Miami drank cocktails ... This was the sort of incisive journalism that the show was brimming with. Sky was half-concerned with making something informative, but also wanted something entertaining. I was entirely concerned with making an entertaining romp around the globe with the occasional dig at travel shows. My informative side stretched to the revelation that wherever you went in the world, someone made a disgusting local spirit that they claimed had aphrodisiacal qualities.

The Sky lawyers were also a bit concerned about the fact we were making a show about alcohol at all. We were told in no uncertain terms that we should 'Not glorify the consumption of alcohol. Not drink in excess. Always drink in context.'

This made us howl with laughter. We used to drunkenly ring the Sky lawyer in the middle of the night from various bars to announce that I was having my seventh vodka and that I was worried about the context ... She stopped taking our calls after a bit. I'm sorry. We were probably really annoying.

We left Miami and drove off to look for America proper. We met some hillbillies in the Appalachian Mountains. Barney Barnwell, an unintelligible hillbilly who made his own potent strain of moonshine, was telly gold. I'd always heard about moonshine, a clear spirit made in illegal stills by people whose basic beef was that they resented having to pay duty on their alcohol – to them it was 'un-American', and who was I to argue? Barney fitted the description of a moonshiner: long white beard, silly hat, faded dungarees and a possum called George Jones, who lived on his shoulder.

He'd organised some of his friends to come round that evening with their different moonshines so that we could try them all. The friends looked like extras from a Klan rally but were all incredibly kind and polite. Each had their own recipe – PeachShine, ColaShine etc. – and they were all cutely keen for us to sample their wares. I can remember very little of the rest of the evening. Watching the footage shot that night reveals a moment when I ask how strong the Shine was? I was told to spit some on the fire, which I did. The fire flared up as though petrol had just been added. Enough said.

Pete and I wound our way through the Deep South, visiting increasingly strange places. We spent one night at a bed and breakfast in which the owners had built a jail in the basement and stuffed the house full of oversized furniture and creepy dolls. We left very early the next morning.

The most frightening moment never made it onto the screen. We'd made friends with some policemen in Jackson, Mississippi, and they allowed us to tag along as they set up random roadblocks and checked for drunk drivers. When we'd finished filming, one of the troopers offered to show Pete and me round the local jail on the condition that we didn't film.

We left the crew at the door and entered what I can only describe as the most terrifying place I have ever been to. We were taken down a corridor, where a guard sat on a chair facing into an open cell. From within came the most terrible screaming I'd ever heard. As we passed by I glanced in to see an inmate sitting on the floor, restrained by some sort of straitjacket. He was wild-eyed, foaming at the mouth and had the look of a man who was not unused to extreme violence. He was on suicide watch. Quite how he could even attempt suicide while in a straitjacket was a matter that I never got to the bottom of. This was not a place for glib questions.

We were taken into a large bare room with a table and two benches that were built into the ground so that nothing could be ripped up and used as a weapon. Around the top of the room was a balcony with a row of individual cells. At the press of a button from a guard in a control room behind thick glass, the cell doors swung open and the inmates were released. We were being shown around by the sheriff, an enormous bear of a man with whom you clearly did not argue. He shouted at the inmates to come down and sit.

'Listen to me, we've got some important visitors from the BeeBeeCeee in the YoooKayyy. If they ask you a question then you answer respectfully ... Am I clear?!!'

The inmates all nodded nervously. I thought it best not to tell the sheriff that we were Sky not BBC – the BBC opened all doors abroad. I looked at the inmates – they were nearly all under twenty, some as young as fourteen. A few were wearing white overalls, while most were in red. I asked the sheriff what the difference was?

'Those in red are in here for murder.' Pete and I nodded and looked at each other nervously. The sheriff got us to ask the kids (for that's what they were, and all black) some questions. We felt woefully inadequate for the task and asked a couple of inane things, both of us wanting to get out of this hellhole, this cul-de-sac of despair, as quickly as possible. After about half an hour we were out and back in the car with the crew.

'How was it? Did you get bum-raped?' asked one. For probably the first and only time on a shoot, we didn't laugh or even respond. That night I had terrible dreams ... Truly the stuff of nightmares.

Our arrival in New Orleans was like driving onto the set of *Escape from New York*. This was eight months after Hurricane Katrina had devastated the city, but it seemed that not much had been done to repair the place. We approached the city down streets and streets of abandoned houses, entire abandoned neighbourhoods, dark and ominous due to lack of electricity. It was creepy as hell. The centre of town wasn't that much better. Electricity there was irregular, no air conditioning worked and it was insanely hot. The whole city was suffocating, angry and heartbroken – it was an unsettling place to be. Wandering late at night down a backstreet of the French Quarter, the maudlin strains of a lone blues guitarist took on a completely new meaning: a paean to a sunken city.

We were told that the Ninth Ward was the worst-hit area and we drove out there the next morning. It was an astonishing sight to behold: vast swathes of a First-World city completely deserted, utterly devastated. Houses had messages painted on them in panicked scripts – 3 *people alive*, or 1 *dead*, or *Atlanta*.

We went into a couple of the houses. You could see where the waterline had reached up to. It was nearly at the ceiling of the first floor. We reconvened in the street to film a piece to camera when three police cars screeched up next to us, and the officers got out brandishing guns and made us all get on the floor and 'spread 'em', in what seemed to be a slightly unnecessary manner. They were really aggressive and accused us of being looters. We tried to explain that it would be a bit weird to do this with a film crew in tow but this didn't go down well.

'Don't get smart with me, boy, or I'll break your face . . .'

I piped down slightly.

After twenty minutes, once we'd shown them papers and filming permits, they relaxed a bit.

'If you guys had gone into any of these houses we would have busted your asses and you'd have been going down for a long time . . .' said the most aggressive of them.

We all looked at each other as though the idea of going into any of these houses was utterly ridiculous. I prayed that they wouldn't want to check our footage or we would probably be heading for a place similar to the hellhole we'd just visited in Jackson, and we all definitely didn't want that to happen. They eventually let us go but told us to get out of Dodge, and we needed no urging. I didn't blame the police – what we were doing was disaster tourism and if I had been a local I would have got annoyed as well. It was time to leave America before something bad happened – it was only a matter of time.

Much as I adored travel, making *Happy Hour* was tough. This was mostly because what I usually loved about travel telly was going out with the crew after a hard day's work. On *Happy Hour*, Pete and I were normally so wasted that we'd retire to our hotel rooms with black coffee and codeine.

Coming home was hard, as I would be physically and mentally wiped out. I just wanted to sleep and do nothing. Unsurprisingly, Stacey wanted some help. She was home alone, looking after two young kids while I gallivanted around the world. She wanted someone to take over. She wanted to go out and have some fun. What I was doing *was* work but it was a difficult one to justify.

You're just travelling the world getting pissed and having a laugh. Don't come home and tell me it's tough . . .' Stacey would look at me accusingly.

'But it *is* work . . .' I'd reply truthfully.

'Yeah, work you enjoy and have a great time doing.' Stacey was not having it.

'So, it's only work if I don't have a good time doing it? I'm sorry that I've chosen a career that involves me doing things that I enjoy. Maybe I should be a coal miner, would that make you happier?' I was on a hiding to nothing and I knew it.

'Just don't pretend that what you do is hard . . .' Stacey was not letting go.

My job *was* hard, but it was also enjoyable and liberating. I tried to put myself in Stacey's shoes: what if she was roaming around the world and I was at home looking after two little kids?

I remembered what my mum used to say about my dad when he travelled. She used to really miss him and long for him to come home. When he came home, however, he wasn't the person she had been looking forward to seeing. I think I was fast becoming that person but didn't realise it.

Our next destination was Russia. For serious drinkers this had to be the mother lode. Russians like to drink, really drink. Curiously, for a nation of alcoholics there were remarkably few bars. This turned out to be because Russians didn't really want to waste time with comfy chairs, soft music, a pleasant ambience – they just want to neck a bottle of vodka and pass out in the street. This was a country where beer was a legal soft drink.

When Gorbachev tried to ban vodka because alcoholism was so affecting productivity, the locals took to drinking perfume or making samogon, a kind of moonshine vodka that had the effects of liquid rocket fuel. I sampled some in a flat somewhere near St Petersburg. It was ninety-seven per cent proof. I think I had three shots. After the second one I briefly imagined myself to be the ruler of the free world and fully understood the Soviet urge for world domination. On this stuff the world was most definitely yours. The third shot killed me off. I have no memory of the fifteen or so hours that followed.

Blurry footage taken by an equally drunk crew showed me in a minibus somewhere hurling abuse at passers-by. At some stage I arrived at a hotel in central St Petersburg where, for some reason, I started a small fire in the lobby as a form of greeting. I definitely got to a room and somehow got online because my garbled messages to Stacey back in the UK were so incoherent that she got the staff to break into my room to check that I was not dead. Whoever came in would have found me naked and unconscious on the floor and clearly thought it best to leave me, as that was where I woke up. On the plus side, I had zero hangover. The samogon was so concentrated and without any of the usual impurities that cause the headaches and mood swings. Russia was quite a trip.

We flew to Moscow, a schizophrenic city caked in grime and dirt but topped with elaborate, gleaming gold cupolas and crucifixes. The population was very similar: 'New Russians' who'd suddenly made vast amounts of money and were in a mood to spend. Large, shiny black cars zoomed around the all-mod-cons city centre at great speed. They took their oligarchs from high-end shop to extortionate hotel restaurant, spraying dirty snow onto the general population that stood hunched and weather-beaten, gazing at their strange new world in resigned disbelief.

New Moscow was no longer the city of empty shelves and bread queues. Anything you wanted – and I mean anything – was available for the right price. To highlight this, we visited a place we saw advertised where you could get your hair cut by 'Nice Russian ladies without any pants or other clothes'.

This was no false advertising. We were ushered into a fully

141

functioning salon where a naked woman did her best to cut my hair before I decided that enough was enough and that I hadn't signed up to present *Eurotrash*. As the TV crew and I attempted to exit, like pious *News of the World* reporters, we were faced with a corridor full of scantily clad women beckoning us into dimly lit rooms with dingy mattresses. We scarpered sharpish and collapsed giggling in our car, having done our bit to further the British reputation abroad as emotionally crippled homosexuals.

It was at moments like these when phoning home was tricky.

'How's the filming going?' asked Stacey.

'Fine ... all going well,' I'd reply.

'What have you been up to?' she'd continue.

'Oh, this and that, you know ... Getting my hair cut by a nude woman in a brothel ... Oh, and I saw Red Square today ... How are the kids?'

Leaving Moscow, we headed out onto the Russian steppes. We would drive and drive and drive towards the infinite horizon. For hours and hours and then days and days we'd motor on, gaining a tiny understanding of what foreign invaders had faced when trying to conquer this behemoth of a country.

Everywhere we stopped we were ushered into places where industrial amounts of vodka were produced and we'd have to go through an unbelievably elaborate ritual of toasts. Most started with one to our parents, then to our family, then to our hosts, then to us as guests and then ... to pretty much everyone in the world, shot by shot. The key was to distract the host by pointing at something and then dumping the vodka in a nearby flowerpot. This method allowed me to dispose of about one in three of my drinks but still left me semi-conscious after every encounter. It made you very wary of meeting anyone. Upon arrival in any new town we tended to duck down in the car or hide behind corners whenever anyone approached us. It was like being hunted by alcohol snipers.

If this wasn't bad enough, we had a fairly unusual interpreter along with us for the ride. Her name was Natasha and to say that she was not a 'New Russian' was something of an understatement. She described Stalin as a 'genius' who might have been a bit 'firm' in running Russia but did a far better job than the 'Jews and Germans' who were apparently now in the driving seat.

One morning she ventured that Ivan the Terrible was not really that terrible, more 'Ivan the not-so-bad'. I gave up arguing with her – despite her vehement views, it was actually quite interesting to be so confined with someone holding such a diametrically opposite world view to your own.

Natasha was the first in a series of local fixers who became characters in the series. She was particularly brilliant because she was very stern, with no discernible sense of humour. My favourite moment with her was actually rather poignant. We were standing by a statue of Peter the Great, a location where newlyweds paid a visit for good luck. As wedding party after wedding party came and went, I couldn't help noticing that the girls were all rather tall and beautiful while the men were all short, fat and particularly unattractive. I mentioned this to Natasha, who sighed, 'Yes, this is because for the last hundred years we have lost all the best men to war – our male gene pool is now very shallow and stinky ...'

Drinking was deep in the Russian soul and sat side by side with the national melancholia.

I returned home and slept for a week, much to Stacey's disgust. My only consolation was that Pete's wife Michelle probably had it a lot worse. She'd been left alone in Newfoundland looking after his *four* young daughters *and* he was being paid in shirts. Fortunately, I decided against using this line of argument with Stacey.

I couldn't quite shake the feeling that that was probably not the way Michael Palin conducted his business.

Stacey had started to get used to me being away and had established a routine that my return only served to disrupt. I was starting to feel like an unwelcome lodger in my own home. Recently she admitted that she 'hated' me during this period. I can't say that I blame her. She was a fantastic mum to our kids while I was mucking about/working around the globe.

Next up was Mexico. Our first stop was at a *corrida*, a Mexican rodeo where the director thought we might get some nice shots. I hadn't quite anticipated what he had in mind.

I'm not really a horsey person. Living in the Cotswolds, you'd think I might have taken up polo or fox hunting but I have always been more of a 'lying in front of the TV' man. That's not to say that I couldn't ride. When I was young, growing up in the Lebanon I had my own horse. She was called Calamity Jane and I spent a brief period rather fancying myself as some sort of Levantine cowboy. During the Lebanese Civil War, when petrol got very scarce, I even rode to school on a couple of occasions. This would have been cool if my mum hadn't insisted on accompanying me, leading Calamity Jane on a rope. You wouldn't have found Billy the Kid doing that sort of thing and my interest in equine pursuits quickly dwindled, as I became the butt of many a school joke.

All this flashed through my mind as the director of the TV show asked me whether I could ride.

'I'm something of an accomplished horseman,' I lied, quick as a flash.

'Good,' he replied, 'because we need you to dress up as a Mexican cowboy and take part in the event.'

I necked a couple of stiff tequilas and tried to remember which bit was the saddle. Sometimes I should just have kept my mouth shut. An hour later and I found myself squeezed into some tight leather chaps, sporting a pair of spurs and an enormous sombrero. There was no going back now. I was given a sprightly looking horse that registered a panicked look as it saw me waddle towards it. Horses smell fear, I remembered, so I tried to look as nonchalant as possible but I think that we both knew that I stank of terror.

I mounted my steed and cantered into the arena slightly faster than I'd anticipated. After a tentative couple of minutes, however, I actually started feeling quite comfortable. Over the Tannoy, the commentator informed the large local crowd that I was a guest rider from 'Inglaterra' and I got a huge cheer that dangerously boosted my confidence. I was starting to strut my stuff a little bit and even managed to gallop the full length of the arena before pulling up sharply right by the stands. A sexy Mexican woman wolf-whistled and a portly, moustachioed man proffered a bottle of tequila. I grabbed it and tried to gulp some down in a suitably macho manner. Things were going well and the crew seemed to be getting some good shots.

'How are you feeling?' asked the director.

'Great, piece of cake,' I replied.

'Good,' he said, 'now they want you to chase a bull, grab its tail and try to flip it over.'

I nodded and tried some deep breathing. I was in too deep. I couldn't back down now. The sexy Mexican lady was winking at me and the tequila had hit me hard. I was directed to the very top of the ring where revolving metal gates led into the bullpen. The cameraman was laughing his head off. He knew that he was about to film gold dust.

A cowboy screamed instructions at me in Spanish. I didn't understand a word but nodded and hugged the saddle with my thighs as tightly as I could. Mexicans ride with one hand on the reins, the other one must always be in the air, unless tipping a bull, in which case it should be on a bull. There was a crash and suddenly there was El Toro. He took one look at me, snorted in derision and shot off towards the stands. I kicked my horse hard and it bolted after the horned monster. I managed to get level with it, adrenaline pulsating through my veins like crack cocaine. I was going to do this and become a local folk hero: El Inglés, the man who came and conquered the bull. I steadied myself and leant down to my right, trying to grab the bull's tail. I made two attempts and then suddenly I had it. At least, I thought I had it. I felt a warm sticky sensation. I'd inadvertently stuck my hand up the bull's arse. It shot off in a different direction in some discomfort and I was left alone raising my bullshit-covered hand to my horrified face.

The crowd howled with laughter and I limped out of the *corrida* trying to wipe the stuff off onto my leather chaps. By the time we'd finished filming, the story had spread like wildfire and every Mexican I passed waved their fingers at me in delight. '¡*Ay caramba!*' as Speedy Gonzales would say. It took me months to live the 'Shitfingers' moniker down. It was a gift to the crew and not one that they were going to forget soon.

We headed off up into the Sierra Madre to a ghost town called Real de Catorce, an old silver-mining town that had been deserted when the mines closed. Over the years, a group of people had returned and restored some of the houses to live in and the place was becoming popular in Hollywood as a film location. Locals couldn't stop telling us about how Brad Pitt had been there for two weeks very recently.

We were going to film a peyote scene. Peyote is an incredibly potent hallucinogenic used by local Indians and visiting hippies for powerful trips. This wasn't exactly alcohol but we never much worried about that on the show if it got in the way of a laugh. We used a local vegetable called chayote as a prop for the filming and had a lot of fun making a paranoid dream sequence in the desert. When we'd finished we headed back into the ghost town for a drink. A local who had been showing us some of the best locations asked us whether we wanted any real peyote? I definitely didn't but I did want to see it. He handed us a bit that looked like the end of a cactus. Pete put it in his pocket, joking that his night was 'sorted'. We forgot about it and ended up in a makeshift bar in town. At one point, Pete and I wandered outside and sat on the steps nursing our beers. Pete took out the peyote bulb and joked about dropping it in his beer. At that very moment a Toyota Land Cruiser drove past us on the dusty central street. I looked at the car and saw that it contained four Mexican policemen and they were all looking at us suspiciously. The man on the passenger side was staring hard at Pete's hand ... The hand with the peyote in it. Before we knew what was happening, the vehicle had stopped and the police had jumped out and were all over Pete. He was spread-eagled on the floor and the peyote was ripped from his hand and held up for the others to see. I suddenly realised that we had a big problem on our hands. How was I going to get out of town quickly without being arrested myself? Sorry – I meant how was I going to get Pete out of this sticky situation?

He was arrested for possession of hallucinogens and taken to the makeshift police station that we didn't know even existed. For a ghost town this place was seriously organised. Pete was locked up and looking rather nervous. I went in with the fixer and started trying to negotiate. We told the police that he was holding the peyote as a prop for a filming sequence but they were having none of it. They told us that he was to be transported to the state capital where he would be put in prison until a trial. The guide told us that they were talking months followed by a serious prison sentence. The normally intensely relaxed Pete, a man described by his training officer when he unbelievably once tried to be in the army as 'so laid-back he could be a duvet', was looking very unsettled. We asked the head honcho whether there was anything that we could do to sort this matter out between ourselves. He laughed as though the idea of a Mexican policeman taking a bribe was an insult to his entire nation.

I went outside and discussed matters with the crew and Alphonso, our wig-sporting Mexican fixer. Alphonso then went back in and had a private chat with the police chief. He came back out looking very serious.

'He will not move – Pete will go to the trial. They are very serious about peyote here. They want to make an example of him. He will go to prison for very long time.'

We all looked at each other in disbelief.

'Bloody hell, Alphonso ... Don't sugar-coat the pill, will you?' I was really worried.

I went in to have a word with Pete.

'How's it looking, Tiger?' he asked me nervously.

'Fine, it's looking fine. Alphonso is dealing with it and we'll have you out very soon ...' I smiled weakly at him while trying to suppress a strong mental image of him in a small prison cell, meeting a giant hairy man called El Bubba.

A couple of hours passed as we kept going in and out of the police station. They were enjoying the drama and were in no hurry to sort anything out. They were now saying that the transport to the state capital was not going to come until the following day. We had a big meeting in the bar. We pooled all the money we had, both personal and from the production kitty. I think we got about $700 together. I went back into the police station with Alphonso. We sat down with the police chief and told him that we were so upset that our filming had caused such problems for him. We were also worried that the arrest of the mega-famous performer Peter would have international repercussions when the press got hold of the story. Nobody wanted the hassle of this and we wondered whether we could maybe sort out the misunderstanding over what was a filming prop with us donating something to the town restoration fund? I passed over an envelope with the money inside. The police chief looked inside the envelope for a moment and then looked back at us. For a terrible moment I thought we were about to be arrested as well. Then the police chief smiled for the first time since we'd met him. He announced that there had indeed been a terrible misunderstanding and that, if we signed a couple of forms, we could leave with Pete but we were to leave the state immediately. We signed about seven forms. I had no idea what they said. I didn't care. I just wanted out, and for Pete or me not to shack up with El Bubba.

Twenty minutes later we were out and running through the streets with Pete. We grabbed our stuff in record time and sped out of town with Pete looking nervously in the rear-view mirror. We only relaxed when we crossed the state line about an hour later. Catorce had suddenly got a little too Real for our liking.

'Dad, are those *Simpsons* clouds?' We were speeding across a flat-calm Lake Rosseau towards Port Carling, intent on a hearty Canadian breakfast of pancakes, bacon and lashings of maple syrup. I looked up from the gleaming controls of my speedboat, my tanned torso taut with tension as my muscular arms guided the vessel expertly between two pine-wooded islands. I turned languidly to my family, who must all have been thinking just how lucky they were to have such a great, uber-manly husband and father in total control of this boat. I was about to agree with my daughter that, yes, the clouds did actually look just like those in *The Simpsons* title sequence, but I hit the wake from a passing pleasure boat and was flung violently overboard. The emergency cord attached to my wrist cut the motor automatically. The boat came to an immediate stop but Superdad's ego was seriously dented. Luckily, we were in Canada and no one had a clue that I was a very important UK minor celebrity on my annual Canadian summer holiday.

This annual holiday was and is my lifeline. I'd flown home from Mexico and tried to rejoin the normal family routine, but I knew that we had a mammoth double filming trip to Australia and then India coming up. I couldn't quite pluck up the courage to tell Stacey this. Luckily, the Canada break was already booked and came just at the right time.

My Canadian summer holiday has always been the subject of much questioning by bemused UK inhabitants. 'Summer ... in Canada? Ooh, better take some warm clothes and hot chocolate ...' Little do these ignoramuses know that Toronto is on the same latitude as St Tropez and enjoys scorching hot summers, rarely dipping under thirty degrees centigrade. I don't hold this against them. After all, I was once like them.

The first couple of times that I visited were at Christmas, and all my preconceptions were confirmed – blizzards, ice, drinks freezing solid inside the car, most of Toronto appeared to live underground in an enormous network of tunnels containing thousands of shops – this was not the place for me. Why hadn't I married a Brazilian, or a Bahamian, or a Maldivian?

No, I had to choose a Canadian, a polite American, a Ned Flanders to the USA's Homer Simpson. What was I thinking? Then Stacey started to suggest that we spend our precious summers in Canada. I drew my line in the sand.

'There is absolutely no way in the world that I am wasting my summer by going to igloo land. I want to go to the South of France or ... anywhere ... hot, but not Canada. Freezing my nuts off in winter is bad enough but there is NO WAY THAT WE ARE GOING THERE FOR SUMMER, AND THAT'S FINAL.'

Two weeks later we were all on an Air Canada flight bound for Toronto (official motto 'Diversity our strength', although it should be 'Jeez, it's cold and windy here, eh?'). I hated not being in control of my life. Having said that, it turned out to be the best decision that I never took – so what do I know?

Ninety per cent of Canadians live within *one* hour of the US border. This, in the second largest country in the world. It doesn't take a geographer to realise that this leaves a lot of empty space to play around in. Canadians, therefore, like to get back in touch with their pioneer heritage by going 'up north' and getting back to nature – fishing, hunting, canoeing and playing charades . . . a lot of charades. Or that's how it used to be anyway. Things have changed a bit since the early twentieth century, when you were in danger of a bear attack if you visited the outhouse. Nowadays, most cottages come with satellite TV, high-speed broadband, industrial barbecues and posh lakeside restaurants. It's wilderness but with lattes.

From the moment I arrived, I was smitten. For posh old Canadian hands, it was not quite the simple, elegant destination that it once was. For me, however, it was utter heaven. Three spectacular lakes dotted with pine-covered islands and gargantuan granite rocks – it was a kind of Canadian *Swallows and Amazons*. Things got even better when I discovered speedboats and water toys.

I am now glad that I married a Canadian. Every year I pick up my rented speedboat as, for the next three weeks, I'm barely off the water. By boat I can go shopping, out to eat, visit three top golf courses and, of course, swim and play to my little heart's content. All my kids' various Canadian cousins join us for our vacation and so I'm kept busy hurling them round the lake all day. When we tire of this, the braver ones join me in a spot of what is known in the UK as 'tombstoning'. We know it simply as cliff jumping. I've got it down to a fine science. I spot a suitable rock, I bring the boat in as close as possible and use the depth finder to check the landing area. When I'm happy, I anchor up – we all clamber up the cliffs and hurl ourselves screaming into the void. This is what summers are all about.

Even the Canadian 'lifestyle' starts to rub off on me as well. I start to wave back at passing boats, I say hello to strangers in the street. I smile at assistants in shops. If I behaved like this back in the UK I'd be savagely beaten. In Muskoka, however, it's par for the course and I start to get used to it. I almost like being nice. This is clearly very unhealthy but there seems to be little that I can do. This is the place where I am most blissfully and perfectly happy. Every year we talk about moving there permanently. Then Stacey, who emigrated from the country for a reason, reminds me that for nine months of the year the temperature is about minus twenty and we quickly decide to just keep going there on holiday.

Anyway, after three weeks of perfect summer we had re-bonded as a family and I felt able to tell Stacey about the mega-filming trip I had coming up. She was as cool as she could be in the circumstances. We flew home and I was there for two days. The TV juggernaut waited for no man and my next stop was Darwin, Australia.

I'd never been to Australia before. I'd always thought I wouldn't like it. I was wrong. I bloody loved it, from the tropical remoteness of Darwin to the dust-red of the Outback. I think that I'm at my happiest in deserts. I could have happily spent two months driving around the place.

We had found a superb character for a guide – he was called Harry. He made his living by taking tourists on trips in his boat, from which he dangled large bits of steak off sticks and made enormous crocodiles jump out of the water to grab them. Harry was almost a cartoon Aussie – big beard, Outback outfit and a wicked sense of humour. When we returned to Darwin from our great expedition into the Red Centre, he invited us to his local pub for our last night up north. The pub was called The Humpty Doo and was not for the faint-hearted. When Harry turned up in 'civvies', it turned out that he was a member of the Hells Angels Motorcycle Club. The Humpty Doo was a hangout for hard-drinking bikers, and we had quite the evening. It started with Pete and me having to down a 'Darwin Stubby', which was a giant bottle of beer. We moved on to rum and then things get a bit hazy. Footage reveals that at one stage I was in the bar on a horse while Pete had somehow got astride a water buffalo. Then two Hells Angels drove into the bar on their motorbikes and started doing wheel burns so that, pretty soon, the entire bar was thick with smoke. I remember very little of any of this, which is a shame as it was certainly a night to remember.

We flew from Melbourne to Mumbai. I rang home from the airport. Parker, by now a smart 6-year-old girl, answered the phone. She'd just helped her school raise some money for a leper colony and was now convinced that I'd catch the disease.

'If you get it, Daddy, what will fall off first? Will it be your nose or your ears?'

I professed ignorance and tried to change the subject but she was insistent.

'I think it will be your ears, then your nose, then maybe your arms.'

I tried to interest her in the news that I would be riding an elephant upon my arrival in Mumbai but Dora the Explorer had apparently done that quite some time ago.

'If you lose your legs, will you be able to swim?'

I told Parker that I had to go. I had important research to do in the bar. She left me with this positive thought:

'The good thing is that the tigers won't eat you because they won't want to catch leprosy.'

Mumbai was quite the culture shock. To ease the pain we stayed in the sumptuous Taj Mahal Palace hotel, the place that, just eighteen months later, would be attacked by terrorists in an orgy of hideous violence. We filmed a surreal scene in which we arrived at the hotel dressed in Raj-era uniforms on the back of a large elephant. It was hotter than an oven and on several occasions I worried that I might actually die of heatstroke on the back of this magnificent beast.

The same thing happened when we filmed a weird dream sequence in Goa in which Pete was, once again, on an elephant and was hunting me through the jungle. I was dressed in a furry tiger suit and so hot that I needed medical assistance and immediate rehydration at the end of the scene. India was not the place to film in. Everything needed to be done very slowly so as not to heat up. This was tricky because the moment I arrived in Goa, I wanted to get the hell out of the place as fast as I could. I was tired and run-down from the constant travelling and drinking.

We'd taken a hellish eleven-hour train journey down to Goa only to find yet another kind of hell awaited us: hippies. If there was one tribe that I detested in my youth, it was the Boomshanka Brigade, the public school idiots who went off to India and Thailand to take mushrooms and go on and on about how 'really amaaaaazing' everything was. They'd return home in stinky hippy garb speaking a weird form of pidgin English in which they'd constantly implore you to 'Take a chill pill' or 'Mellow out, dude'. The number of times that I longed to kick these culture jumpers unconscious eludes me, but it was an awful shock to arrive in Anjuna only to find that they were all still at it.

We travelled on to Hampi. This was a very special place – a secret river valley dotted with staggering ruined temples and opulent palaces. It looked like the real-life set of *The Jungle Book* and somehow we were in King Louie's palace. We made our way through the narrow, worn stone streets towards the river. We met an elephant that, when given a banana, tapped you on the head with his trunk as a blessing. Once at the river, cool stone steps led us down to a little bamboo coracle that glided us across the river. As I watched the tall towers and boulders of Hampi slip away behind us, somewhere, far above us, a temple bell rang. I was in the footsteps of E. M. Forster. I was the last great Indian explorer. Jesus, I was fast turning into a hippy.

We reached the far shore and disembarked, camera crew in tow. A loathsome-looking German hippy in plastic sandals was waiting for the ferry. He stared at our cameras with obvious displeasure.

'You are totally ruining the purity of our existence by coming here,' he said.

I was so blown away by the sheer banality of his statement that I made him repeat it. He didn't because he had more to say ...

'Television is the work of the devil and you are all lizards ...'

The crew and I looked at each other, shrugged and then trudged off towards the next location. He probably had a point.

We flew home from India – Pete, to Newfoundland and me to the Cotswolds. We knew that we still had one more show to film but I wasn't sure how we were going to cope. It was going to be a European road trip from London to Prague and we were leaving in two weeks' time.

While home, *Fifth Gear*, Channel 5's answer to *Top Gear*, contacted me. They wanted to see if I'd be interested in road-testing a tank for them. I couldn't resist and the road-legal behemoth was delivered to my house the following day. The villagers looked suspiciously out of their windows as it was offloaded into my drive. This clearly confirmed their suspicions that it was only a matter of time before I started behaving like Keith Moon.

The director wanted me to go on a mission in the tank and I suggested that I might do the school run in the thing. They loved the idea, and so after a little practice I set off to pick my kids up. It all went quite well until I started up the imposing school drive. The tank then developed a leak and started spewing oil all over the place under the horrified gaze of the headmaster. Unfazed, I parked up outside the building and enjoyed watching the faces of my kids as they came out. My daughter, Parker, was mortified and immediately went back inside and hid. My son, Jackson, however, was in seventh heaven and I ended up driving him and a friend home with him popping out of the turret and waving to his friends. I felt like a good dad for once.

Sadly, the following day I went to pick him up in my usual car and he came out only to burst into tears when he saw it.

'But ... where's the tank?' he wailed.

Being Superdad was not always easy.

Speaking of motor vehicles, Princess Productions, with whom most communication had now broken down because of the different directions we wanted the show to go in, had got us a Lotus Esprit in which to do the Prague trip. I had other ideas and managed to blag an enormously luxurious Jaguar XJ8. I'd been reviewing it for the *Sunday Times* and they'd kindly extended the loan.

Pete and I had both lived in Prague. I'd been working there as a diplomat for the European Commission in the early Nineties during my short-lived 'serious' period. Pete had come out to visit me and ended up moving there to become a full-time slacker/novelist. This final show was probably one too many. We had a new director, a woman who had very strong ideas about how she wanted the show to be. Not only did I disagree with this vision, but we had been making the show for so long that we sort of directed it ourselves and it must have been very hard for her to deal with. It all ended in tears in a hotel room in

Munich with Peter dressed as a woman and me in lederhosen. It wasn't very pleasant. I wish I could have handled it better.

To make things weirder we had a production coordinator, Lora, who, for some wonderfully odd reason, had a phobia of pylons, windmills and bridges. This made our progress through Europe very tricky. She would be driving the crew vehicle when she would suddenly spot something like a wind turbine ('Like evil triffids,' she would mutter), and she would freeze and bring the van to a halt by the side of the road. The only way we could continue was to put her in the back and completely cover her with a blanket before driving out of the danger zone. Our curious cortege wound its way across the Continent.

We started off in Belgium. I adore Belgium and seem to always end up filming there. The Belgian tourist board had also noticed this and contacted me to see if I'd be interested in some free holidays in their country in return for me writing about the place? I declined but offered them a new slogan: 'Belgium – it's not as shit as you think.' I never heard anything back.

We raced the sedate Jaguar around the Nürburgring like it was a Formula One car. In Bavaria we found a brewery that allowed people to come and bathe in vast vats of beer. We couldn't turn this opportunity down but I wish we had. Not only was swimming in beer not quite as pleasant as I'd imagined, but four locals in tight Speedos unexpectedly joined us. I suspected that they had rather been looking forward to a little 'schwinging' session and it all got a bit awkward. Pete and I made our excuses and slipped away into the night.

Upon our arrival in Pilsen, home of the mega-brewery of the same name, we immediately got to work on a rare scene that I'd actually thought about back in the UK. Normally we'd have organised things to visit and then we would make up the scenario as we went. This one, I felt, was a winner. We wandered around town posting big signs that read:

PISS-UP
TONIGHT
AT THE BREWERY
ENTRANCE FREE

Then we set up a party room in the middle of the labyrinth of cellars and tunnels underneath the brewery where they kept the beer. We had party balloons, streamers the whole shebang. Nobody turned up. It was galling to learn for absolute certain that we couldn't organise a piss-up in a brewery.

Pete and I finally rolled into Prague with a heavy heart. This was the last show in the series and, hard as it had been, we had persevered and made what I thought was a really original and funny series. I remain exceptionally proud of it and very annoyed that we couldn't use the original music on the DVD. I did briefly toy with the idea of pitching a drugs sequel called *Dom Joly's Bad Trips*. Stacey finally put her foot down. This was probably a good thing, as I would now be dead.

Chapter 8

Reality Bites

In full camouflage gear, we started yomping across fields towards the rear of Elizabeth Hurley's property. Ingrid was huffing and puffing and it was all good stuff. When we got to a fence near the edge of the property we hunkered down to wait. Suddenly, there was movement in the Hurley household and the lady herself, plus assorted hangers-on, came out into the very field we were hidden beside. Hurley and her mates were attempting to round up some cows. This made for great piccies – it was real *City Slickers* stuff.

Suddenly, someone in the Hurley group looked our way. I ducked down but he must have spotted something as he started striding towards us. Ingrid, the camera crew and myself all lay as still as possible in the trench – we were partially covered by bushes but not brilliantly. The guy came right up to the other side of the fence. There was silence. Finally, I had to look up – he was staring at me in total confusion.

'Hello,' I said.

'There are people hiding in this ditch,' he shouted incredulously back to the group.

'RUN!' I shouted.

Ingrid, the camera crew and I stood up and legged it back across the fields to our car, while I heard someone on the Hurley side shout for security. It was total chaos. We finally got to our car and jumped in and zoomed off. About a minute down the road a large 4x4 went racing past us with two thuggish-looking guys inside. We'd got away, but only just.

When we'd been driving around London in the Toyota Previa for months on end filming *Trigger Happy TV*, there had been an in-joke about my potential second career. Everyone was certain that I should be a paparazzo, as I seemed to have an innate ability to spot a celebrity face, however minor, at a hundred metres, in a crowd. It was not an ability that I was particularly proud of, but it was what it was. I also happened to love taking photographs, although mostly of the travel variety. So when I was asked whether I wanted to be in a show called *Deadline*, in which a bunch of celebs would become paparazzi, I was interested.

It was a typically telly idea: gamekeeper turned poacher etc. In hindsight, as with most of these things, I should have dug a little deeper, or indeed just thought – ITV2 ... *Nein danke*. I did try to find out who the other celebrities might be, but they wouldn't let on. I knew that Janet Street-Porter was to be the editor figure in the show. I liked Janet, despite her being a monumental egotist, so I took a punt and signed up.

We all had to meet up in a boardroom just off Soho Square, like nervous schoolchildren on the first day of term. I was the last to arrive and, as I walked into the room, I desperately scanned it for a familiar face. I was to be disappointed. It would be fair to say that the cast was not a stellar one. In no particular order they were: Abi Titmuss, Dean Holdsworth, Chris Parker, Yvette Fielding, Iwan Thomas, Imogen Lloyd Webber, Lisa I'Anson, Ingrid Tarrant and Blair McDonough. I had fallen far and fast.

The only two I recognised were the former Olympic athlete Iwan Thomas and the DJ Lisa I'Anson. I knew I'Anson because, while filming a character in *Trigger Happy TV*, I'd targeted her.

I had this really fat, stupid American character called Dwayne, who wandered around London stopping passers-by and giving them a story about how his tour group had left him behind and asking them whether he and his dog, Jensen, could come and stay with them for a while. For the beauty, I put an announcement in the PR sheet, *London at Large*, that the winner of 'America's Stupidest Man' was in town and available for interviews. I'Anson's radio show were the only people to get in touch and so I went off to be interviewed by her. What followed was an excruciatingly awkward encounter in which she tried to ask me questions that I continually and purposefully failed to understand. She never worked out it was me and I wasn't going to tell her now.

She only lasted a couple of days. Our first job was to snap people coming out of the Met Bar. I was determined to find a fire exit and sneak into the back. She started bleating about how this was really embarrassing as she and all her friends went to the Met Bar socially ... I asked her whether she might have thought about this before signing up. She had a meltdown. The following day she left the show.

It turned out that we were to be overseen not just by Janet Street-Porter, but also by a curiously dressed, porky Australian called Darryn Lyons, who ran one of the UK's biggest photo agencies. To say that he was a larger than life character would do a disservice to him. I think Charlie Brooker's *Guardian* review of the show (that we gleefully passed around the office secretly) sums him up the best:

The set-up: a bunch of glittering stars try their hand at producing a weekly celebrity magazine under the aegis of Janet

Street-Porter, the Fleet Street legend famous for sounding like she's rolling five broken dice in her mouth whenever she speaks.

Each week, there's a tense showdown in the boardroom (sorry, 'meeting room') during which she fires someone (although she doesn't actually say 'you're fired', she says 'clear your desk', thereby convincing the viewer what they're watching is in no way similar to *The Apprentice*).

Janet's assisted by two deputies: Darryn Lyons and Joe Mott. Mott (played by a young Kenny Everett) spends most of his time quietly moping at the edge of frame in a stupid flat cap, a bit like Jack Tweedy in this year's *Celebrity Big Brother*. He seems almost depressed, which is possibly something to do with having to share an office with paparazzi supremo Darryn Lyons, a monumental bell-end who looks precisely (and I mean precisely) like Mel Smith playing a King's Road comedy punk, circa 1981.

This being a fabricated telly job, the bosses will have been instructed to behave like rude, uncompromising, dick-swinging bastards throughout – an opportunity Lyons gleefully seizes with both hands. He struts, he barks, he bollocks, and he bangs on and on about how important it all is, in the dullest and most macho manner possible, as though he's single-handedly leading an SAS task force into Syria. It can't be much fun being bellowed at by a man who looks like a 46-year-old Woody Woodpecker impersonator under-going a messy divorce, especially when he's shouting at you just because you failed to get a decent photograph of Pete Doherty – something the world needs like increased carbon emissions.

Yes, because unlike a real editorial team, the celebrity trainees are expected to take their own photos as well as writing copy, which makes it about as accurate a depiction of the magazine production process as an episode of *Ugly Betty*. Of the trainees, only Dom Joly, who seems to have turned the whole thing into some surreal personal adventure, shows any promise whatsoever. The rest just mill around bumping into each other like blind chickens. Considering this, and the fact that 50 per cent of the job (i.e. typing) isn't very televisual, the end result is far more entertaining than it has any right to be.

Reading a review of a show that you are currently in could often be fatal but I think that I was too far gone for that. I actually got off on the paparazzo element but the weird, fake dynamic of the 'office' drove me to the pub far more often than usual. I think I was pretty much drunk from start to finish of the show. It was the only way to cope. 'Reality' TV is often very tempting to the 'resting' celeb as it normally pays good money to do something unusual and exciting. Unfortunately, the actual reality of doing 'reality' is that you always end up feeling rather cheap and abused – that's what makes good telly after all. Also I had had my own little experience of being papped and doorstepped and I'd never enjoyed it. The *Mail* once decided to try and dig up some dirt on me and started doorstepping my family around the world. My sister set the dogs on them in Lebanon but my dad, from whom I was estranged, probably thought he was doing me a favour when he invited the pushy reporter into his house in France. Luckily the only thing he got out of him was an embarrassing photo of me on a horse. When the story eventually 'splashed' it was a bit of a damp squib – 'Trigger Happy TV Star Is Middle Class' was the genuine headline.

I wrote to them to insist on 'upper-middle' but they never replied. I buried whatever scruples remained and dived into the world of celeb-hunting.

I spent a lot of time outside Kate Moss's London home. I'd have two cameras slung over my shoulders and an emergency compact version in my trouser pocket – the adrenaline was high. Despite my attempts to blend in by wearing a weird woolly hat and a scruffy mac, the other paps quickly recognised me and there was a sudden minor feeding frenzy, like hungry goldfish around a solitary plankton. I was photographed from every possible angle, powerless to do anything about it until their hunger was sated, which it quickly was, as my photo wasn't worth much in the celeb market unless they could pitch it as:

> Has Celebrity Stalker Dom Joly gone mental? Comedian spotted looking like a down-and-out hanging outside Kate Moss's house ... An unnamed friend says that he is worried for the former funnyman's state of mind ...

Paparazzi are many things, but they are the only truly honest yardstick of where you stand in show business. If they can sell your picture, they'll snap you. If they can't, you'll be ignored, although they'll always get a 'death snap' – one snap of anybody they even remotely recognise – this is in case they suddenly die. The 'last' photo of anybody, however lowly in the celeb food chain, is very valuable.

I'll never forget – having just recovered from a serious bout of pneumonia brought about by filming all day in a Welsh coal-mine (proof, if it be needed, that I was never cut out for proper work) – answering my door in Quenington to see a rat-like personage staring at me intently. He was taking not-very-surreptitious photos with a camera half-hidden in his left hand. I was in my dressing gown and looking like I'd just got out of bed, which I had.

'Can I help you?' I asked the rat-man.

'Are you ill?' The rat-man was clearly assessing my physical state.

'Sorry ...' I replied, confused ...

'Are you ill? We read you were in hospital with pneumonia.' The rat-man appeared to be concerned that I wasn't on my deathbed.

'Sorry, who the fuck are you?' I was angry now.

'I'm from the *Daily Express*, we got a report you were dying ...'

I lost it and kicked the guy in the arse as hard as I could while 'helping' him off my property. It was like being circled by a badly dressed vulture ...

Back on *Deadline* duty, I asked a pap in Kate Moss's road which celebrity he disliked the most. He didn't hesitate: Jude Law. He nearly spat the name out. Around me every pap agreed. They all hated Jude Law and they all seemed to have stories about him.

'His real name is Dave,' said a very young pap with slightly crossed eyes. 'Do you know he's actually from Lewisham? When he turns up to premieres we all shout, "Oi, Dave, over here!!" and he ignores us. It's really funny.'

Everyone started blurting out their Jude Law stories. One quietish guy in a van with a little dog at his side told me a blinder: 'I spotted Jude Law walking around Primrose Hill and I started taking pictures of him. Suddenly this elderly resident runs up to me. She starts telling me to leave him alone etc. I tell her to calm down, he's a celebrity after all, and he's in a public place and I'm only taking his picture, it's not the Third World War. Suddenly Jude Law runs up to me, he's been listening in and his face is twisted with rage. He shouts, "I'M AN ACTOR, NOT A CELEBRITY!!" From then on he's known by all us "paps" as Celebrity Dave.'

Another pap piped up about David Walliams.

'He hates us,' says the first guy. 'He was desperate for fame and now he's got it he resents us.'

His partner interrupted: 'Once, he came out of his house

pointing back at it, saying, "See this house. I live in it because I'm rich and successful, unlike you arseholes."'

It rapidly became a therapy session and everyone wanted to pour their hearts out.

On another day I decided that I wanted to get some photographs of Harry Potter, aka Daniel Radcliffe, who was appearing in the play *Equus* at a nearby West End theatre. I could have just waited outside the stage door and snapped some shots but this wasn't terribly televisual, so I went and rented a chef's outfit. I then repeatedly tried to gain entrance into the theatre by claiming to be Radcliffe's personal chef. This was funny but both the theatre and Radcliffe freaked out – they thought I was some kind of homicidal stalker and extra security was added.

My next plan was to hang around the theatre dressed as a street cleaner. This was going well until the comedian Alan Carr happened to walk past me. He recognised me and I could see by his face that he had just witnessed what he thought was the sheer horror of show business: one moment a successful comedian, the next a street cleaner. He marched on without saying anything but clearly determined to work even harder to avoid my fate ... Eventually Radcliffe's 'people' found out that I was linked to the *Deadline* show and they brought pressure to bear on the production company to make me leave him alone. Man up, Radcliffe, it was only a bit of fun.

I had a bit of a run-in with James Bond as well. I was hanging around the rather sumptuous Mandarin Oriental in Knightsbridge waiting for someone (I can't remember who) when Pierce Brosnan stepped out of the building. I seized my opportunity.

'Hey, Mr Brosnan, could I get your photograph?' I asked politely.

'Why don't you fuck off?' came the unnecessarily aggressive reply.

Brosnan started to cross the road towards Harvey Nichols. I had the bit between my teeth now, so I crossed the road fast and nearly got hit by a taxi. I lifted my camera and tried to get some more shots of Pierce Grumpy. Brosnan shot me a look of pure hatred and marched over to me. He stamped on my foot hard and kept me pinned to the spot. He leant in very close, so close that there was no way I could get a photograph.

'You're a persistent little fat fuck, aren't you?' growled Brosnan in a rather surprisingly sinister manner.

I assumed that I'd caught him on an off day but a little internet research showed that Pierce was a persistent paparazzo antagonist. There was footage aplenty of him having a go at several snappers in the US.

Ingrid Tarrant turned out to be the ex-wife of Chris Tarrant, and she took an instant dislike to me. The feeling was mutual. We would almost always be sent out in pairs and she clearly loathed being put with me. This, of course, made the show do it all the more often as (I've said it before) telly loves tension.

So, the show paired me up with Ingrid and we were sent to get the photos of Liz Hurley that ended up with me lying in a ditch. This was particularly embarrassing as she was my neighbour – but I had lost all sense of right and wrong by now. Somehow, I had gone from having a US TV show, being nominated for three British Comedy Awards and the Golden Rose of Montreux, to sneaking into my neighbour's garden to try and get photos of her for a magazine that didn't really exist, while accompanied by Chris Tarrant's annoying ex-wife. As falls from grace went, this one was pretty up there ...

Ingrid Tarrant had the most cringeworthy moment on the show (and that was quite an accolade). She was chasing people at some film premiere and saw the late Peaches Geldof getting into a limo. She chased Peaches, shouting something like, 'Peaches, please, I knew your mother ...'

Bringing up the name of Peaches' troubled, dead mother was not the classiest thing to do and Peaches Geldof snapped back, 'For God's sake, have some dignity ...'

Now, at that particular time, when Peaches Geldof told you off about dignity then you knew you were in trouble. Years later I was asked onto her short-lived chat show. The producers plied me with wine before I went on and I was steaming drunk by the time the cameras rolled. I was interviewed by some weird wet-wipe who had something to do with producing the Chris Moyles breakfast show. The whole thing was so inane that I started taking the piss, loudly. After this disaster they then made the mistake (or was it?) of sitting me directly behind Peaches while she interviewed people dressed in furry costumes. It would be safe to say that I interjected quite a bit. For the next week or so I got slammed by the Chris Moyles radio sycophant gang, but the *Sun* TV reviewer admitted that I was probably speaking for the nation. Personally, I can't remember too much, which is probably for the best.

I spent my last day on the job chasing Lily Allen around the East End and ended up getting a great photo of her trying to playfully punch me in the face. Job done, I retired to the Groucho Club to get wasted and try to forget about the whole experience. I was about an hour into festivities when in walked Lily Allen. My knee-jerk reaction was to try and snap her but then I remembered that I was demobbed, in my own club, and that I could behave normally. Lily sat down next to me and we started chatting. She was at the peak of her success, with a hit album and another one on the way. She started grumbling about all the work she had to do and how she had now agreed to write a book. It all seemed too much for the pop princess. Slightly oiled, I decided to play the role of mildly elder states-man of show business. It was crazy how quickly I'd forgotten my recent foray into alternative careers. Now I was back, a middle-aged statesman of comedy giving wise advice to a young novice.

'Lily,' I said. 'My advice is don't spread yourself too thin. You're at the top of your game so concentrate on what you do well and don't start getting distracted by other stuff.'

I could have been talking to a younger version of myself.

'Why would you bother to start doing a book when you've got the music going so well right now?' I asked gently.

'They've offered me £700,000 to do it . . .' said Lily, sipping on her drink casually.

I sat there silenced. That seemed to me a very good reason to write a book. I looked up towards the bar while trying to think of something else to say. Lily's dad, the very intimidating Keith Allen, was standing there nursing a drink and giving me a look I would long remember in my nightmares. I took the hint and slipped away to the smoking terrace. I needed some fresh air.

Chapter 9

Wanderlust

With my brief career as a paparazzo over, I was starting to get wanderlust again. I decided it might be time to take up the *Sunday Times* on their kind offer. I became a kind of international gonzo correspondent. It was my dream job and a lot easier to negotiate with Stacey, as I was able to balance the home/away periods better.

I went everywhere: the USA, Malaysia, South Africa, Zanzibar, Costa Rica, Bosnia-Herzegovina, Dominica, Jamaica, Norway, Turkey, Armenia, Uzbekistan, Canada, the Arctic Circle, Kazakhstan, Croatia, Serbia, Hungary, Austria, Germany, Denmark, the Czech Republic, Morocco, Italy, France, Spain, Vietnam, Belgium, Mexico, Thailand, Corsica ... even Scotland.

I'd just think of somewhere to go, ring the paper, ask them to sort it out and then go and have fun. I realised just how lucky I was to have got to this position and I was determined to make the very most of it. For instance, I was flicking through a magazine when I saw a photograph of a weird rocket contraption that hung on a wire over a valley somewhere in the South Island of New Zealand. The moment I saw it, I knew that I just had to try this thing. So I did.

I flew to Auckland and then to Queenstown via Los Angeles. Big mistake. This was when I first started to get real problems due to the fact that I was born in Beirut, Lebanon, one of the twenty-five countries that US Homeland Security had designated to be a bad place to have been born in, whatever your actual nationality. The 'bad' countries in question were: Afghanistan, Algeria, Bahrain, Bangladesh, Egypt, Eritrea, Indonesia, Iran, Iraq, Jordan, Kuwait, Lebanon, Libya, Morocco, North Korea, Oman, Pakistan, Qatar, Saudi Arabia, Somalia, Sudan, Syria, Tunisia, United Arab Emirates and Yemen.

Anyone born in one of these places was subjected to NSEERS (National Security Entry/Exit Registration System, sometimes called Special Registration), one of the most explicitly racist, under-reported initiatives in post-9/11 America.

I didn't want to enter the States. I didn't even really want to get off the plane, but we were given no choice. We had to go through US immigration before being allowed back on to continue on to Auckland. I was taken aside when they saw that I was born in Beirut. I was marched off to the bureaucratic hell that was the NSEER special room. It was always the same in every US airport. A room full of tired travellers faced with rude, uninterested immigration officials who paid little heed to the signs on the wall that told you about your rights to be treated with courtesy and respect. I was held for an hour without being able to talk to anyone. I kept trying to tell them that I had to get back on my plane but they were not interested. Finally, I was summoned into an interrogation room, where I was repeatedly asked why I wanted to enter the United States. However many times I tried to explain that I didn't, and that I just wanted to get back on my plane and go to New Zealand, they just didn't get it. It was crazy. I'd show them my ticket, my boarding pass etc., but they just couldn't compute. Eventually, I was saved by a kind air hostess who went above and beyond the call of duty to come and get me and harass the officials. They wished me a good trip to New Zealand as I was exiting. I thought it best not to mention the rocket – never has a 'security' policy turned so many potentially pro-Americans into enemies. Thankfully, Obama eventually repealed this ludicrous system.

Queenstown was the world capital of adrenaline adventure. A pretty little town on the South Island, nestled on the edge of a forbidding-looking lake and surrounded by a stunning range of mountains, it was originally a popular ski destination. But something must have got into the water because in the early 1980s everything changed.

First, they invented bungee jumping: you could still jump off the bridge where the first jumps ever were attempted. But they didn't stop there. As I'd wander down a street in the town I would be deluged with offers of White-Water Rafting, Jet-Boating, Zorbing, Paragliding, Canyon-Swinging, Quad-Bike Safaris, Hot-Air Ballooning, Skydiving – the list was endless. What made New Zealanders indulge in these high-adrenaline activities? Actually, if you looked a bit closer, it didn't actually seem to be the locals doing any of the activities. They just invented them and then charged gullible fools like me to partake. It was the tourists who were hurling themselves off precipices and rolling down steep hills in giant, spherical, plastic vomit buckets. The locals were just counting the money.

I rang the number I'd got for the Rocket Man and a monosyllabic voice gave me some GPS coordinates and told me to meet him there in three hours' time. I drove up high into the hills behind Queenstown and eventually turned off the little road onto a dusty track. I parked my rental car next to a little sign in the middle of a very big field. The local residents, a flock of merino sheep, eyed me suspiciously before continuing on with whatever it is that sheep do.

Two hundred yards away, the lush green field dropped dramatically out of sight into the Shotover River. I could hear the screams of the passengers on one of the jet-boats that hurtled suicidally through its narrow gorges. Beyond the river, the jagged, snowcapped peaks of the wonderfully named Remarkables mountain range pierced the clear blue sky. The scene was not unlike the Cotswolds, except that someone appeared to have plonked both the Alps and the Colorado River slap-bang in the middle of it.

A beaten-up Land Rover hurtled down the track and screeched to a halt next to me.

'You Dom?' enquired the rugged-looking driver.

'That's me,' I replied, trying to sound nonchalant.

'Hop in, mate,' ordered the Kiwi, and hop in I did.

My driver was a man of few words as we bumped and bounced up a very rough track, higher and higher into the forbidding hills. At the top of the track he took a sharp left turn and we started a precarious descent into a steep-sided valley. Strung across the valley was a set of steel wires. An even thicker wire dropped down from these wires to a platform on top of a hut. As we approached said hut I could see that the central wire was attached to a rocket-like device with handlebars at the front and an imposing propeller at the rear.

'You ready, mate?' said my near-mute accomplice.

'I think so,' I replied, again trying to look relaxed. A thin bead of sweat started to make its way down my back.

'Right, let's get you strapped in.'

He offered me a helmet that wouldn't have protected me from strong rain and a pair of goggles that had a whiff of Biggles about them. I lay down on my stomach and grabbed the rudimentary handlebars as he strapped me into the machine with a series of what looked like old airplane seat belts.

'Right, mate, when I press a button, the rocket will be slowly winched backwards up the side of the valley until it reaches its full height. When it stops, pull that left handbrake lever to release yourself and keep your hand tight on the right-hand one. That's your gas. If you get it right, you should reach speeds of up to 105mph. You've got a six-minute flight. Enjoy it, mate.'

He gave me the thumbs up and pressed a button on a yellow plastic controller, and I felt the rocket lurch backwards. I was being dragged up the valley walls, getting higher and higher, with the front pointing down into the abyss. It was obviously far too late, but only now did I really begin to wonder, *how had I got myself into this situation: just me and a monosyllabic Kiwi, alone together, miles from anywhere in the hills high above Queenstown, New Zealand, me strapped to a rocket?* If I died here, nobody would be any the wiser. He could have just got back into his Land Rover and trundled off to start a new venture. If asked, he could have said that I'd never turned up. A shepherd might find some scorch marks in the side of the valley wall one day, but would he manage to put two and two together? I thought not.

The rocket reached the end of its climb and I heard an audible click, like the hammer of a pistol, as the release mechanism was engaged – and then there was total silence, save for my futile attempts to control my panic by deep breathing. I looked down into the abyss of the valley and instantly understood the whole drowning-man's-life-flashing-before-him concept. More through resignation than determination, I pulled the left-hand lever with my quivering wrist. It was a hundred times worse than I'd imagined.

I screeched down into the valley, towards the ground and straight over my impassive Kiwi friend – the only witness to my impending death – who was holding an enormous sign over his head that read 'MORE GAS'. I screamed and screamed until there was no breath left in my body and my only choice was to breathe or expire. The rocket started to climb up the other side of the valley and I remember thinking I was going to vomit, and then feeling a peculiar dampness down my left leg, and then blackness. I think I blacked out; certainly there were no more signs, just a light at the end of a beautiful tunnel where seven icy blondes were beckoning to me and they were holding beers ... Six minutes later, the rocket came to a gradual stop and the man unstrapped me. I got in the Land Rover and, again in silence, we trundled back down to my car. As he drove away I was left alone with the sheep and my thoughts, wondering whether any of it had actually happened.

Sam Cadman suddenly came back into my life. He had won the Green Card lottery and moved out to live in LA. He was working as an ad director but kept getting a lot of love when people found out he'd done *Trigger Happy TV*. People kept telling him that we should do a movie. Sam contacted me and asked me what I thought. I was all for it, but was it really feasible? We were very clear what we wanted to make: a ninety-minute cinematic spectacular shot in the USA. *Trigger Happy: The Movie*. We wanted to make the *Ben-Hur* of hidden camera movies: epic stunts with hundreds of people involved. Sam had already been in touch with Charlie Todd from Improv Everywhere in New York to see whether we could borrow his impressive online list of people who'd signed up to do huge scenes. We figured that not only would these guys be up for being extras in our movie, but that it was a very cool way of getting big numbers of people inexpensively. The basic pitch was: if you like *Trigger Happy TV*, don't just watch it, come and be in it.

The irony was that when *Trigger Happy TV* had been airing in the UK, several movie companies who wanted us to make a film had approached us and we'd given them fairly short shrift. Our view of TV comedy shows that turned into films was that they were almost always awful. They always had some narrative arc shoehorned in and we really wanted to make a big, dumb, non-linear movie. We were terrified of ending up with a movie in which suddenly the Big Mobile guy went on a 'journey' to find the lost battery for his big phone and ended up in all sorts of wacky adventures . . . I hated those sorts of movies. We wanted to stay true to what we wanted to do and that meant no movies. In the time between, however, the success of *Jackass* and their subsequent 'no story' movies meant that possibly the time was right for us to make the movie we'd wanted to make. Sam and I got together online and started writing up ideas.

After we'd got a pitch together, I flew out to LA and we headed off on a road trip into the Mojave Desert. This was how we always came up with our best stuff and it worked well. Not only that but Sam had rented a whole lot of costumes and we shot some stills of me in various scenarios: me jogging through Death Valley and a motorcycle cop having a nervous breakdown on a roadside rock. The photos were funny and we hoped they'd help people visualise our idea.

Once back in LA, we set up some meetings in which to pitch the project. Our big hope was that Comedy Central, who'd aired our original series and had a development deal with Paramount, would like the idea and help us realise it. We set up a meeting and they sounded very enthusiastic, but then again everyone sounded very enthusiastic in LA. Come the big day, Sam and I drove downtown, practising our pitch in his car. We got to the building and announced ourselves to the receptionist in the foyer, who was looking at Sam and his homeless-person-style beard with some distaste. We told her that we had a very important meeting with the guys at Comedy Central. She called up and then spent quite a long time on the phone. Eventually it turned out that we had got the date wrong and that the meeting had been scheduled for the previous day. We were so embarrassed. We got in the car and called them up and made some ridiculous excuses and managed to reschedule for the next day.

The receptionist was still suspicious of us when we turned up the following afternoon, but she called up and we got the green light to ascend to their offices. She gave us a weird fob that we assumed was to register our presence in the building. We reached the bank of lifts and got into one that some sharp-suited guy had just got out of. The door closed behind us and we waited ... and waited, but nothing happened. We pressed the buttons but the lift wouldn't move. We tried to open the doors but they wouldn't budge. We laughed at how stupid this was and pressed all the buttons again. Nothing. We were stuck.

Then, to make matters worse, the light inside the lift went off. We were now imprisoned in a lift in LA with no idea of what to do. Sam wanted to ring Comedy Central upstairs and let them know of our plight. I told him that this was a bad idea. We already looked really dumb for getting the day wrong – now this would confirm our total loser status. We were in the lift for more than an hour until somehow the door opened and a man stood staring at us in an accusatory manner. Someone had spotted us on CCTV cameras and had called the police, thinking we were demonstrators of some sort. I think it was Sam's beard. We found out that we'd needed to swipe the fob the receptionist had given us over some metal board in the lift. When she rang up Comedy Central, the people we were meeting with were 'unavailable'. I can't say I blamed them. We must have looked like muppets. LA didn't jump at the chance of making our movie and I returned to the UK determined to approach it from another angle.

Meanwhile, a trip to Vietnam had made me start thinking

about my curious predilection for travelling to dodgy places. This would subsequently lead to my first travel book: *The Dark Tourist*. I was particularly taken with a visit to a set of Viet Cong tunnels a couple of hours outside Ho Chi Minh. A group of ex-Viet Cong ran the site and proudly showed me all the tricks in their dark little handbook.

First up was a series of quite sublimely awful booby traps that involved hinged bamboos with sadistic pointy bits ready to stick into every part of an unwary GI's body. Then there was the man making flip-flops out of old car tyres. I'd see these sort of flip-flops again in *The Dark Tourist*, when a war criminal tried to sell me Pol Pot's shoes. There was also a firing range where, for roughly a dollar a bullet, you could fire an AK47 at some chickens – as in a later trip to Cambodia, where I was offered the opportunity to blow up a cow with an RPG, I declined.

The best was kept for last: the tunnels. It would be fair to say that the Viet Cong were a hardy bunch. They used this fact to great effect by building a labyrinthine complex of tunnels all over the country. They would live full-time in these claustrophobic, cramped rat-runs, only emerging at night to attack the enemy before disappearing back into their deadly mole holes. These particular tunnels were built right under an enormous American base. This allowed the Cong to enter and terrorise the US soldiers at will. The tiny entrances to the tunnels were brilliantly camouflaged so that you could actually step on one and have no idea. Even ventilation shafts for the cooking smoke would be built so that it exited three, four hundred metres from any entrance. Some of the tunnels had been widened so that corpulent dark tourists like myself could have a look. Once inside, however, I got hideously claustrophobic and had a total panic attack. I was trapped and had to force myself to relax before I could work my way back out. The idea that these were widened and that people had lived and fought in these tunnels was beyond my comprehension. The Americans never had a chance them.

Back in the UK, I had spoken to various people and told them about my and Sam's idea for a *Trigger Happy* movie. We organised a series of meetings with all the big movie honchos in London. Sam flew over from LA. We didn't need Americans. We were going to make the big British breakout movie of the summer. What followed was profoundly depressing. Sam and I would turn up to meet some big cheese in the film world. They would almost invariably be wearing black polo necks and doing a lot of invisible-goatee stroking. We would explain our idea and there would be a lot of uuhming and aahing before the words 'narrative arc' would appear. 'Can we see a script, please?' was always the next question. Sam and I would then launch into our spiel about there being no script, as this was hidden camera and all impromptu – we had ideas though? We could see them start to glaze over and lose interest. Pretty soon, desperate as we were to please, Sam and I were pitching ludicrous storylines to beef up what had been our pure, original idea.

'So, the Big Mobile guy has lost the magic battery to his machine ... It gives him power ... Angelina Jolie, Dom's girl-friend in the movie ...' We were doing anything to retain interest, but of course they were more interested in this fictional fantasy than the one we wanted to make. We eventually got a good development deal, but by now there was a script and the whole thing was so far away from the original film that we wanted to make that we started to actually hope nobody would ever greenlight it. It was embarrassing.

If you ever want to empty your mind of everyday worries, a trip to explore the legendary Empty Quarter, the vast desert area on the end of the Arabian Peninsula, will do the trick. I got the well-timed opportunity to do so, guided by some ex-SAS men who had served with the Omani army in the Seventies when fighting against Marxist rebels. The SAS guys were keen to set up a company that took people round the Empty Quarter, and as such had organised a tour for me. I managed to get on with them very well and dealt with desert conditions without embarrassing myself ... until the last night.

It was yet another crystal-clear night and we were eating outside, under the stars, in our final camp. The stars were like an IMAX experience – you felt compelled to put your hand up and try to touch them. As the first course arrived I noticed something white moving right next to my open-toe sandals. I looked down only to spot a large scorpion about two inches away from me. Very calmly, I lifted my leg and watched the beast scurry on past me and away. I was very pleased with myself for such sangfroid. I glugged some wine down in what I considered to be a macho manner and rejoined the conversation with gusto.

After supper, we sat around a roaring campfire swapping manly stories about travel and adventure. I was one of them, an adventurer, an explorer, a soldier ... Suddenly, out of the corner of my eye I spotted something scuttling towards me. It was a ginormous, hairy camel spider and it wasn't alone. There were about six of them and they moved in that horrible, fast, scuttling way that ginormous, hairy spiders do. I lost it. I went mental with fear and jumped onto my chair and started gibbering like a baby. My military escorts were beside themselves. They nearly fell off their chairs laughing as I stood there pleading with them to do something. They just laughed and the spiders seemed to sense their indifference and gain courage. One scuttled up the leg of my chair while the others encircled me like a lonely wagon train. I was screaming now. I was out of control. Arachnophobia, as I would later discover in the Australian jungle, is my Achilles heel – it is utterly irrational and impossible to control. My military companions were actually on the floor laughing so much. Finally, one of them took pity on me and started grabbing the spiders and hurling them into the fire, where they hissed and popped like angry chestnuts. Maybe I wasn't cut out to be in the SAS after all?

Back in the UK, my social circle had changed. As a fellow *Indy* writer, I had met Alex James from Blur on several occasions and become friendly with him. This led to Stacey and me being invited to several social functions at his farm in Kingham, about thirty minutes away from where I lived. We were based in the south Cotswolds – Hurley/Winslet Country. Alex lived in Clarkson Country. Unbeknownst to me at the time, I was venturing into the Chipping Norton set.

There was always an eclectic mix of people hanging around: Rebekah Wade/Brooks, the ill-fated CEO of News International, lived next door with her husband Charlie, and David Cameron, not yet prime minister, would often pop by for drinks. It was at Alex James's that I met Jeremy Clarkson. There then followed invitations to his house for New Year's Eve. Stacey and I went along there and didn't really know anybody. We tucked into the free booze and eventually got some food from the buffet and sat down at a table. It was only then that I noticed we'd plonked ourselves right next to Cameron. I was quite pissed by this stage and thought I'd be amusing by teasing him about keeping a diary of his journey towards becoming PM. I told him that should it all go pear-shaped he'd have a lovely nest egg from eager publishers. I then launched into my views on how he would eventually be unseated by Boris. It would be fair to say that we did not have an instant rapport and I could see Cameron longing for some way to escape this arsehole seated next to him.

Suddenly Clarkson appeared through a door. He was holding a very realistic-looking replica AK47, and unbeknownst to the future PM he proceeded to point it at Cameron's head. I instantly reached for my iPhone in my pocket, hoping to grab a photo that would hopefully buy me a retirement home in the South of France, but the moment was gone before I could act.

I think that it was soon noted that I was probably not the most desirable guest in the 'set' and the invitations dried up as media attention heightened; with both the election and the subsequent Hackinggate looming, they started to close ranks and batten down the hatches. This was annoying as I was ploughing my random insider knowledge into a spoof column that I was now writing for the *Independent*.

I had come up with a fake persona called Cooper Brown, a horrible, right-wing American film executive who was now in the UK doing a sort of reverse Piers Morgan. In the column, Cooper was married to a posh Brit with impeccable Tory connections that allowed him access to political salons, and he dished the dirt in no uncertain terms. I knew that the column was working when the *Indy* letters pages started filling up with disgruntled lefties announcing that they would be scrapping their subscription to the paper if this 'horrible Nazi' wasn't fired immediately. Cooper Brown lasted a couple of years and was then resuscitated in the *i*. I was very fond of him.

A couple of years later, a reporter from the *Mail* rang me up. He had found out that I had been present at a party at Alex James's house when some monumental conversation had apparently taken place between Cameron and Rebekah Brooks. Had I noticed anything of this that night? asked the reporter. Sadly, all I could remember was that two other members of Blur had been there and we were just a Damon Albarn away from a full house . . . This was not the scoop that the reporter wanted.

Meanwhile, my wanderlust had not gone unnoticed by television channels. I started to get offers of travel shows, some terrible, others just awful. Then one day the phone rang with an offer to film an episode of *Rough Guide Extreme*.

'Do you want to go film something in Nicaragua?' The caller

was a little fuzzy-sounding on the phone and I couldn't really hear her that well. I was in the Cotswolds *dead zone* for mobiles and I was just managing to retain one bar by being perched halfway up an old willow tree hanging over the River Coln.

'Sure . . . Sounds like fun . . .' I was cut off and half-fell out of the tree simultaneously.

Looking back, this was probably a sign, but I ignored it. I continued my long, contemplative walk alongside my two dogs, Oscar and Huxley. Huxley looked troubled – he worried a lot about stuff and was a very wise old dog. 'Nicaragua?' he growled. 'Sounds dodgy. Did you ask her what you were going to be doing out there?' (*Uh-oh: talking dog alert . . .*)

I ignored him, but he was right: I hadn't got a clue and I should have known by now never to accept random TV shows without reading the small print. I emailed the producers the moment I got back home but it was too late – I was committed. I asked them to get me a schedule of what we would be doing. It arrived half an hour later:

Day One – Look round Managua (so far so good)
Day Two – Visit old capital of Leon (this is great)
Day Three – Climb volcano (uh-oh!!!!)

I stopped reading and started to panic. I was not the fittest man in the world and at that time tended to avoid all forms of physical exercise apart from my daily dog walk. The phone rang – it was the show's director – this lot didn't hang about . . .

'We're so excited that you're going to be doing this . . . We've found another really fun thing to do – can you snowboard? It's just that there's another volcano that you can board down on the ashes, and we thought that it would make really good telly . . .'

This was getting a lot worse. Luckily, I had my failsafe escape clause.

'No, I'm afraid that I can't snowboard, let alone ashboard – I'm a skier, always have been ...'

I breathed an inaudible sigh of relief.

'No problem,' said the unstoppable director. 'We'll ship some skis and boots out – what size are you? This is going to be great ...'

Two weeks later, I was in the quite stupidly hot customs shed in central Managua, trying to negotiate the pick-up of said skis and boots. Opposing me in this venture were about a hundred different officials who all needed forms signing and palms greased. My skis were, apparently, the very first pair ever to be imported into the country and customs were sure that this was some elaborate gringo reverse-cocaine-smuggling scam. (The term gringo, by the way, comes from old Mexico. When the US invaded in the early nineteenth century they wore green uniforms. Angry locals used to write 'green go home' on the walls everywhere – interesting fact, no?) But I digress.

It had been difficult enough to even find the customs shed. Managua, it turned out, was a city where the streets literally *have no name*. Everything was directed from a tree in the rough centre of the city. So you were given directions like, *it's two blocks towards the lake (South) from the tree and then three blocks up (East) and then five blocks towards the hills (North)*. To make matters even more complicated, someone in a big truck knocked the tree over about twenty years ago, so Managuans then had to do their directions *from where the tree used to be* – but this got too confusing, even for Managuans, so they planted a new one.

The ominous-looking Cerro Negro, whose smoking black hulk was visible from my hotel window, was the youngest and most active of all Nicaragua's volcanoes. It had erupted so recently that, unlike all the others, it hadn't even had time to allow any greenery to grow on it. It just looked mean, like a big school bully waiting to give me a good kicking and steal all my lunch money.

With my skis on my back, I set off on the hour-and-a-half climb to the summit of the bully. It wasn't too arduous and I started to feel a little cocky as I cleared the top of the jagged lava flow and reached the bottom of the long ridge that would eventually take us to my 'departure point', as my guide insisted on calling it. Half an hour later and I was looking down a fifty-degree slope made up entirely of little sharp black rocks. To me, ash conjured up an image of sandy soft stuff, but something must have been lost in translation. As I contemplated the descent and the cameras started to set up, smelling blood, we were joined by two boarders from Leon. The boards in question were not snowboards, more metal toboggans, and the astonished looks that they gave my skis – and me – made me realise that I was in big trouble.

It was too late, however – the cameras were ready and I was a professional ... Except I wasn't. I looked down the black slope and had a moment of complete panic. I'd seen this scene before somewhere on something called *When TV Goes Tits-Up*. I knew that I really shouldn't do any more thinking. I turned my skis to face the slope. I started to move ... just ... I slipped down about three metres and then the skis stuck fast on the rocky ground and I went arse over tit, cutting up my face as I planted it hard into the sharp little rocks. Then I felt the whole slope starting to slip downwards: an *ashalanche*. Did these even exist? I stuck my skis hard into the moving shale and managed to stop my descent. So there I was, stuck to the slopes of a live Nicaraguan volcano in full ski gear while the cameras rolled – I really should have listened to my dog.

It was clear that there was no way you could ski down this thing, and I managed to get this salient fact over to the director along with quite a few choice expletives regarding his 'research'.

186

My guide managed to clamber down to me and together we got my skis off and he gave me one of the toboggans that we should have used in the first place. I gingerly tried to launch myself down the slope on this new vehicle, hoping to recover some adrenaline-credibility on camera. Sadly, I kicked it too hard and the foot board came flying off, which made the front of the thing bury itself into the stones and I came to another embarrassing halt. As this was happening, several boarders zoomed past me whooping loudly in a *no fear* kind of way and I realised that any plans to attend the BAFTAs with this particular programme were going to have to be shelved. Eventually, I managed to roll and stumble down to the bottom of the nightmarish lunarscape and headed off to find our vehicle, bleeding and bruised – this had not been my finest hour.

Our final Nicaraguan destination was a pretty little seaside town called San Juan del Sur, just north of the Costa Rican border. The crew and I were spending a couple of days relaxing there at the end of the shoot. On our first evening in town, we headed off down to the beach for a spot of supper. We found the perfect-looking seaside restaurant and I'd just ordered a ceviche and a chilled bottle of Chilean wine – all was well with the world.

It was then that I noticed the guy on the beach. He was shirtless, had one of those torches that you wear on your head and he was stumbling around, looking for his flip-flop. I knew this because he kept shouting, 'Where's my goddam flip-flop?' in a soft Texan accent. It was clear that the guy was pretty wasted. He was having quite the problem standing up. He eventually gave up on his quest and staggered towards our restaurant. He tried to negotiate the low wall dividing the dining area from the beach but this proved to be way too much of a problem and he tripped and fell into our table, sending everything flying. We all jumped up as the drunken guy stood up unsteadily and mumbled apologies, before crashing into another table and going down again. It was at this moment that I recognised him. It was Matthew McConaughey. This was way before his recent McConnaissance and Oscar redemption. This was very much in the middle of his *lean against a door frame with my shirt off and a wry smile*, rom-com period.

San Juan del Sur was an up-and-coming surf destination and it seemed that McConaughey would make a rubbish film, cash the cheque and head down there for six months, bumming around. I was about to tell him how much I admired his life choices but he was off. He staggered out of the restaurant, narrowly avoiding being run over by a motorbike before disappearing into the fragile night. As I was about to explain my star-spot to the crew, a British couple sitting nearby, who had seen the commotion and recognised me, came over to say hello. I told them that they'd just missed a far bigger fish, but they didn't believe me – it's the problem with being a prankster: all my best stories are ignored. I later searched out the actor online and found out that his night had ended with a couple of locals giving him a lift home and stealing his mobile and a couple of thousand dollars. I'm unaware of what happened to his flip-flop, but I should have asked him to be in our ill-fated movie project.

We edited the show together and it was pretty good. It appeared, however, that Channel 5 thought otherwise as, despite them paying for six different celebs to travel the world being 'extreme', they never aired the series. I contacted them several times to at least try and get some reason for this curious decision but never received any form of satisfactory reply. I was seriously pissed off. I was keen to make my name as a 'travel guy' and had risked life and limb, all so that Channel 5 could just forget about it. It wasn't as though Channel 5 had the luxury of too many good shows and were forced to shelve some.

Maybe the whole thing was some complicated tax dodge set up by Jimmy Carr and Gary Barlow? Who knows? Like much else in television, it just didn't make any sense.

Ticking off yet another celeb cliché, I had rediscovered golf. I used to play the game as a kid but hadn't done so for ages. I wasn't much good but couldn't resist invitations on trips abroad with friends. Simon Kelner was a golf fanatic and we would often head off to distant climes together, taking on all comers.

I could go into detail about our trip to Marrakesh with Piers Morgan but for everybody's sake I'll keep it short.

'What is Piers Morgan like?' I asked Simon just before I met him.

'Shameless,' he replied.

He was bang on. This was after he'd been sacked from the *Mirror* and before he'd headed off to America to get sacked over there. On the plane over to Marrakesh he was only interested in who would make the headlines should the plane crash. Once in Morocco, he spent most of the time wandering around the pool of the Mamounia with a copy of his just-released (and rather good) book *The Insider* clearly visible in a see-through bag, for all to see and admire . . .

I once found myself on a trip to Gran Canaria (my idea of utter hell) for a golf tournament that included the chef Mark Hix, a man who manages to combine a staggering consumption of alcohol with some magnificent cooking. Most of our group had been into town for a night out. They returned in taxis at around midnight, as we had an early tee-time the following morning. Sadly, some had not had enough and hit the hotel bar for a couple more hours. At about two-thirty in the morning they had a second wind and decided to revisit the town for more shenanigans. They ordered a taxi to take them back in. Imagine their surprise when the cab arrived and they tried to jump into the back seat, only to find an unconscious Mark Hix sprawled over it. The driver had not noticed the intoxicated chef and had been driving his comatose body around town for a couple of hours. Hix was awoken and evicted from the cab so that the die-hards could hit the town once again. Unbelievably, he played very well the following day.

The pinnacle was probably a mammoth California trip with Simon Kelner and the actor Jimmy Nesbitt. It started at Pebble Beach and ended up at the Four Seasons in Los Angeles. I was getting rather too used to this lifestyle and was worried what my wife was going to say when I got home and rang down for room service and a monogrammed towelling robe. I sat in the lobby bar preparing the first draft of the new movie screenplay that would make my name in the City of Angels. I nodded in an overly familiar fashion to Vince Neil, the ex-lead singer of Mötley Crüe, who was looking reassuringly dazed and confused. Mickey Rourke wandered in. He had the look of a man who had done some serious playing with matches. Suddenly, there was a shout of recognition from another corner of the lobby – it was TV's hardest man: Ross Kemp. He had been married to Rebekah Brooks and was now another recent evictee from the Chipping Norton set.

He came over and gave me a very showbizzy kiss on both cheeks. Ross, the hardest man on telly, was in town filming some extremely hard-core scenes with the Mexican Mafia in the badlands of LA. We invited him out for a restorative game of golf the next day – he looked like he could use it. It was shaping up to look like a star-studded match – Jimmy Nesbitt took a phone call from Max Beesley, who was thinking of playing golf with Robbie Williams ... Should we meet up? Donald Trump's course? This was pure LA ...

The following morning, we all assembled in the car park out front to meet our LA golf host, Richard Schiff (Toby from *The West Wing*). Beesley and Robbie hadn't made it, but the rest of us were raring to go. Richard announced that we were off to a place called the Lost Canyons and that we were to follow him. I made the error of getting a lift with him. Big mistake. It turned out that before Richard became an award-winning actor, he had been a New York cab driver.

Now, I've driven in some of the world's hairiest places – Beirut, Naples, Swindon – but nothing, and I mean *nothing*, could prepare me for this man's driving. As we screeched in and out of other terrified cars on the six-lane freeway leaving the city, at over one hundred and fifty miles an hour, I began to wonder whether we might be featuring in some sort of weird movie ourselves – surely this man couldn't drive this way in normal life? But he did. Unbelievably, and with what seemed like a hint of disappointment in Richard's eyes, we made it to the Lost Canyons for our round of golf. There was a look of post-orgasmic pleasure on his face as he kicked his feet through the thick pile of litter that was half a metre high in the footwell. I hitched a lift back to LA with someone else.

That evening we were guests of the hotel and they had really pushed the boat out. We were outside on a long table on the ter-race where some famous chef had been brought in to cook for us. I arrived late and sat opposite Ross Kemp (the toughest bloke on the box), who was looking very distracted. I tried to make polite conversation but Ross (a TV hard man) was not with us. He just sat with a thousand-yard stare. It was all very awkward. Eventually I had to deal with it head-on.

'Ross, are you OK, you seem ... troubled?'

Ross looked up at me with big, sad, worried eyes.

'It's just ...'

He stopped for a second with the look of a man who had seen terrible, terrible things ... and once been married to Rebekah Brooks.

'It's just that we're sitting here having an amazing time,

enjoying ourselves and all carefree, and yet just three miles away there's some serious violent shit going down ...'

Ross stopped again and looked very upset.

I was about to say something when Jimmy Nesbitt, who was sitting two seats up from Ross, closed the whole thing down.

'Well, stick to fucking panto then ...' he shouted. There was total silence around the table. I downed a glass of wine and excused myself.

Hole in one ...

Chapter 10

Help Wanted

G rowing up, I always wanted to be a foreign correspondent. In 2008, I got the opportunity. The *Independent* sent me to Beijing as their special Olympic correspondent. I'd always dreamed of going to an Olympic Games, but to get to go to one in Beijing, as a reporter, was a double bonus. My shtick was going to be ignorance. People who reported from these kinds of events always tended to be experts in their field. I wanted to report on the Games from a layman's point of view. What was it like to be a Joe Normal at the Games? What the hell went on in the Olympic Village? Who watches walking races? I was like a kid in a sweet shop. I stayed in a hotel bang in the middle of the Olympic Park. Every day I'd wander down to the bus terminal, peruse the different events on offer and decide what I was going to watch that day. I was soon explaining the Olympics to the folks back in the UK. Here was my informative breakdown of Greco-Roman wrestling.

A brief history and explanation of Greco-Roman wrestling

Greco-Roman wrestling is the world's oldest known sport. Yet most Brits don't seem to have much of a clue about the sport. Fortunately, help is at hand. In every venue is a 'media lounge', and these provide the lazy or ignorant journalist with more than enough information with which to write a very good article. I popped in to see a couple of bouts and found this leaflet invaluable – I attach it here below to give you, the readers, the same kind of insight that we top sports journalists get ... It's only fair.

Eligibility

1. Only countries that end in 'an' or 'a' are eligible to take part in the sport.
2. Contestants must be shorter than five feet five and have full body hair (front and back).
3. Contestants must at all times be accompanied, and regularly berated by, a 300lb trainer who resembles an angry bear that has been caught trying on lady bear outfits by his best bear buddies.
4. Competing nations must organise and bring along a rowdy bunch of short, aggressive-looking spectators – preferably with some sort of shady military background. They will deal with any border infractions of the segregated seating areas.
5. Contestants must be able to ignore any abuse from hostile crowds as to how homoerotic the whole affair is.

Rules

1. Contestants have to stand in a red and yellow target and then grapple with each other for prolonged periods of time, while wearing very tight leotards.
2. Occasionally, a referee will stop the match, dip his hand in a black sack and pull out a coloured ball. If the colour of the ball matches your outfit then your opponent must kneel on all fours in the central circle and you can attack him like a dog.

3. Contestants are discouraged, although not specifically banned, from consuming copious amounts of garlic and onions for breakfast.

4. Contestants must feign complete indifference to circumstances when they find themselves in a 'hold' that incorporates the opponent's hairy testicles being squashed against the contestant's face.

5. 'Holds' can only be from the waist up so 'wedgies' are illegal – contestants opting to not wear pants must get consent of opponent.

6. Contestants are not permitted to use their goats at any time during the contest except in the situation of a tie – then goats are allowed.

7. The flying of the Olympic flag is not intended as an affront to the integrity of any of the nations taking part. Flag-burning is strictly illegal and will result in a forfeit of two fighting cocks.

8. Contestants must, under no circumstances, rip off their leotard, simulate the wiping of their anuses on said leotard and then shove in referee's face – the official's decision is always final.

9. No Australians allowed (hygiene ruling).

10. Contestants must be prepared for a random drug test – the so-called 'cock in the pot'. The tester will need to actually see the penis and is required by Olympic rules to check for prosthetics. Please do not take this personally or as an affront to your manliness ...

History

Greco-Roman wrestling has been popular somewhere since the dawn of time. Obviously, it was first made really popular by the Grecos and the Romans. They would regularly organise inter-empire 'meets', where contestants would wrestle with each other for periods of up to two months before a result was declared.

The sport became so popular in Greco that it was used to settle the equivalent of 'gazumping'. Were two buyers of a house to be in conflict, they would wrestle for the property.

Under the reign of the Sun King Louis XIV, the sport was made illegal in France. Louis felt that the sport was far too sexually provocative and admitted that he 'liked to watch it … almost too much'. It was only re-legalised in France in 1976, after a submission to the Ministry of Justice by world-famous mime artist and passionate wrestling fan Marcel Marceau.

Oscar Wilde once went to a Greco-Roman bout at Yale while on a lecture tour of the USA. On leaving seven hours later, he remarked that sport had never really been his thing but if it was compulsory then 'surely this must be the one'.

Conspiracy theorists even believe that Greco-Roman wrestling rights might be behind the Russian invasion of Georgia. Russian hardman Vladimir Putin is a keen Greco-Roman wrestler and there is a theory that the actual Russian objective is the Georgian training school in Gori, where they keep their training goats.

It was quite the two weeks. I saw almost every sport known to man. Under the nervous gaze of Radio 5 Live's Peter Allen, I harangued the American basketball team for queue-barging on a trip to the Great Wall of China. I visited a restaurant that only served meat from every part (and I mean *every* part) of the donkey. I even found myself just seven metres above the finishing line as Usain Bolt smashed both the 100m and the 200m sprint records. I was doing that rare thing – being a witness to history. All too soon, however, it was over and, as the firework display to end all firework displays exploded over the Chinese capital, I fought my way through the world's biggest traffic jam to attend the British Closing Ceremony party.

The myth that you can see the Great Wall of China from space is just that, a myth, but that night, thanks to a Chinese invention – fireworks – I was pretty sure that you could have seen Beijing from the Moon. For fifteen minutes, as Boris Johnson was awkwardly waving the Olympic flag in the stadium, the Chinese capital came to a standstill as it was lit up by the most impressive firework display since the US lit up Baghdad.

I was in a taxi, and all the traffic just stopped and everybody got out of their cars and gazed upwards as though some fiery comet was headed towards earth. I abandoned my cabbie and walked the rest of the way. I was headed for London House, a private members' club in the popular Houhai district where the Beijing handover party was taking place. It was a real *B*-list event – Boris, Beckham and Brown (Gordon) were expected, and security was tight. Inside, champagne was flowing and miniature bowls of fish and chips were being circulated by puzzled-looking local waitresses.

I bumped into an old acquaintance – the editor of *Beijing Time Out*. He told me that the original plans for the handover had been far more grandiose. An initial guest list of 2,500 had to be rapidly culled to 600 and many embarrassing, last-minute phone calls had been made, rescinding invites. Subsequently, the local expat community were not, it would be fair to say, big Boris fans.

His jingoistic speech, however, treading all over diplomatic niceties and having a pop at the French as well as claiming pretty much all of sport as British, got a drunken ovation from the audience and mild applause from a slightly embarrassed-looking Prime Minister Gordon Brown. It was a stupidly humid night, and the garden was really heating up. I suddenly found myself live on Sky News, being interviewed alongside a rather gorgeous and still ridiculously shy Leona Lewis. To my right, I could see Jimmy Page and Jackie Chan. To my left was David Beckham, talking live on the BBC – it was all very surreal.

The competing groups of security and press officers were going mental as they tried to shield their protégés from over-excitable revellers. Beckham had a man-mountain of a security guard with him whereas the prime minister's security detail looked far less intimidating, but they all did that talking-into-your sleeve thing that the American secret service always do when hustling Bush about. I said hello to Beckham and asked him whether he was enjoying Beijing?

'Yeah ... It's gweat ...' he replied. Possibly the most unin-spired question and answer session of the whole Olympics ... What can I say? I was new to being a reporter.

My contact within the prime minister's entourage asked me whether I wanted my picture taken with The Boss? I briefly thought Bruce Springsteen had arrived but then, out of nowhere, Gordon Brown appeared in front of me.

'Hello, Dom, how are you enjoying Beijing?' This was clearly the question *du soir* so I followed Beckham's lead: 'Yeah ... It's gweat.'

Brown nodded and smiled his big awkward smile.

The prime minister looked hot and sweaty. I looked unbe-lievably hot and sweaty. This was going to be a distinctly unattractive photograph.

I looked around for someone to take the photo and Brown pointed out Mark Byford, the deputy head of the BBC, in charge of all its journalism.

'He'll know what he's doing,' laughed the prime minister and I handed my camera over. Byford took two photos and handed it back – they were badly out of focus.

Sarah Brown had a look and snorted: 'That's the problem when everyone's drunk, give the camera to me.' She grabbed

her husband, placed him next to me again and took a great picture.

Thank God for sober First Ladies.

I returned home triumphant. I'd been a foreign correspondent
and not completely screwed it up. Sure, it's not like I'd been in
a war zone or covered a famine, but it was a big tick on the
bucket list.

By now my travel writing had attracted publishers and Simon
& Schuster offered me a deal to write a couple of travel books. I
immediately set about planning my first one, documenting my
love of travel to slightly dodgy destinations. Using a contact I
had made while in Beijing, I was off to North Korea as well as
Cambodia's Killing Fields, skiing in Iran and a weekend in
Chernobyl. I couldn't wait.

Travel writing is, in my opinion, the best job in the world, but
it didn't pay very well. I had a wife, a life and two kids to pay
for, and they needed to be kept in the style to which they had
become accustomed.

It was at this moment that I got my annual offer to appear on
I'm a Celebrity ... Get Me Out of Here! The selection process for
this show seems to be that they ask pretty much everyone in
showbiz whether they are interested. They see who says yes.
Then they try and cast a perfect TV storm. American celeb?
Check. Ageing actor? Check. Blonde girl in bikini? Check.
Hunky but simple male? Check. Troubled personality? Check.
Misunderstood sports star? Check. Chubby comedian? Check.

Everyone I knew and trusted in my life told me not to do it.
So I said yes, because I'm a contrary old bastard. Also, I have
very few actual life skills but the one thing I do possess is the
ability to ad-lib and to be funny on the hoof. Most comedy is
scripted and tightly controlled. I'm rubbish at that. My comedy
is about reacting to events and firing off other people. This
leaves me with very few formats that fit the bill. *I'm a Celeb*

could be a fantastic window-display for me. It could also be a place where everything went terribly wrong. What if my black dog returned? What if there was a thick, tattooed footballer in there? What if I went mental and took the whole camp hostage and started to eat human flesh? It was too late. I had signed up: '*Alea iacta est.*'

It was all very cloak and dagger. I had travelled secretly to Brisbane under the ironic code name of *Happy*. Very hush-hush, except for the paparazzi who greeted us at Brisbane airport. To be honest, they rather spoiled the hush-hush element but we were still moved around as though we were on some form of Cold War spy exchange.

I was transferred by my security detail to a hotel about twenty minutes away from the hideous Gold Coast, with only a chaperone for company. I had to inform said chaperone of my whereabouts in the hotel at all times and I had to hand in my mobile phone and laptop, as we weren't allowed to use the internet. Fortunately, my Australian chaperone seemed blissfully unaware of iPads so I had full use of the web for the duration of my stay. I was also not allowed to leave the grounds of the hotel unless it was in a prearranged convoy. To be honest, the security was intense and a little over the top. It very much felt like my guards hadn't quite made the cut for the army and rather resented the fact that this was all they were good for.

The weather was good and I lay by the pool all day reading books, and slowly started to forget that I was in Australia to do anything but have a holiday. When the day of my 'entry' actually came, I was surprisingly resentful. First came 'Dr Bob', the show's bearded doctor, who gave me a quick once-over and talked me through some of the deadlier types of 'critters' that I might encounter. The chat left me terrified, as he rattled through the long list of things that could kill me. I'd tried to keep my arachnophobia a secret but it wouldn't be for too long. They'd actually asked me on a form, 'What do you fear most?' As though I was going to assist them in my torture ...

I wrote that I had a pathological fear of good food and comfy pillows.

Speaking of pillows, the only personal things I was allowed to take in were three pairs of underwear, three pairs of swimming trunks and one luxury item. I hummed and haahed for ages about what to take. Most people take photos or pillows. One person took a pillow with a photo printed on the pillowcase. Jenny Eclair took in fake tan, Aggro Santos, the rapper, took in a bottle of after-shave shaped like a gold ingot ...

The rules stated that you were not allowed furniture, games or anything electronic.

I eventually opted for a disposable camera. They were terrified of anything that could allow you to internalise, this being a recipe for bad telly. They wanted you bored, irritable and vocal – anybody sleeping in the day was woken up immediately and if they did not comply, then the whole group was punished.

Back in the hotel, all my personal belongings were taken off me and signed for one by one. The atmosphere in the room was quite tense – I felt like a condemned man on the morning of his execution. It was crazy. I was just off to muck around on telly, not headed for the scaffold, but your head started to play tricks with you. I was walked to a car in an underground basement and driven to the coast where we drove around randomly for ages while whispered conversations were had over walkie-talkies. Nobody would tell me anything about what was going on – it was a sackable offence. I was entering the bubble and was decidedly not prepared for it. In shows I'd made before, you did the job and then you could have a chat with the crew, josh around a bit – it made the whole thing fun. Not in this show. From first contact, I realised that this was going to be different. The isolation element was an integral part of the experience.

'Time is a luxury,' said one of the producers to me when I asked him the time. Everybody I came into contact with, including Ant and Dec, had strips of gaffer tape over their watches. Any question or light-hearted greeting was met with silence and stony indifference. It was very dispiriting and dehumanising – just as it was meant to be.

Finally the call came through to the 12-year-old producer in the car, and I was driven to a helipad. There I was joined by an equally dazed Jenny Eclair, who had just got off the plane from London. 'I met you once in the Groucho . . .' These were her first words to me on camera. Our fates were sealed. We were celebrity arseholes and deserved everything we were about to get.

We were choppered for forty-five minutes into a different world. When we landed, everybody was in combat gear and it looked like we'd just been taken prisoner by some Colombian terrorist group. We were ordered into canoes and set off into the unknown. Jenny and I tried to josh with each other but it was hollow talk – we were both a lot more nervous than we were prepared to admit. I assumed that we were heading for the main camp but the evil masterminds behind the show had other ideas. We arrived in an isolated campsite at dusk. The sounds from the jungle army of insects were ear-splittingly loud – I started to feel a bit panicky, disorientated. I looked to the crew for support but they looked back blankly – we were in this alone. I was knackered – the adrenaline comedown was enormous and I just wanted to sleep on one of the two camp beds by the makeshift fire. The production had other plans. We had to earn stars to get meals for our future camp-mates. We were ushered into the Shack of Terror.

The first thing I saw in the tiny shack was three stupidly large spiders on the table in front of us. It was classic fight or flight psychology, and my instincts were screaming FLIGHT!

Fortunately, Jenny was made of sterner stuff and she bullied and cajoled me into staying for the whole experience, as more and more heinous 'critters' were deposited into the shack during our four-hour ordeal. I managed to work out the time by snatching a glimpse of a time code on one of the cameras – it was a tiny moment but it felt like an enormous victory. Jenny and I eventually crashed out on our beds and fell asleep. By that stage, I would have been able to sleep on a bed of spiders, but fortunately the producers hadn't thought of that idea ... yet.

The following morning we were awoken at dawn, and handed a phone. We had to phone the camp and request that two celebs of our choice come to rescue us. This was our first glimpse of the cast. (I had to pretend that I didn't know the list – I'd been checking online.) Unlike many previous years, I actually recognised quite a few names – Britt Ekland, Nigel Havers, Shaun Ryder, Lembit Opik, Linford Christie ... There were a couple of people whom I'd never heard of but it wasn't quite as low-rent as most years. There was a pleasing lack of soap-stars for one thing. Jenny and I opted for Havers and Ryder to come and 'save' us. An hour later and we were led to a jungle clearing, where a helicopter landed and our two 'saviours' got out nervously. They had already been in the jungle for four days and were showing clear signs of institutionalisation. They were terrified that they were about to be subjected to some new torture and were incredibly mistrustful of us. Havers, who had never seen the show before coming in, was in a state of almost perpetual shock. It was becoming more and more difficult to remember that we were in a 'light entertainment' programme.

On the flight towards the camp we introduced ourselves – Shaun Ryder, who hated small talk, was quite silent and I shall never forget the look of sheer terror in Nigel Havers' eyes. What the hell was going on in this camp?

The first person I saw when I entered was Gillian McKeith, who stared at me with the sullen, hostile eyes of the schoolyard madam. Others were more friendly – I recognised Stacey Solomon, a sweet ugly duckling with a good singing voice from *The X Factor*. I sat on my damp hammock and tried to control the rising feelings of panic. This had been a terrible mistake . . .

It's incredible how quickly the human spirit adapts to unpleasant situations. Pretty soon, camp was home and I dreaded being taken out of it to some unknown destination and task. It was classic hostage psychology that wouldn't have been out of place in Guantánamo Bay. We were being controlled by an all-seeing power, and most people quickly fell into line.

Everybody in camp was pretty open and friendly – some, like Lembit Opik, overly so. I was quickly filled in about the 'Gillian situation'. It turned out that 'Dr' Gillian McKeith – a woman famous for analysing people's stools on television (and not being a doctor) – was afraid of everything and behaving like a selfish harridan. The public had smelt fear and, like a blood-thirsty crowd at the Colosseum, were baying for her blood. Gillian didn't help herself – she had a medical excuse for every-thing and behaved like a spoilt child around the camp. My favourite fact about her was that her husband (poor man) had been unable to join her children in Australia . . . because he had a phobia of flying . . . What a family.

Before we got on the show, we were sent to a psychiatrist in North London to be evaluated. It's a catch 22 for these types of shows. They don't want to be criticised for making money out of exploiting vulnerable, mentally unstable celebs . . . On the other hand, it's vulnerable, mentally unstable celebs that make the best telly. The solution is to give people a psych test that, just by the fact that Gillian McKeith passed, is clearly utterly useless. Nevertheless, this then gives the production company a defence that we have all been intensively screened psychologically and everything is in hand. I got nervous before mine and consumed an entire bottle of champagne for lunch in a fish restaurant just down the road. So I was in a good mood when I arrived and thought that I dealt with the shrink's probing questions with both humour and aplomb. When it was over I asked her jokingly whether I had 'passed'.

She looked at me for quite a while in that disconcerting manner that shrinks do, before telling me that I had indeed passed . . . but that she felt that I would really benefit from seeing someone regularly when this was all over. She even gave me the number of someone to ring. I left her office sheepishly and wandered off down the road muttering to myself about how there was nothing wrong with me, nothing I couldn't sort out myself . . . Maybe I should have taken her up on the offer?

Back in the jungle, if we were taken out of camp to do a trial we would be marched silently over precarious rope bridges before being bundled into blacked-out vans that we termed 'Beirut buses'. This was more hostage stuff, and I rapidly gained a tiny insight into what people like John McCarthy must go through (obviously without the all-important fear of death) and how you clung to anything that provided a sense of stability or continuity.

I was moved to a 'prison' about four days after entering camp and I longed to return to my uncomfortable damp hammock that had so freaked me out on arrival. I got incredibly close to Jenny Eclair, whom I loved. Others were more of a disappointment. I was expecting Britt Ekland, a woman who had lived a seriously interesting life, to be brimming with stories. She was dull as ditchwater and the only interesting fact we got out of her was that she jogged backwards every day (because Mick Jagger did the same). Lembit Opik was a man so out of touch with reality that it hurt. He was considering running for London Mayor. Nobody bothered to tell him how utterly ludicrous the idea was. When we got out, we found that he'd been ditched by a Cheeky Girl and had a young girlfriend who would drape herself around him in some seriously hideous public displays of affection. Nigel Havers became more and more agitated by the whole experience and turned increasingly to me for guidance as to what was happening. For instance, a trial would be announced – it would be called something like The Creepy Tunnel of Doom:

'What do you think it is, old boy?' Nigel would ask nervously.

'I think it's a dark tunnel that you have to crawl through while they pour insects all over you,' I'd reply.

'Monstrous ... simply monstrous, what kind of show is this?' Nigel would say with a thousand-yard stare.

Nigel eventually cracked when we were all trooped down to an area where we were put into makeshift docks and had electrodes attached to our bodies. The idea was that we would be electrocuted every time we got a question wrong. I knew that we would not really be electrocuted, as Health and Safety would not allow it. The electrodes would just give us an annoying buzz that would make the nerves judder. Nevertheless, I surreptitiously put my hand under my shirt and removed one of said electrodes. Sadly, I was too far away from Nigel to tell him to do the same. He had a wonderful hissy fit and stormed out of the enclosure, where he proceeded to have a screaming row with a producer.

'I will not sit here and be electrocuted. This is inhuman. This has gone too far, we're not animals ...'

The next day he upped and left us. It was not a place for him. Shaun Ryder, however, was enjoying himself more and more and coming out of his shell. I loved Shaun; he was smart and funny and very entertaining. He loathed Gillian McKeith as much as the rest of us. Time after time, she would be chosen to do a trial and she would freak out and come back with no stars. People were getting seriously hungry and very irritable. She would jump out of her skin at the sight of a micro-bug and a leaf falling would send her into a fit.

One morning I woke up early and wandered down to tend the fire and sip on a cup of hot, smoky water. I looked up to see Shaun waking up. He nodded at me and then looked down below him to where McKeith was asleep, cocooned in a large sleeping bag. Shaun looked at me and grinned. He produced a long stick that he kept under his bed and subtly prodded the sleeping McKeith before quickly hiding the stick. She went mental, jumping up and screaming hysterically about animal attacks and bolted to the telegraph room. He'd been doing this regularly every night. We howled with laughter – the jungle had turned us into cruel creatures.

I often wondered what my family was up to while I was on the show. It turned out that they were living in the hideous Versace hotel (a place that looks like Elton John has vomited all over it) and being bussed out on the hour-long drive to the set every morning at the crack of dawn to watch the show in a tent. Stacey told me that they would sit and watch the thing, praying that I hadn't been mean to anybody, as things then became very tense with whichever relative or friend of that person was there. If there was no major incident and I wasn't chucked out, then they would be bussed back to the Versace and have the day to play around in at the pool. They had an absolute blast and would have stayed for another month if asked. Meanwhile back home, my lovely mum, who normally pooh-poohs any of these sorts of programmes, became hooked and watched every episode and became almost proud of the notoriety that my being on the show caused in her Shepherd's Bush street.

People often ask whether the jungle experience is as bad as it seems on telly.

'I bet it's fixed and is much better than it seems,' they'd say confidently.

Curiously, I think it was worse than it appeared on the telly. You didn't see the hours and hours of terminal boredom. You could never really get the sense of creeping paranoia that hit you when the public vote approached. However bravely you faced the thing, it was a very unsettling experience having the UK population decide whether you were an arse or not. When McKeith wasn't initially voted out, we all freaked out. Maybe we'd completely got it wrong and she was somehow popular or liked? Stranger things have happened in showbiz but thankfully it turned out that people were just voting intelligently to keep her in so that she could be tormented more. She, of course, misunderstood this completely and started to think she was queen bee. It didn't seem humanly possible, but she actually started to behave even worse than before.

Despite all the deprivations, paranoia and McKeith, I found myself loving the experience. It was something to do with the total detachment from modern life. All one's daily stresses were removed and all you had to worry about was the day ahead of you. The jungle experience was one that, even if you had all the money in the world, you could not replicate. To be thrown into a hostile rainforest with a random bunch of high-achieving personalities with a crew of about three hundred running the entire experience ... I didn't regret my decision for a moment, although I was very relieved to get out and find that I hadn't embarrassed my wife or kids too much. When I got out, it was to find them babysitting Stacey Solomon's kid and hanging out with the Ryder clan. My son was even wearing a Happy Mondays T-shirt. It was all very hard to adjust to.

Best of all for me was the long-forgotten feeling of going clothes shopping and selecting a slim-fit shirt that actually fitted. I don't think I took the damn thing off for about three weeks, until it started to physically fall apart. I lost two-and-a-half stone during my time in the jungle (actually not a jungle – a rainforest – but I'm quibbling). People pay vast sums of money to go to places where they are starved and pummelled into better shape. *I'm a Celebrity* provided me with the same service, paid me handsomely, and as a bonus I wasn't surrounded by the rich, hairy Russians who normally frequent international health clinics. Result.

Chapter 11

Now What?

Back in the UK, I was inundated with weird requests on the back of my jungle 'performance'. Two of them synergised rather wonderfully. I had long wanted to visit Patagonia and Antarctica, and I got an offer from a friend who ran a posh travel company to accompany him down through Argentina and onto a boat that would take us to explore the edge of the Frozen Continent. I'd already agreed when another came in – would I like to do *Total Wipeout*, the curiously addictive TV assault course? My kids were avid fans of the show and demanded that I do it. I was unsure until I read further and found that filming took place just outside Buenos Aires, and they would cover a business class return flight to the Argentinian capital. This was a no-brainer. Fly to Buenos Aires, become *Total Wipeout* champion and then move on to explore Antarctica. I said yes immediately.

I normally check, if I can, to see who is on these sorts of shows as there is usually someone I have pissed off in the past and it's best to be prepared, but I didn't bother on this occasion and turned up at Gatwick, wondering what awaited me. Once in the business lounge, it turned out that what awaited me was a large and entertaining piss-up. Everybody was either nervous of meeting each other or of flying, and we all got gloriously pissed on free champagne. The first person I saw was Simon Day, a fantastically funny comedian who was in *The Fast Show*. He was instantly friendly and welcoming, and I relaxed. He told me that he didn't drink any more, but then appeared to forget all about it five minutes later and joined in with everyone else.

I looked around the table – there was the imposing presence of Razor Ruddock (a footballer with quite a reputation), Lady Sovereign (the poster girl for chav rappers), a couple of Olympians (Gail Emms and Dalton Grant), a 'glamour girl' called Nicola McLean, a *Big Brother* winner (Brian Belo) and various other minor celeb types. It was one of those weird showbiz happenings that gathered a stupidly disparate group together. It quickly went a bit pear-shaped. Lady Sovereign nearly got thrown off the plane for getting ludicrously drunk, trying to smoke and then starting a food fight. Razor Ruddock, Simon Day and I huddled together and drank more – it was going to be a long trip. As it turned out it was a rather short one.

Come the day of filming and I should have seen the signs. Why did Endemol, the production company that made the programme, decide to film it in Argentina of all places? One of the reasons was that they'd bought a piece of land about half an hour outside the capital where the set had been built. I surmised that, with the recent Argentinian economic problems, the land had probably been dirt-cheap. Once the set had been built, the company simply flew in competitors from each different country like human sausages. One week it was France, then Germany, then the UK etc. Once the initial start-up had been paid off, it was a licence to print money. More importantly, I think that health and safety laws were a little laxer in Argentina than Europe. I should have taken the hint when I spotted two ambulances parked by the course but I was too adrenalised by then.

We were all keen to try and get over the Big Red Balls that the show was so famous for. It was stricter than we thought – we weren't allowed to watch anybody else compete and the course was soaked before every run so that it was extra slippery. I don't remember too much except that I was doing really well. I was past the Big Red Balls and onto the last obstacle when it happened. I was on a platform in front of a revolving circle that had shapes cut into it. My plan was to soar effortlessly through the air, land in one of the holes, crouch until the circle reached the top and then hop off onto the winning podium. That was the plan. The reality was I jumped and landed inelegantly in a hole with the full weight of my body crushing my left foot. I was in shock and tumbled down into the water. The pain was excruciating but everyone was cheering and adrenaline forced me on. I reached the ladder, somehow climbed up and finished. I had the second fastest time. This was scant recompense, however, as I then collapsed and fell into the water. I was dragged to the shore where the presenter interviewed me with my shorts halfway down my legs.

'I'm in a lot of pain,' I remember saying before blacking out.

I awoke in a hospital with a foot the size of my head. I got my mobile and rang the family back home. My son answered:

'Hey Dad, did you win *Total Wipeout* – are you the champion?'

'Not exactly, no ...' I replied. 'Is Mum there?' I had broken three metatarsals in my foot. I would not be going to Antarctica. I would be going straight home for an operation.

The irony of me getting a 'footballing' injury in Argentina, despite my loathing of the game, was not lost on me. Every cab driver would ask me what was wrong with my foot. 'Metatarsal,' I would reply. 'Ahh, Rooney, Beckham ...' they would smile sympathetically as though my top international football career was on hold for a while.

On the plus side, being on the show did give me a great idea for a film script. Here's the pitch:

A disparate gang of minor celebs are in a Third-World country to compete on a cruel TV game show, in which one of them will get the chance to revive their flagging career. Unfortunately, a revolution breaks out in said country while they are there. The celebs have to park their egos and insecurities and use their multifarious and obscure skills to help each other escape the disintegrating and increasingly violent situation.

This is probably a more in-depth pitch than the one Stallone did for *Rocky* and look how well that turned out. It's a smash hit – trust me. *Copyright Dom Joly.*

I was flown back to the UK to have quite a major operation on my foot. I was going to be in a cast for at least three months. This was a problem. I'd just agreed to have a go at doing some sort of live show with a view to touring the UK. This was my biggest phobia. Everyone you ever tell that you're a comedian instantly assumes that you mean stand-up and that you're very confident in front of a crowd. This couldn't be further from the truth. I had only ever done stand-up once in my life, and that was for a joke. I'd got major prosthetics put on for the first time and then went on stage at The Comedy Store in London. Nobody recognised me and I just said the first thing that came into my head for as long as I could until I was booed off. I lasted fifteen minutes, as people assumed I was doing some clever set-up with a great punchline.

It never came.

Anyway, in character I'm ballsy and can approach strangers and interact, but the idea of standing on stage as myself is utterly terrifying. So I thought I'd try and face my demons. In a movie, I would be freaking out, having panic attacks until the moment before I went on stage, when suddenly I would find some inner strength and I would slowly win the audience around, finishing with a standing ovation and triumph over adversity ... This did not happen. I was awful. I had no experience of having to work a crowd and, for a lot of the tour, had no crowd to work.

In honour of Stacey Solomon throwing a stone at my face on *I'm a Celebrity ... Get Me Out of Here!* I had someone selling cloth stones for a pound a go in the foyer. At the end of the show, I got the audience to pelt me with the stones and then all get up and run screaming out of the theatre. I filmed this on an infra-red camera that I was holding. The idea I'd had was to take this footage of people running screaming out of theatre after theatre and use it as the trailer for the movie that Sam and I seemed destined never to make. It would have been good – a cinemagoer would hear one of those big movie voice-over voices:

'From the people who brought you *Trigger Happy TV* and other slightly less successful shows, the hidden camera movie that is taking the country by storm ...'

This, while they watched scenes of mass, unexplained panic in about fifty theatres. It would have been brilliant ... I still hope we make the film one day. I want to call it *Scenes From a Movie That We Never Made.* That should kill the box office stone dead.

The tour was crazy, though – I was doing seventy dates and often the shows were in vast venues. When this happened and nobody showed up it was incredibly dispiriting, but there seemed to be no rhyme or reason to the numbers. One night I'd be in Shrewsbury and have a sell-out to 800 people, and the next night I'd be in Hull playing to an audience of twelve. I could never anticipate whether I'd sell out or die, as the tour took me crisscrossing all over the country on a schedule that looked like a drunken spider had designed it. Fortunately, I had a wonderful Kiwi called Kylie who tour-managed for me and patiently put up with my fear and loathing while she drove me up and down the country from gig to gig, often with me unconscious in the back.

My dad died suddenly about a week into the tour. I had to break off and fly to Lebanon for his funeral.

He was a good man who served in the Fleet Air Arm in the Second World War and then went to Oxford, before settling down to run the family business in Beirut. He was separated by two generations from me and we had a rocky relationship. He wrote several books during his life and I think that, given the choice, he would have loved to have been an author instead of feeling obliged to take over the family business. Unfortunately for his generation, duty was everything, and he made the best of what he was supposed to do. I always got the feeling that he perhaps subconsciously resented the fact that I set off to do exactly what I wanted, even if it took me some considerable time find out what that was.

He never, ever spoke of my success. He never once congratulated me on anything that I'd achieved. Part of me used to put it down to the fact that he lived abroad and simply wasn't aware of what I did, but this can't have been the case. There were several times when I would be with him, having an awkward meal somewhere and someone would come up to me and ask for an autograph or say hello. He never acknowledged these weird incidents. It was all very peculiar. It had always been peculiar, however, ever since he and my mother divorced when I was eighteen.

I think that he never really approved of me. Somehow I didn't seem to live up to whatever personal benchmarks he had set for the perfect son.

In the self-indulgence fest that was *Being Dom Joly*, there was a long, almost uncut scene in which I meet my fictional dad for lunch. It is so toe-curlingly awkward and stilted and pretty much reflects every meeting that I had with him. We had a bit of a rapprochement in the years before he died, but this was mainly because he started to lose his marbles a little. He became a very sweet old man with none of the moody, stressed underside that used to be ever-present. I developed quite a nice, simple relationship with this man, but sadly he wasn't my father. My father had departed quite some time previously, leaving this pleasant shadow to live out the rest of his life, playing golf every day and drinking wine in the evening before falling asleep in front of the cricket.

My dad, like myself, was born in Beirut to British parents and was always somehow stuck in some curious expat time bubble. I got the feeling that every time he returned to Britain he understood it less and less. His was a post-war Britain of codified rules and sunny days at Test matches. Despite my having been conceived in 1967, the entire Sixties movement and the subsequent youth culture takeover of the country had almost entirely passed him by.

When he'd been a boy, his parents had sent him to boarding school in England. This having been during the war, he was forced to stay in the UK with relatives and would only return home to Lebanon once a year. He loathed every second of it. Being British, however, he decided to send me to the very same school (Haileybury College). I never quite understood this thought process.

He grew up with the feeling, prevalent in his generation, that you should choose a career and stick at it whatever the difficulties. Work was work and then you could do the things you enjoyed. I was always determined that work would be what I enjoyed. Otherwise I would suck at it. He was a deeply honest and decent man, emotionally crippled by boarding school and the subsequent shock of war. I don't think he ever truly recovered. He was unable to express himself emotionally to me, he loathed conflict, and yet this was a man who successfully ran a family business in Beirut throughout the civil war. He was brave and stubborn. I remember as a boy, when the house was being shelled night after night and we were all sleeping on mattresses in the basement, my dad would refuse to leave his bed on the exposed, top corner of the house. He was awarded the OBE in the Seventies. He was a bundle of contradictions, and my real sadness is that I'm actually rather similar to him but he never seemed to see that.

We buried him in Beirut. The service was in the church in which I was christened. It used to sit on the seafront on St George's Bay in Beirut but it was now surrounded by new glass high-rises and was quite a way inland, as the bay had been filled in with rubble from the ruins of old Beirut. It was a curious ceremony. For me, I had lost my father a long time ago, when he divorced my mother. We'd never really had a relationship since then and I had done my grieving throughout my twenties. I was very sad he was gone and it made me feel immensely mortal. I flew back to Britain in a curious state.

I'd only missed two dates of the tour, but I was, not surprisingly, in a really bad place. I was not really in the right frame of mind to be doing my first live comedy tour. It was the secret to good comedy . . . timing.

The show had to go on, however, and I was now surviving on a curious cocktail of vodka, Red Bull and Berocca that I would down before I went on stage. I felt empty, listless and seriously unhappy. I wasn't sure if I could carry on but I couldn't bear the idea of giving up. Then, about three-quarters of the way through the tour, something happened. I started to feel better and find my live feet a bit. I cut the show length down by a quarter, started to experiment and change it up every night. By the last couple of shows in London's Bloomsbury Theatre, I had cracked it. I did seventy-two gigs in under three months. I was pleased that I'd seen it through. I would never, ever undertake something that was out of my comfort zone again. I needed to stick to what I was good at, whatever that was.

Chapter 12

Fool Britannia

With the tour over, I set off round the world hunting monsters for my second travel book, *Scary Monsters and Super Creeps.* I had no qualification to be a monster hunter except that I had a business card printed off that read:

Dom Joly – Monster Hunter

I travelled to Hiroshima, Northern California, Nepal, the Congo and British Columbia. It was as close as I'd get to actually becoming Tintin. Actually, that's not strictly true. A couple of years previously I'd made a documentary about *Tintin and the Black Island* and had gone the whole hog – dyeing my hair ginger, donning the Belgian reporter's costume and eventually landing on the beach in Barra, an Outer Hebridean island where Hergé got a lot of his inspiration from. For a while I roamed Scotland, a portly Tintin with a badly dyed Snowy as a companion. We'd hired a Snowy for the production and it was only when it started raining that we realised that the bastards had dyed the poor dog white. It was all very odd.

I was at my happiest travelling the world on weird and wonderful wild-goose chases. This was what I loved. This was what I should be doing. The lure of television, however, works in mysterious ways. I'd just returned from the Congo when I got an email asking me to go and see ITV. I was intrigued. ITV had never really been my kind of channel and I was curious as to what they might want. It turned out to be rather interesting. Harry Hill had stopped making his fabulous *TV Burp* and they needed something to replace it. They were looking for a family-friendly, Saturday 6.30pm show. Because I'd been on *I'm a Celebrity*, they felt that I was now a familiar face to ITV viewers and wouldn't frighten them too much. It was weird – I'd never gone on the show with a view that it might help anything other than my bank balance and my waistline. Somehow, it had paid off handsomely.

This was the TV mother lode. If you could crack that slot then the world was yours. ITV had this idea about a show that used archive footage of old ITV prank shows and then had me recreating them today. The idea was to do a sort of pseudo-scientific, *Are we as gullible today as in the old days?*-type show. This didn't interest me too much but I was certainly up for having a crack at that time slot. I pitched a show on the spot, basically a kind of *Trigger Happy-Lite* that we would film all round Great Britain. My friend Adam Longworth gave me the ideal title one drunken night in the Groucho Club: *Fool Britannia.*

ITV were interested and commissioned a pilot. I thought it might be cool to form a little prankster team so that I didn't have to do everything myself. We found a couple of people online who were doing some innovative stuff and we started to film the pilot.

The first character I had in mind was a vicar behaving badly. Institutional figures are great for hidden camera as people naturally trust them and the reaction was heightened when they behaved badly. My vicar was a very simple fellow but he ran his parish (we filmed in Bourton-on-the-Water) with a rod of iron. The scene we filmed for the pilot was him waffling on to a couple of Japanese tourists before wandering off and pushing a stunt man dressed as an old woman off a bridge into the river. 'Clumsy me!' he screamed in delight, before walking off.

I'm at my best when I dress up as a character, approach strangers and engage them in conversation, before starting to turn it all a bit odd and surreal. For ITV Saturday night purposes, however, we needed something more obvious and mainstream to finish it off. So the vicar would always do something like pepper-spray a cyclist, steal an ambulance etc. For me, it was all about the pre-conversations. The vicar would always ask people where they were from and then politely launch into a tirade of abuse about their homeland. People didn't know how to take it. The best vicar moment was quite subtle. I had an actress and her daughter sit on a bench by the river in Bourton. The little girl was holding a balloon. I waited until I spotted a real couple walking along the river towards me and then timed my entrance so that I could nonchalantly cut the little girl's balloon string with a pair of scissors while putting my finger to my lips demanding *omertà* from the horrified couple.

One of the most common questions I'm asked re hidden camera is whether I've ever been beaten up? The answer, I'm afraid, is no ... Doing hidden camera has given me a very acute sense of imminent danger. So many times have I approached a stranger and started to talk to them when I've nipped it in the bud and walked away. It's all in the eyes. Sometimes you look into somebody's dead eyes that tell you immediately that this person has been released from Broadmoor and that you are in trouble. I've developed a traffic light system for judging people. Green is the perfect subject. They will believe everything you tell them – carry on. Amber is trickier – they are a touch suspicious and you must proceed carefully. Red is danger – they are potential serial killers and you must extricate yourself immediately and run away.

A nun assaulted me once. It was when we were making *Trigger Happy TV* and we'd taken over the Tannoy system in a supermarket in Notting Hill Gate. The joke was that the Tannoy would describe a customer – 'aisle three, red trousers, blue shirt, he's back . . .' – and I would appear as a very suspicious security guard and follow them around. We were doing this when a nun entered the store. We all looked at each other, unsure as to whether we should or not? In the end I nodded and the Tannoy boomed out: 'The nun is back and she's acting shifty by the yoghurts.' I appeared round the corner to stare at the nun, who went mental. She started hurling cans of beans at me while swearing like a trucker. She eventually stormed out, having run out of ammunition to chuck. We never found out whether she was a genuine sweary nun or a stripagram.

The closest I've ever got to actually being punched was while playing the vicar. I was chatting to some American tourists and being quietly rude about their country when an actor we'd organised started busking on a bridge behind me. The vicar did not like any disturbances in 'his' village and therefore excused himself to go and deal with the fellow. I grabbed the guitar and smashed it to pieces before hurling it into the river and then returning to chat with the shocked Americans as though nothing had happened.

Out of the blue a very angry, shaven-headed passer-by got involved. He'd seen the incident and, rightly, had been incensed. He came up close to me, eyeballing me and demanding to know what I was up to. I tried to say something funny but he got even more aggressive and I was pretty certain he was about to clock me. I could feel the crew in two minds: on the one hand, this was great telly; but on the other, I might be kicked to bits. Finally, after what seemed like an eternity, an AP appeared and started to explain what was going on. The guy changed tack immediately and started howling with laughter. It turned out he was a big fan and thought the whole thing was hilarious – he couldn't believe he'd been fooled. We asked him whether he would sign a release form and he was initially happy to do so. Something suddenly struck him, however, and he stopped in his tracks ...

'You mean this will go out on the telly?' he asked, looking very nervous. I wondered whether he was on parole or suchlike. We said that yes, this would definitely go out on the telly as it was very funny. He leant in and started whispering and pointing to a woman who was waiting for him: 'Fing is, right, that lady is not my wife ... We're on a bit of a dirty break, if you catch my drift ... I don't fink it would be the best idea, putting us on the box ...' It was so frustrating but there was nothing we could do about it – we had to roll again and try to get something as good, but we knew we never would.

We cut a pilot show together and it went down very well back at ITV – well, my bits did anyway. It turned out that they weren't so keen on the other performers. I tried to look upset by this but actually I was pretty chuffed, as it meant I got my own Saturday night show on ITV without looking like I was desperate for it. To be fair, I had my doubts. To me, Saturday nights on ITV had been the epitome of naff – cheesy, lowbrow entertainment and not really where I had ever wanted to end up. I had no interest in becoming another Jeremy Beadle. On the other hand, I was filling the boots of Harry Hill's *TV Burp*, an amazingly funny and surreal show that had opened up all sorts of possibilities for that slot. I didn't want to make another *Trigger Happy TV* for now. *Trigger Happy* was made for my mates and me – it was what made us laugh. To have a hit Saturday night show on

ITV, you had to do the hardest thing in telly – make a show that appealed across the board, grandpa, mum and dad, and the kids – all this without making it too dumbed-down. It was a tricky challenge.

After much pondering, ITV finally commissioned a full series of *Fool Britannia*. My first job was to find a director. I was given the name of the current go-to guy in hidden camera. Paul Young had directed everything in the genre from *Banzai* to *Balls of Steel*. I immediately recognised the name and suddenly felt very old. Paul had been my runner on Series One of *Trigger Happy TV* and now he was going to be the director. In TV, it's not policemen who appear younger and younger – it's directors. He had a stupidly annoying, high-pitched laugh that I would constantly hear through my earpiece when we were filming, but it was a good thing, though. My main job on set was to make the cameramen and Paul laugh. If you can make the crew laugh, then you're halfway there, because those bastards are a dour lot ...

ITV brought in a producer called Greg Bower, who had worked on the *Trigger Happy* homage, *Fonejacker*. He was to be the 'grown-up' of the show and the conduit between ITV and me. I'd never really got on with producers and I was very aware that I would have to play the game right if ITV and I were going to work. To say that Greg was a man of few words would be an insult to mutes. I don't think he actually said a single thing in our first four meetings. It was only when I ordered a beer during one of our working lunches in ITV Towers that he expressed surprise. Greg was quite fantastically antisocial. When we were on shoots, we would all go out together in the evening to blow off a bit of steam, have supper and a couple of drinks. Greg very much preferred his own company and would either remain in his room with an attractive bottle of red wine or be occasionally spotted dining with a friend in a dive bar. He was not a team player, but he also didn't try to be my friend and stood up to me, which is what a producer should do. It meant that I didn't have total control (which is always a good thing) and I worked far harder than I would have normally done. Greg, however, really liked to control things from his end. This was bad, as it meant that the show started to get divided between ideas that Greg and his 'writing room' came up with and the ideas that Paul and I had. Ours were always a lot more instinctive:

'Give me a garden gnome costume and we'll do something,' I'd tell Greg.

'What exactly would you be doing with the gnome costume?' Greg would ask nervously.

'Oh, I don't know, but it will be funny . . .'

Greg would look unconvinced and we'd often have an awkward standoff.

The problem was that I hated committing to plans as I'd never worked that way before, but Greg was right in that we needed to have some sort of structure and some end point to a gag. If I were to be left to my own devices then we would have ended up with a lot of weird and funny bits that would be difficult to mesh together without confusing Middle Britain.

We eventually filmed the garden gnomes in Weymouth and it was very funny, if slightly odd compared to the rest of the show. We were filming on the coast, in somebody's front garden that faced right onto a pathway. I leant on the garden gate and engaged with whoever happened to walk past. Things went rather well, the weather held, and we got some good stuff. After about an hour or so we cut for a break and I sat in a chair in the garden drinking a very welcome cup of coffee. That was when I noticed the estate agent showing a family around the house next door, which was for sale. They came into the seafront garden and the agent was busy describing the merits of the place. The family, however, were not listening. They were all staring at me, a six-foot human garden gnome in the neighbouring garden.

There was no crew about – it was just my potential new neighbours and me.

I couldn't resist.

'Hello,' I said, waving a little too frantically, 'moving in, are you? I've got a hot tub ...' They smiled politely and backed away into the safety of the house that they would now clearly never buy.

As usual, most of the funniest stuff was in between takes when I was arsing around for the crew – more of my and Sam's *for the beauty* stuff. I particularly used to enjoy trying to sell drugs while dressed as the vicar. I'd sidle up to someone and whisper, 'What do you need? I've got Hash, Whizz, Uppers, Downers, Purples, Blues, Horse, Peyote ...'

The bemused passer-by would turn around and give a double take, but I would press on.

'If you're looking for shooters then I'm totally tooled-up back at the vicarage. But we'll have to meet there 'cos the filth are watching me like hawks ... Pretend we haven't had this chat and I'll meet you there in ten ...'

I'd wander off, leaving them standing and staring at me in astonishment with Paul's hyena cackle ringing in my ear.

We only had one unfortunate incident. We'd set up for one shoot around the river and a couple of our cameramen were using one of their favourite tricks, the Pramcam. This involved hiding a camera in a pram and covering it with a blanket. The cameraman then leant over the 'baby' and filmed the action while pretending to be a doting parent. Beautiful as this scene of fatherly devotion was, it started to raise some suspicion. The sight of a man leaning into a pram for hours on end can cause some misunderstanding. I'd often hear the words 'Camera Two, need a wife ...' in my ears. Paul would have realised that one of the cameramen had been staring into his pram for too long and was starting to attract attention. A female AP or runner would be dispatched to join the cameraman in staring at their non-existent baby. It looked a bit more normal.

Sometimes, however, we were too late, especially when we happened to have set up outside a bank. Concerned staff in the establishment, believing that an elaborate bank heist was about to take place, called the Cotswold SWAT team that we'd met many years before. We carried on filming, unaware of any problems until Operation Bacon swung into action. Once we had explained the situation and confirmed that the Pramcam operators were neither exhibitionist paedophiles nor part of some sophisticated stakeout, the police alert was reduced to a code amber.

We filmed a sketch that I adored down in Padstow, in Cornwall. I was dressed in a long coat, inside which the art department had pinned about forty different types of cake in little plastic boxes (so that they wouldn't get crushed). The crew set up on the other side of the harbour and filmed across the water to me hanging around and looking very suspicious. I would then approach people seated on benches, open my coat and surreptitiously enquire as to whether they 'wanted any cake?' They would look surprised and refuse, and I would then reel off the longest list of cakes that I could remember. I was a 'cake dealer'. It was basically getting a Class A drug deal joke onto Saturday night family TV. It made me laugh anyway.

I loved the *Bet you're wondering what happened to me?* character. This was myself in a wheelchair, covered in plaster and looking like I'd broken every bone in my body. I'd be left by my 'nurse' (the wonderful Naomi) next to a couple on a bench and wait for them to ask what happened. I would then launch into a long and fantastical story that got more implausible every time: 'I'm a Devon/Dorset honey smuggler and got attacked by a bear' or 'I'm a scientist and got drunk at the office party and fell into the Hadron Collider'. My best story was a recurring joke about Alan

Titchmarsh having a terrible temper. I told a couple that I'd been at the Chelsea Flower Show and had happened to mention that I didn't think Titchmarsh's garden was quite as good as his one the previous year, and 'he went mental'.

We repeated this joke in Croydon at a big sports store, where I set myself up as a bouncer. I told people wanting to go in that the store was temporarily closed so that Alan Titchmarsh could select his summer foot wardrobe. 'He doesn't like ordinary people seeing his feet...' I said. People went predictably ballistic.

I had a bit of history with Titchmarsh. In one of the last *Trigger Happy TV* celebrity interviews, I'd lured him down an alley near Broadcasting House. I was about to interview him, while dressed as a down-and-out Santa, when his PR person clicked that something was wrong and started dragging him away. He looked very confused. I was so annoyed that we'd been rumbled that I then behaved very badly to a national treasure. As we exited the alley, Sir Paul McCartney was leaving Broadcasting House and, spotting Father Christmas, gave him the obligatory thumbs up. I am ashamed to say that I returned the greeting with a rigid digit. The look on Macca's face was priceless.

I did my bit to encourage Scottish secession from the Union. We spent a week filming in Glasgow and the environs. One of the scenes we filmed was me approaching Scots in George Square while dressed as a tweedy English professor, accompanied by my Scottish 'interpreter'. The joke was simple – the interpreter would ask the Scot something in a broad Scottish accent and then repeat the answer to me in exactly the same words but in an English accent. I would then ask a question in English and the interpreter would repeat it in a Scottish accent despite the Scot announcing that he was speaking English too. We ramped it up a bit when I produced an orange and some toothpaste and asked the interpreter to ask the Scot whether he had any idea what these objects were? One particular guy went berserk, and I was very lucky to escape without the traditional Scottish appreciation of bad comedy: a Glasgow Kiss.

It wouldn't have been one of my TV shows if I hadn't managed to blag a week or so away filming somewhere hot. I suggested various places like Cannes, Rimini, Miami, but ITV decided that this might alienate their core audience and insisted on ... Benidorm. This didn't fill me with pleasure but still, a trip's a trip, and I really will go anywhere that I haven't been before – it's an addiction.

Benidorm was, if anything, worse than I could have expected. What was probably once a rather lovely little village nestled in a spectacular bay and blessed with a long, golden beach was now Sodom and Gomorrah. You all know what it looks like: a beach packed tight with tattoos in front of a long row of hideous apartment blocks. What really summed it up for me was when I spotted a long line of dangerously drunk teenage girls queuing up to ride an enormous Bucking Penis – this truly was the decline and fall of Western civilisation before my eyes. Or maybe I was just getting old? Looking back from the admittedly rather wonderful beach you'd see nothing but row after row of soulless tower blocks designed, it seemed, by architects with a visceral hatred of form and beauty, and this in a country that had produced the Alhambra. We were staying in a curious golf resort in the hills just behind the town. The owners, perhaps shamed by what had happened below, had decided to turn their establishment into the Spanish equivalent of Portmeirion. Every building in the vast and rather empty complex was an exact replica of real, prominent buildings in the Costa Brava. The place was supposed to have the feel of a Spanish village but was actually more like the set of *The Truman Show*. There was a mock central square that we sat in for coffee but unfortunately the owners, in their infinite wisdom, had decided that people didn't want to sit in tranquillity, soaking up the dying rays of the sun while sipping on sangria. No, they felt that what we really wanted was a mini-disco in which hugely powerful, hidden speakers blared out 'The Hokey Cokey' in Spanish while a demented woman in a jumpsuit cavorted around screaming into a microphone and trying to get the two or three children hanging about to dance. It was a scene that *The Fast Show* would have passed on for being too unrealistic.

I decided to go for a late swim but changed my mind when I got to the pool, as a gentleman of a certain age was being 'relieved' by a rather enthusiastic hooker in the shallow end.

The following morning we were up bright and early and down into town, ready to start filming. We were constantly in danger of being mown down by the quite ridiculous number of 'disability' scooters zooming around the place. In Benidorm, these were not the exclusive domain of the disabled but seemingly the popular choice of transportation for every visitor. I saw whole families drive past in convoys with the drivers' ages ranging from six to sixty. It appeared that they were cheaper to rent than mopeds, and of course you could drive them into shops so no need for that knackering use of legs when you were purchasing your beer, fags and condoms.

Halfway through the afternoon and trouble started. A very large and irate Neapolitan swaggered into the bar where we were filming and claimed that one of our crew had knocked him off his moped, and that I had then sworn at him (completely untrue). He announced that he had been 'disrespected', that 'nobody a-disrespect a-somebody from a-Napoli', and that he was going to 'a-kill a-someone'. His angry eyes scanned our rather nervous group before settling on me. I was clearly the chosen one. This was unfortunate, as I happened to be dressed as a Spanish lothario complete with medallions, leather trousers and an abundance of chest hair. The barman whispered to us

232

that the protagonist was 'local Mafia'. I nodded at him in a manner that conveyed that this was not reassuring news. The Neapolitan, already a visitor himself to Benidorm, took one look at me and clearly assumed that a Colombian gang was trying to muscle in on his action. I happened to look like Pablo Escobar's mad brother, which helped. He squared up to me with his tattooed plumage on full display. I noticed a handgun in the back of his jeans. That was enough for both ITV and myself, and I was whisked away to the safety of our hotel for a day off spent lounging in the cleanest of the three pools.

It was sadly only towards the end of our stay that we discovered the tiny section of Old Benidorm, with its winding streets, local bars and great little restaurants. There wasn't a Brit in sight, which made it even better. We were a little gang – Paul and me, Kit and Jess who did my make-up and prosthetics every day. Those three months of the first series of *Fool Britannia* were probably the most fun I'd ever had filming. Like all good things in telly, however, it could never last.

With the series in the can, we started the long edit. Normally this was my forte but ITV wouldn't let me use the editor I wanted and refused to pay for me to fully edit the series. I had to pop in and out and try to either influence or polish things up that other people were editing. Then an edict came from on high that canned laughter was to be added to the series. A little part of me died. Canned laughter is such a curious thing. There is a rumour that all the laughter you hear over comedy shows was recorded back in the Sixties and is used over and over again. Most people who seem to turn up for TV show audiences tend to be quite elderly. This means that when you listen to canned laughter, you are listening to the sound of dead people laughing. Spooky.

Series One was a passable first attempt. I wasn't able to edit it the way I'd have liked and the addition of a cheesy voice-over and a laughter track had killed any semblance of credibility, but I was pursuing the golden calf: the early evening Saturday audience. Maybe this was what you had to do to get it?

It wasn't. It did well but wasn't a huge breakout hit. The vicar definitely made an impression and I knew we had a really strong character. I wasn't too downhearted, as I had always been looking at the first series as an experiment to see what worked and what didn't. I wanted to learn the lessons from it and start to get it right in the second series. Harry Hill had not got *TV Burp* right until about the fourth series and ITV would definitely give me the time to get the thing right, that's how TV works, right? Wrong.

There was a very long and awkward silence from the powers-that-be until they finally recommissioned the series. It was hardly a strong vote of confidence, but then I thought back to Kevin Lygo at Channel 4 uuhhmming and aahhing over a second series of *Trigger Happy TV* when we were the biggest show on the telly. So I shrugged my shoulders and prepared to make a cracking second series.

Then came the meeting. A new suit at ITV brought myself and a couple of others together to discuss what the second series should be like. After an hour I wanted to shoot myself. The upshot was that I was too posh and that my voice-over should go (I was thrilled), and that the show should be 'warmer' (that means less funny), and that we should have more 'traditional' set-ups ('Can we do some Beadle-type things?'), and that I should not be in every sketch ('Get some young people in').

I made a terrible decision. Rather than fighting them with everything I had, I caved in. I thought back to *World Shut Your Mouth* on BBC One, when I'd ignored everyone else and done exactly what I'd wanted. It had been a good show but so wrong for the channel, and I'd been chucked out of the Beeb. This was my chance to show that I could listen, that I could learn from my mistakes. So I decided not to fight, as we would just end up with a show that was pulling in two directions and pleasing nobody. Maybe these people did know better? It was their job after all. It was their channel. Maybe it would be brilliant?

Besides, I had other things to worry about. I'd been approached by ITV to do yet another reality show, called *Splash*. Weird as it might sound, I'd always rather fancied myself as a bit of a diver. I'd been flinging myself off cliffs into rivers and lakes in Lebanon and Canada ever since I was a kid. This was an opportunity to be taught by Olympic diver Tom Daley, as well as to play the 'keep the channel happy' game. So I said yes.

I'd made another terrible decision. Daley was barely involved – he'd show up for ten minutes to be filmed pretending to teach us before leaving. I was doing a five-hour drive there and back every day to the training sessions in Essex. Initially I was OK and I was the first one to go off the terrifying ten-metre board. Every part of you is screaming, 'Go back, stop, you're going to die!' as you stand on the edge of that board. I did it, though, over and over, and got some pretty good, very basic dives in. My arms ached from them being ripped back in their sockets from the pressure of entering the water but I was pretty sure that I'd be OK.

Then came the big night when I was squeezed into some weird 1920s bathing costume and I realised that I'd been spectacularly miscast in some homoerotic *TOWIE* spin-off. The communal caravan in which we all sat beforehand was a show in itself, a minor celebrity gumbo with Joey Essex managing to get stuck in the bathroom and Donna Air and me smuggling in champagne and getting pissed.

I just wanted the whole thing to be over. When my moment finally came, and I climbed the diving platform up to the very top to meet Vernon Kay and the camera crew, I was in an out-of-body-type mode. I went to pieces on fear, shame, adrenaline and champagne. I can't remember any of it except that I launched myself too far out and could feel myself rotating in midair. I remember everything going into slo-mo and thinking that this was how it was all going to end – I was going to break my back live on national TV in front of my whole family. My bowels would probably collapse and I would soil myself as the final indignity as, once again, I would be dragged out of a pool in front of the nation . . .

The pain of the impact was unbelievable and I can still feel it. The good news was that I wasn't paralysed. The bad news was that this meant that I had to continue with the show and be interviewed by Gabby Logan. I looked up to the audience to see my daughter looking at me in as supportive a manner as she could . . . I had to stop doing reality TV.

Chapter 13

Here We Go Again

So by now I'd gone up, then down and was now up again, and about as mainstream as I'd ever thought possible. Not only was I making a Saturday night ITV show, but I was also starring in an ad campaign for Stena Ferries. The ad company had approached me and I'd assumed that they had done so because of my travel pedigree. After a while I was not so sure. We filmed it in Belfast, a city that I loved. The ad people were really nice, but it was when I saw my wardrobe that I hesitated. I'd presumed that they wanted the traveller 'Dom Joly' in the ad. Looking at the outfit, however, it appeared that they wanted my Home Counties, paedophile doppelgänger instead. I was offered chinos, yellow shirt, loud jumper and ... to top it all off ... leather driving gloves. I thought that there must be some comedic angle to this outfit that I hadn't picked up in the script and so got dressed without much protest. As the filming progressed, however, it became clear that there was no subtext. In fact, there seemed no reason whatsoever for me to be dressed like Ronnie Corbett's golfing partner. So, for the last couple of years, as I've tried to steer people away from my ITV mainstream stuff towards my more 'serious' writing side, I've regularly had to look out of the window to see an enormous billboard of me stuffing a suitcase into the back of some car on my way for a Car-cation. This always kills any attempt to convince people of my artistic seriousness. I recently drove my family to Istanbul and back over the Easter holidays, and we took a Stena ferry from Harwich to the Hook of Holland. As I wandered around the ship I got some serious stares from bemused passengers. It must have been a bit like finding Lenny Henry in your Premier Inn bathroom. I think they all assumed that contractually I was forced to spend most of my time on a Stena ferry, just going back and forth while smiling at the good people on board. For the record – it was very nice.

I'm not even going to mention the online poker ad I did in Israel, dressed in swimming trunks . . . Bugger . . . I just did. Ads are incredibly tempting for the impecunious celeb. The average ad spends in thirty seconds what I'd spend in six half-hours of *Trigger Happy TV*, and this is a very depressing but also rather attractive fact. It is therefore a stronger man than me who says no to an offer to do an ad – what Bill Hicks called 'sucking the devil's cock'. Sometimes, however, I really should pay attention to the fine print.

I had to fly to Israel to film the aforementioned online poker ad, as this was where the company was based. This was an added bonus for me as I'd never visited the place and really wanted to have a look around. Unfortunately, the feeling wasn't mutual. At the airport, my passport caught the attention of a very aggressive and suspicious Shin Bet officer. First he spotted that I was born in Lebanon, then he saw my visas to Iran and North Korea . . . the final straw, he was strangely perturbed by the fact that one of my middle names was Romulus.

'Where is this name from?' he shouted at me in the little room into which I'd been taken.

'It's from Romulus and Remus, the founders of Rome. I was conceived there, room 13, Hotel D'Inghilterra, if you really want to know . . .'

This was pretty specific detail.

'Is not Arab name?' shouted the Shin Bet officer.

'Not that I'm aware of . . .' I said, rapidly losing my cool.

The officer went through my passport again and stopped on the Iranian visa.

'Why you go to Iran?' he yelled.

This was an exact replay of when I'd tried to enter the States and a dim immigration official had become obsessed with this question. Just as in the States, the tone of the question annoyed me so much that I gave them the answer I knew would not help matters.

'I went skiing there . . .' I said.

The Shin Bet officer looked like he was about to have an aneurysm.

'Skiing! Skiing! There is no skiing in Iran. You are lying.'

I took my laptop out and opened my iPhoto. I scrolled down to the section where I went to Iran and started showing the official photos of me skiing in Iran. He pretended not to be interested but I could see that he was utterly fascinated by these holiday photos from the country that so regularly threatened to drive his own into the sea. The Shin Bet man calmed down a little and we started to scroll through my photos as though I was showing them to a relative. When I'd finished he appeared to be content that I had gone to Iran to ski as opposed to undergo intensive training in how to drive Israelis into salt water. He was still not happy about my coming into the country, however. I gave him a fax I'd received from the ad company. It was in Hebrew so I didn't know what it said, but it was surely proof that I was there for work? It did the job. His attitude totally changed and I was soon allowed in. When I had the thing translated I found out why. The fax informed whomsoever it concerned that I was *an international film star of great repute and much acclaimed for my work. I was coming to Israel to do some of this acclaimed work that would only reflect well on the country.* There was no mention of the fact that I was going to be dressed in a bathing suit, advertising online poker while being slowly buried up to my neck in a shower of gold coins ... but I guess that's advertising for you.

Filming started on the second series of *Fool Britannia*, and I decided to concentrate on a single strand and just turn up on autopilot for the rest of the show. In the first series, we'd done something called Half-Time Entertainment, in which I'd come onto the Twickenham pitch at half-time and be introduced as someone who'd won the chance to sing to the crowd. The joke was that I kept missing my cue and having to restart the song while getting more and more irritated. It worked brilliantly. Half the crowd had their heads in their hands while the other half hurled abuse. I loved it because it had scale. We decided that we would make this a regular strand in the second series. I also decided to get rid of all the old characters apart from the vicar and start afresh. I think I knew the second series was going to be a turkey and I'd already subconsciously started to distance myself from it.

On one of the Half-Time Entertainments we got access to film at the Rose Bowl, home of Hampshire cricket. I was introduced between innings with Slipper, my performing dog. The crew set up an assault course and I ran on in a silver spangly suit with Slipper on a lead. I looked like a cross between Liberace and Desperate Dan, and made an impassioned speech to the crowd about how I'd found Slipper on the streets of Paris and how, over the last five years, we had developed a show together that pushed the boundaries of communication between man and beast. The music started and I let Slipper off the lead, at which point, as arranged, he legged it straight out of the stadium, leaving me to have to mime and act out what he would have done, had he been there ... The crowd winced in embarrassment for me. I could actually feel their discomfort in the air, it was very curious.

The Manchester Opera House let me come on before a production of *Ghost: The Musical*, where I was introduced as 'The World's Best Mind Reader'. I did a spiel about how I was going to 'burgle' the audience's minds but that they should not worry, as I would be careful and put everything back ... I then asked for a volunteer to stand up – a girl in the fifth row did so. I told her to think about where she was born and I would then tell the audience. I proceeded to reel off a never-ending list of places, from Kampala and Ulan Bator to Chipping Sodbury and Kettering, that the poor girl had to shake her head to, one by one. Out of the corner of my eye, I could see a woman in the front row nearly dying of embarrassment ... for me. I really wanted to let her know that it was OK.

These moments – plus some great prosthetics from Millennium FX for a strand called *Where's Joly*, in which I was turned into a watermelon and a doner kebab (among others) – were fun. For the doner, I was a kebab in a kebab stall. All that was visible of me within the kebab were my eyes when I opened them. I'd watch kids walking past holding their parents' hands and then suddenly spotting the kebab looking at them. I'd quickly shut my eyes and try not to laugh as they would scream at their parents, 'Mum, Dad, the kebab was looking at me ...' It was funny, but not as good as it should have been. I wanted to do it in some dodgy kebab bar and target drunken midnight customers. This was considered 'not very ITV' and so we ended up doing it, rather incongruously, in the middle of the afternoon in a shopping centre in South London.

The rest of the show was careering towards a brick wall at a hundred miles an hour. They'd even started filming scenes without me actually being there – never a good sign on your own show.

A series of seriously ill-thought-through and unfunny 'big' scenarios had been set up. They were nothing more than bad Beadle pastiches, but without either the budget or the imagination. The lowest moment for me was driving three hours to somewhere in Kent to don a uniform and a false beard and turn up at the end of a terrible hit on some builders and a dog in cement to 'reveal' that it was all a big joke. There were about thirty people involved in this thing, from actors to builders, dog handlers to production crew. How had I gone from doing a great show with five people to making a crap one with fifty?

It reminded me of the great Tom Green talking about the move from his anarchic Canadian low-fi TV show to MTV. He was used to just wandering the streets of Ottawa with one cameraman. Then, when he filmed his first thing for MTV, he described a moment when he looked behind him and saw about forty people following him with clipboards and headphones and all the other pointless paraphernalia of TV overkill. Bigger is not always better. I loved Tom Green – he, Dennis Pennis and Andy Kaufman are my all-time comedy heroes.

Back in *Fool Britannia* land, the crap rolled on. I was suddenly in another big set-up in Nottingham involving some girl setting up her sister, who was getting married. A Sacha Baron Cohen wannabe played the part of a wedding planner with an obsession for gay innuendo and smut. I not only had to interview the sister and ask her how she felt, but the only thing I did on the joke was walk in at the end and remove my fake moustache to 'reveal' it was me. If there had been a handgun available, I'd have used it.

The shoot picked up a little towards the end when we filmed at my local festival, Cornbury. This is the sort of family music festival that die-hards would hate. It had cashpoints, fine cuisine, and David Cameron goes every year. It was a perfect place to film. We filmed some stuff with the ASBO vicar. He pretty much wandered around the festival being rude about everything. We did a sketch where a stooge jumped the line at a Portaloo and the vicar knocked him over in an apoplectic fit of rage while others in the line watched in astonishment. The problem was that loads of people were recognising the vicar so, by the third take, we had about fifty people seated opposite the Portaloo, munching on sandwiches and drinking wine as though an audience at a show. Flattering as this was, it really didn't help with secret filming, especially when they all decided to applaud after every tipping of the Portaloo.

The highlight of Cornbury was a failed attempt on the prime minister, my old mate 'Dave' Cameron. As I was walking towards our next location, I spotted the PM entering a tent selling silly hippy hats, with one of his kids. I gestured to the cameraman that I was going in. I tapped Cameron on the shoulder and he turned round ... Just as I was about to launch into some patter, I was grabbed from behind and hurled out of the tent by his impressively vigilant security team. It appeared that *Fool Britannia* was on the viewing schedule in Number 10, as they recognised the vicar much earlier than most members of the public who watched in confusion as the PM's bodyguards roughed up a vicar. It would have been a great publicity coup for the show, but it was not to be. Later that evening I was disguised as a new character, after two hours of prosthetics – that of a dodgy-looking roadie. The organisers had given us permission to wander on stage before the band Keane's set and start reading out terrible poetry on the main mike. At the allocated time, I approached the stairs leading up to behind the main stage while being followed by a camera crew when David

Cameron's security team once again grabbed me. He was about to introduce Keane and nobody had told them about my appearance. Cameron had to wait in the wings while I did my shtick ... which was nice ... I don't think we're destined ever to be good buddies.

With filming coming to an end, I pretty much left ITV to do with the show whatever it was that they felt it needed. I had given up, thrown in the towel, waved the white flag. Fittingly, I flew to France and holed myself up in an old manor house in the Ardèche. All I could do was wait ... and fight the curious French law about having to wear Speedos in public pools. The first news was encouraging. ITV had decided to drop the canned laughter. Maybe the fact that long-dead people would no longer be laughing at inappropriate and oddly jarring moments might save the series? But then it was decreed that there would still be a voice-over and that, despite my mass audience-alienating posh voice, I was to do it. I knew things were on the slide. When I finally got back after a blissful month off with my family, it was time to watch the off-line cuts. It was a mishmash of ideas, styles and jokes. It sort of had something for everyone, but nothing for me. It was comedy by committee ... Exactly what comedy should never be.

I had a little screening party for the first show of the second series at home in the Cotswolds. There were about twenty-five people crammed into my TV room. As the show went out, I knew it was doomed. The kids laughed at the visual jokes, but the chatty stuff left them cold, while the adults tried not to be rude about the sub-Beadle elements that the kids neither understood nor much cared about. I stopped watching the series by the third show, something I'd only ever done with the horrific US version of *Trigger Happy TV*. I may have made politically bad decisions at the BBC but at least I'd liked the shows I was making, and that, I've come to learn, is pretty much all you can hope for in the roller-coaster ride that is television.

Three weeks later I got a call from a couple of young Americans. They were interested in optioning a new series of *Trigger Happy TV* in the States. 'We all loved that show, man. We love it and we really want to make some new shows out here. Are you interested?' I was interested. I started jotting down ideas and they began to pour out uncontrollably. I soon had pages and pages, and they made me laugh – really laugh. I got excited. Then we started talking business and I remembered why America was a nightmare. They sent their 'deal' through. I didn't get much past the paragraph that said I'd have to pay for my own flights and accommodation. This was taking the piss, and I sent them packing. It was time to take control and head off to do my own thing – right or wrong.

So that's what I'm off to do next. I'm going to have a crack at cracking America. I'm off in search of my second act ... or is it my third ... or fourth? I have no idea. I've lost count. But whatever, it's in the USA, it's television and I'm in control – what could possibly go wrong?

Epilogue

Oh God, an epilogue. Who reads epilogues? You should read this one, though – it's full of lots of bitty things that I couldn't fit into the rough timeline of this book. Seriously, stick with it.

Here's my *Top Five Most Embarrassing Moments in Showbiz . . .* so far.

1. **Who Wants to Be a Millionaire**. I was watching a Danny Boyle movie called *Millions* the other night. There is a scene in the film in which Jimmy Nesbitt is watching *Who Wants to Be a Millionaire* and getting all the answers right. His character's kids tell him that he should go onto the show, as he would win a million quid. A cold shiver rocketed down my spine. I'd always quite fancied myself on this show. At home I would also sit and answer all the questions while pooh-poohing thick contestants getting the obvious answers wrong. In 2014, I was asked whether I'd like to take part in

a celebrity charity episode? I agreed and suggested that I take part with Jimmy Nesbitt, a friend and a smart man to boot. It was only when we turned up on the night in question that we realised that this was to be the last ever show with Chris Tarrant and that subsequently there would be more than a little extra scrutiny of the show. Jimmy was nervous but I was feeling quietly confident, which always comes before a fall. We'd struggled for ages to find three good, varied Phone-a-Friends and had only confirmed the third about half an hour before recording. We tried to josh about with the other contestants – Sir Chris Hoy (seriously nice man) and Kevin Bridges, one of the Hairy Bikers and Rachel Riley, but everyone was too busy worrying. Finally, we were taken onto the set and Jimmy and I did a run-through in which we did very well. I came off feeling much happier but Jimmy was still nervous. Then we found out that we were to be the first pair on and things started to get serious. Twenty minutes later and we were introduced to the audience and came on to sit on the slightly awkward stools in that very familiar studio. The moment the music started, everything went weird. It was like the first time I'd done *Have I Got News for You* – everything suddenly became way too real. Instantly, you had zero confidence in your answers and paranoia set in, with you starting to see a trap in every answer. I can't remember the first couple of questions, but they were the type that were so easy you went blank for a moment. Nevertheless, we managed to get through to the first barrier – the grand – and I answered a question about what county Bishop's Stortford was in. I knew it was Hertfordshire, as it was near my old school, but started having ridiculous doubts. It was crazy how your mind started playing tricks on you. We began to settle down and even had a Chris Tarrant chat, in which he asked how

Jimmy and I knew each other. He then asked us what our weak areas might be. I said that mine was sport but that Jimmy was excellent in that area. I was looking forward to mentioning to Tarrant that I'd tried to teach his ex-wife to snort vodka through a straw but decided to save this nugget until later. We cracked on and answered two more questions correctly. We were now doing OK and concentrating on getting to the fifty-grand mark which meant that, whatever happened, you went home with that. We hadn't used any of our lifelines. Things were looking good. Then up came the sport question. It was about who had held an Olympic record for the longest. I didn't have a clue, but was drawn to Steve Cram. Before I could say anything, Jimmy whispered that he felt it was Steve Cram. This was a good sign and we started to think about going for it. Suddenly Jimmy got cautious. 'Shall we go fifty–fifty?' he said. For some reason I said, 'No, let's go for it.' Greed is not good in this situation. Jimmy went, 'Steve Cram. Final answer,' and suddenly everything changed. The lights in the studio dimmed, lasers pointed accusingly and Chris Tarrant was going, 'I'm sorry, but it's the wrong answer ... It's Jonathan Edwards ...' and we were being ushered out, walking the long walk of shame, unable to believe that we'd screwed it up without even using a lifeline. Jimmy and I could barely look at each other. Even worse, we now had to sit on a sofa and watch the other contestants and pretend to be supportive. Every time the cameras were not on us we would whisper to each other, 'I can't believe it.' Jimmy looked like he was catatonic. On the screen in front of us, Sir Chris Hoy was doing really well and we had to pretend to clap and look happy. Then, at the fifty-grand question, Hoy and Bridges screwed up and went back down to a grand with us. Jimmy and I both pretended to look really heartbroken

249

for them but the moment the cameras were off us, Jimmy whispered, 'That's got us off the hook ...' It was so wrong but that's exactly how we felt. Thankfully for us, but not for charity, the Hairy Biker and Rachel Riley also crashed and burned. A terrible night for worthy causes but slightly less embarrassing for us, so that was OK then ...

2. *Let's Dance for Comic Relief*. I'm friends with a lovely girl called Georgie Hurford-Jones, who worked for Simon Cowell in LA. Georgie had two sisters, who were both in telly back in the UK. One day, one of the sisters asked for a meeting. We met up, only for me to find out that she was trying to persuade me to take part in *Let's Dance for Comic Relief*, a show that she was producing. I immediately said no. I was an ex-Goth, and dancing was pretty much my least favourite thing to do in the world. Then they pulled out the trump card: 'We thought you might like to do "U Can't Touch This" by MC Hammer.' I stopped protesting for a second. I could see a way out of this. I remembered the video in which 'Hammer' wore the most ludicrous baggy trousers. If I could get the costume woman to make me baggy trousers so big that I couldn't actually dance in them, then it would not only be funny but would solve my non-dancing problem. So, after a little more prompting, I agreed and I started getting a guy from the show coming down to my house three times a week to teach me the moves. I went through the motions of learning but a) I can't dance and b) I knew that I had my humungous-trousers-get-out-of-jail-free card. I'd rung the costume lady and told her my requirements and she seemed absolutely down with it – all was in hand. Three weeks later and the big day came. I was going to be dancing live on national TV. I should have been crapping my pants, but I hadn't put them

on yet. We were filming at Ealing Studios and I got there late afternoon, had a look round, listened to the run-through and then set off to find the wardrobe lady. When I got there she was in good spirits. 'I've had so much fun making these, they're so funny ...' She brought them out and there was total silence. The trousers were silky and shiny and slightly less baggy than the ones that MC Hammer had used. They were very danceable in, and not even that ludicrous. I was screwed. It was too late to do anything. I was dancing live in front of the nation in two hours' time. Now, normally in these kinds of showbiz stories, one pulls oneself together and pulls it out of the fire at the last second. Not me. I can vividly remember an out-of-body experience when I was standing behind the screen with my backing dancers as Claudia Winkleman announced, '... And now, dancing live before the nation, Dom Joly as ... MC Hammer ...' The screen went up and I half-jogged on and desperately tried to remember how the dance was supposed to go. The audience was stony silent – it was as though they were watching an execution. I jumped around in the manner of a man being electrocuted and longed for the track to end. I was sweating, I was dying live on air ... When it was finally over, there was hardly a sound from the audience, the judges were embarrassed, I was embarrassed, MC Hammer was probably embarrassed. When the public votes came in, I was first out. This was actually a relief to me, as the idea of having to do it again was unthinkable. I was aware, however, that normally the comedy act goes through whatever. This was *Comic Relief* after all – just dress as a woman and you're through. Not me ... The public had wisely seen no redeeming feature. I still sometimes wake up at night and hear the words 'Stop ... Hammer Time ...'

3. *Save the Children.* I've realised that most of these embarrassing stories are charity-based. Trust me, this is not a
last-ditch attempt by me to boast about my 'charidee' work.
It's just that charity events give you the opportunity to do
weird things and inevitably they take you right out of your
comfort zone. Some people seem good at coping with this
type of thing. I'm more your Rupert Everett running away
from the *Comic Relief* version of *The Apprentice*. The one
thing I did think I could properly contribute to, charity-
wise, was towards helping the crisis in Syria. I'd grown up
in neighbouring Lebanon, had travelled all over Syria and
so, when Save the Children asked me to help, I agreed. At
last, I would be doing something that was definitely helping and I would actually know what I was talking about.
Save the Children asked me whether I'd become an ambassador for them and whether I'd be prepared to travel to
Jordan to visit a refugee camp on the Jordanian/Syrian
border. I said I'd be delighted and the wheels were set in
motion. The problem with being an 'ambassador' is that
you are expected to be diplomatic, have no political views
and do nothing to embarrass the charity organisation in
question. These have never been my strong points. On the
day of the trip, I turned up at Heathrow and checked into
my economy class seat to Amman. Having gone through
security, I went into my automatic pre-flight routine that is
almost ingrained within me. I am a creature of habit and I
always go to the Salmon Bar to have a prawn cocktail and
a glass of champagne. As far as I was concerned, I was off
duty until I landed in Amman. As usual, I was very early (a
bad habit) and had loads of time to kill, so I started tweet-
ing. In one of my tweets, I took a photo of my meal, saying
that I was off to Jordan and thought no more about it. By
the time I landed in Amman all hell had broken loose.

People had started complaining to Save the Children about my tweet, with the implication that their donations were paying for my glass of champagne and a prawn cocktail. I was a 'luvvie' on a 'luvvie break'. It was untrue. I paid my way, but I was mortified. I should have thought about it more. I didn't look good. I had been an ambassador for about three days and I had already screwed up on a monumental scale. It was time to pass the Ferrero Rochers around and apologise.

4. *The Body Shop*. Occasionally, I get asked to host some award shows. This can be very lucrative but I always have to emphasise that I am *not* a stand-up comedian. This is because the contract always comes through with a phrase like: *8pm guests sit for dinner. 9pm Dom stands up and does 10 mins of material before awards start.* I have to go back to them and point out that I'm happy being there, riffing with the audience, but I don't have 10 mins of material. Normally this is OK, but sometimes it goes very wrong. I was offered the job of hosting The Body Shop Awards. I checked that they didn't want me to do some stand-up and it was fine. I looked at the schedule of events – there was a Seventies disco band on stage, accompanying proceedings, and I just had to turn up, give out awards and compere the evening. It was perfect. I remember being slightly surprised that The Body Shop was having their awards in Birmingham but told myself not to be so discriminatory. The day before the event, I rented a terrible Seventies outfit and wrote some jokes about the different pungent smells that emanate onto the high street from Lush and The Body Shop. I thought I'd do a bit of shtick by pretending to have got the wrong dress code – this also got me out of wearing black tie, which I loathe. So I got to the venue, met the

liaison person, who showed me into my dressing room, and that was that. Come the event and things went disastrously. I was introduced with much fanfare from the stage and I marched into the vast room from the back, winding my way through the diners. There was an awkward silence in the room. Once on stage, I made a lame joke about how everybody seemed to have got the wrong dress code as they were all in black tie. Again, total silence. So, as I felt the floor opening up beneath my feet I launched into some desperate 'jokes' about Lush and The Body Shop and how come employees weren't allowed to work in places where people smoked but somehow it was OK for them to be in the olfactory hellhole that was The Body Shop? There was nothing. I just wanted to die. It was at this moment that my co-compere leant over and quietly let me know that these were the awards for *The Body Shop*, a magazine celebrating panel beaters and car workers in the Midlands . . . I never recovered.

5. ***Richard & Judy***. Not long after *Trigger Happy TV* had aired, I started getting all sorts of media requests. Among these was an offer to go onto *This Morning* to be interviewed by Richard and Judy. Now, at the time, Sam and I were still in our 'punk' stage, where we didn't want to do any normal interviews or telly unless we subverted it somehow. We'd just done a live interview for *T4*, in which I appeared dressed as one of the *Trigger Happy* dogs and Sam had rushed into the studio halfway through the interview and attacked me while dressed as the other dog. We hadn't told the show that we were going to do this and it all ended in glorious chaos. So when the offer for *This Morning* came in, we had a think about what I should do. In the end, I foolishly told Sam that I would faint live on air. We got to ITV

Studios and Sam came with me to make sure that I didn't wimp out. The closer we got to transmission the stronger the urge to run became, but I'd promised Sam ... Finally, I was called onto set only to find that I had got the B team – Fern Britton and John Leslie. Richard and Judy were on holiday. I was livid and wanted to forget the whole thing but Sam insisted that I had to go through with it. I spent the first part of the interview warming up and looking a little woozy before finally crashing to the floor right in the middle of a live bit. I fell into Fern's fulsome, pre-gastric band boobs and she panicked and they cut to a further VT of some *Trigger Happy* clips. Then, unbelievably they came back to the studio where I was pretending to have just come round while Fern nursed me and I apologised to one of her boobs. When they eventually moved off to do another segment I was handed to the ITV nurse, who tried to take me to the little clinic she had in the basement. I bolted at the first opportunity and made my escape out of the back and over a wall. It was all very curious. Over the following years I would do *Richard & Judy* several times; Richard would always be very complimentary about my stuff and was very nice to me. The weird thing, however, was that just before you went onto the show someone would come into the dressing room to tell you that the show was sponsored by Schwartz Herbs, and to remind you not to say anything offensive about that company. Until that very moment you had never thought about Schwartz Herbs but now, you went live on air with nothing but Schwartz Herbs running through your brain like some Tourette's time bomb.

The last fifteen years have not all been total humiliation, how-ever. There have been incredible, exhilarating, mind-blowing moments. Most of all there have been times when I seriously thought I might actually die laughing. So, to conclude a rather therapeutic look back at surely the most unstable fifteen years in the history of showbiz, here is my list of the *Top Five Things That Have Made Me Laugh the Most in the Last Fifteen Years*.

1. *Sheep shagging*. I once made a show called *The Complainers* for Channel 5. The original idea was really funny: find out what annoyed the British public the most and then get revenge on their behalf. It was going to be entertaining and feel-good, so I signed up. Then, as per usual, things went pear-shaped. Channel 5 seem to have a standing policy of changing whoever is in charge of the channel about once a month. The new person changed the idea of the show completely. Instead of a funny revenge show, they now wanted more of a *Watchdog*/consumer rights type of programme. I had not signed up for this and the production was divided between those hired to make funny stuff and new people who came from current affairs and kept telling us that we couldn't legally get away with everything we were coming up with. So the production was a mess, but my little team ploughed on regardless. We wanted to do something about the rise of CCTV in the UK and someone told us about this town that had just spent a fortune on the most hi-tech system in the country. A researcher had been down there and told us that they had everywhere in the town covered. Not only that, they were particularly proud of an incredibly powerful camera that could zoom right in on a hill about a mile above the town. The researcher told us that he had pointed to a speck on the hill and the camera operator had zoomed in to reveal a man walking his dog. Much to the chagrin of the researcher in question, this gave me an idea. Ten days later and I was in the control room of the town in

question, filming an interview with the camera operator. I pointed at the powerful zoom camera screen. 'What's that?' I asked, knowing full well what it was. The operator went into his spiel about how powerful the zoom was. I pointed at a dot on the distant hill and asked him whether he could zoom in on it? He duly did to reveal our researcher with his trousers down by his ankles apparently 'pleasuring' a sheep (a rather realistic fake one that we had made). The operator's face was priceless. He stopped the interview as he tried to contact someone to apprehend the 'suspect behaving in a lewd fashion with an animal on **** Hill ...' We kept rolling with tears of laughter running down my face. That researcher probably runs ITV now.

2. *More sheep*. While we are on the subject of sheep, they have always been something that make me laugh. There is just something intrinsically ridiculous about them. My other favourite sheep-based joke (and a bit of a *Far Side* homage) was right at the end of *World Shut Your Mouth*, when the camera panned away from a sign requesting that walkers did not 'worry' a farmer's flock of sheep. The camera steadily revealed the flock of sheep standing awkwardly in the middle of a field with me in the background, on the other side of a fence holding a megaphone to my mouth. 'Now I don't want to alarm you ...' I boomed at the sheep '... but I was in the pub the other night, and the farmer was in there, and he was quite depressed and talking about jacking in the whole farming thing and doing something else. Now, you don't need me to tell you that this would not be good news for you guys ...' As I 'worried' the sheep, the door of the farm behind me flew open and the farmer himself appeared with a shotgun. I'd assumed that we'd obtained permission to film, but it seemed to have slipped

everybody's mind. The farmer was beyond apoplectic and didn't appear to be aware of the concept of hidden camera comedy when I tried to explain the curious situation at gunpoint. I was lucky to get away unscathed and was warned that, should I be spotted on his land again, he would shoot first and ask questions later.

3. *Art*. My favourite thing to do with my kids is to go to an art gallery and all gather round the fire extinguisher that invariably sits in the corner of every room. We peruse the object as though it was some lost precious masterpiece. It never fails. Pretty soon you are joined by other unsuspecting culture vultures, who will also start to stare and scratch their tiny goatees at this awesome piece of 'installation' art. We then move on, as the 'chain' has started – other gallery-goers will join the last ones etc. As well as making me laugh, I hope it teaches my kids to make their own minds up about what is or isn't to be appreciated in this world. When I first came to the Cotswolds, we moved into a house next door to a beautiful riverside house that curated a biennial sculpture exhibition in their wonderful grounds. Some of the stuff shown was amazing but a lot of it was over-priced dross. Try as I might, I couldn't resist. On the evening of the first day of the show I slipped into the grounds and crossed the bridge over the river into the meadow where some of the bigger exhibits sat. I chose a perfect spot and deposited a smeggy old pair of flip-flops carefully on a little stone plinth. I had made a sign to accompany my 'work'. It was in the same style as the rest of the exhibition. It read: *Shoes of Man, Earthwalker, Destroyer and Saviour – £139,000*. I spent a wonderful next two weeks popping over daily to watch people stop and admire my flip-flops. They were never discovered by the organisers

and stayed right until the end of the exhibition. I never saw them again – possibly a sharp-eyed collector purchased them? Perhaps I won the Turner Prize? I should have checked ...

4. *Joe.* When we flew to New York for a rather pointless filming week during the first series of *Trigger Happy TV*, Sam and I made a pilgrimage to the Carnegie Deli, a tourist trap that served stupidly large open sandwiches that would feed an entire African village. We were checking the menu and looking round at the hundreds of famous signed photos on the wall (my favourite was from Bozo the Clown, who was pictured staring creepily out of a bush in some park – he'd written 'See you around ... like a bagel' on his photo). As we took everything in, the waiter approached our table. He was what you might call a smart alec. He had the whole New Yawk patter and was a bit patronising to the two Brits in front of him. I wanted a salt beef sandwich and asked for one. 'You mean pastrami right, buddy? That's what we call it over here, you Limeys need to learn to speak American ...' He laughed the big laugh of a man who found himself very amusing. Sam and I looked at each other. I stood up and looked at the man intently. 'Sir ... I can only apologise for this misunderstanding, it's just that we are from the UK and only just arrived here. I am mortified by this and can only hope you accept my most sincere apologies.' The waiter looked at me as though facing a mental patient. 'Sure, buddy ... Forget about it ... It's no big deal ...' He wandered off, shaking his head in disbelief. When he returned with the sandwich, I stood up again and formally apologised at length once more. The waiter looked irritated and told us to forget about it. 'Seriously, it's not a big deal ...' When we

finished the meal and were leaving, I went up to him again and apologised. 'I can't stop thinking about it – how could I make such a stupid mistake? I should have done some research and known what words to use ... This has seriously ruined my holiday ...' The waiter was by now convinced that he had a lunatic on his hands and politely said goodbye, telling us that it was 'all OK ... Seriously'. That night we rang the deli from the hotel and asked to speak to the waiter whose name, we knew, was Joe. When he came on the line, I explained that I was having difficulty sleeping because of the embarrassment of the linguistic mix-up that morning. 'Is there anything I can do to make things right?' I asked Joe, who was now rapidly losing his rag. 'Listen, buddy, it's NOT a problem, seriously, get over it, who gives a shit ...' Joe hung up. Over the next week, we rang him about nine further times, sent two letters of apology plus an enormous bouquet of flowers. I still write to him once a year.

5. *Pig/Prawn*. I once had an idea for a sketch after we kept driving past a London caravan that sold fish. The joke was that I would approach the counter and ask the man whether he had crab claws. When he replied in the negative, I would lift my arms above the level of the counter to reveal enormous claws on the end of each of them. 'I have!' I would shout and then run away. It still makes me laugh, it's just so stupid. I'm not sure why we never did it – it was probably something simple like we couldn't find any crab claws to rent. Although we had some costumes made, we were often a bit lazy in this respect. We had the number of every costume shop in London and we would scour them for anything we needed and sometimes for inspiration. We did once rent a prawn costume from a shop in North

London only to find, when it arrived, that it looked like a pig. We rang the store and they assured us that it was a prawn costume. So we took it out on the street and asked passers-by – they almost all said that it looked like a pig. With the certainty of our market research, we returned the costume and refused to pay on the grounds that we'd wanted a prawn and had got a pig. The owner, an irate man, went mental and told us to leave and never come back. From then on, whenever we were bored, we would ring the store and ask whether they had a pig costume for rent? The owner would reply that he unfortunately had no such costume. We would pause for a second before telling him that 'friends' had mentioned that he might have a prawn costume for rent that greatly resembled a pig – might that be available? The owner would go nuclear every time and hurl abuse at us before slamming the phone down. It still makes me laugh ten years on – in fact, I might give him a ring now ...

So here we are at the end of the book. What have we learned about me and show business, apart from the fact that we are most likely ill-suited? I wish there were some clear rules that I could share with you to help if you are just starting out, but the truth is there just aren't any. Do what you love, commit to it and try to retain as much control as possible. All the rest is chance.

I live for the private moments that make me laugh until I can't breathe, moments almost impossible to get onto the screen. I live *for the beauty*. But the things that make me the happiest in life? Family, travel, adventure, new experiences ... Comedy doesn't really come into it.

I was once at Cheltenham Races as a guest of the *Independent*. As we quaffed free champagne in our private box high above the punters, I looked down. Far below, trying to make his way through the crowd was a poor man who had clearly been paid by the racecourse to dress up as the Gold Cup. Punters were laughing at him, knocking him over and throwing drinks at him. 'That's me in a couple of years . . .' I said to Simon Kelner, pointing at the wretch. Simon and the rest of the box laughed a little too hard for my liking.

Who knows . . . For now, I'm just going with Teddy Roosevelt, a man who lost both his wife and mother on the same day but stayed magnificently resilient to the end:

> It is not the critic who counts: not the man who points out how the strong man stumbles, or where the doer of deeds could have done them better. The credit belongs to the man who is actually in the arena, whose face is marred by dust and sweat and blood; who strives valiantly; who errs, who comes short again and again, because there is no effort without error and shortcoming; but who does actually strive to do the deeds; who knows great enthusiasms, the great devotions; who spends himself in a worthy cause; who at the best knows in the end the triumph of high achievement, and who at the worst, if he fails, at least fails while daring greatly, so that his place shall never be with those cold and timid souls who neither know victory nor defeat.

Onwards . . .